Topologies of Sexual Difference

SUNY series in Gender Theory
____
Tina Chanter, editor

Topologies of Sexual Difference

Space in Philosophy and Visual Art After Irigaray

Edited by

LOUISE BURCHILL, REBECCA HILL, *and* JAMES SARES

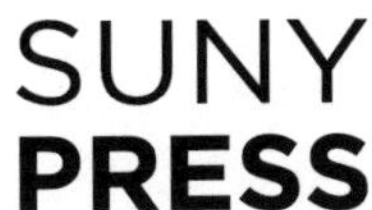

EU GPSR Authorised Representative:
Logos Europe, 9 rue Nicolas Poussin, 17000, La Rochelle, France
contact@logoseurope.eu

For information, contact State University of New York Press, Albany, NY
www.sunypress.edu

Chapter ten originally published in Italian as *Quando il futurismo è donna*
© Francesca Brezzi and Mimesis Edizioni 2009

Library of Congress Cataloging-in-Publication Data

Names: Burchill, Louise, editor. | Hill, Rebecca, 1971– editor. | Sares, James, editor.
Title: Topologies of sexual difference : space in philosophy and visual art after Irigaray / Louise Burchill, Rebecca Hill, and James Sares.
Description: Albany : State University of New York Press, [2025] | Series: SUNY series in gender theory | Includes bibliographical references and index.
Identifiers: LCCN 2025003552 | ISBN 9798855803662 (hardcover : alk. paper) | ISBN 9798855803686 (ebook)
Subjects: LCSH: Irigaray, Luce. | Sex differences—Philosophy. | Feminist theory. | Sex differences in art.
Classification: LCC B2430.I74 T67 2025 | DDC 305.4201—dc23/eng/20250212
LC record available at https://lccn.loc.gov/2025003552

Contents

Part Four: Sexuate Art in the Making

Illustrations

Acknowledgments

Above all, we wish to give thanks to Luce Irigaray for the monumental contribution of her thinking and teaching of sexuate difference. We acknowledge the community of scholars and artists involved in the Luce Irigaray Circle for their friendship and their work. Sabrina Hom and Athena Colman, codirectors of the Luce Irigaray Circle, have our gratitude for their sound advice at a difficult stage of this project. We thank Emanuele Panzera and Glory Scurto, the heirs of Olga Biglieri Scurto (the artist Barbara), for granting authorization to reproduce Barbara's paintings. Lorenzo Rocca, Rights and Permissions Editor of Mimesis Edizioni, equally has our gratitude for his generous support in securing the translation rights for Francesca Brezzi's chapter and the illustration permissions for the examples of Barbara's art, as well as for providing the images.

We thank Elizabeth Presa for allowing us to reproduce a photograph of her *Placental Economy* on this volume's cover. The artist's statement:

> As a way of giving a material form to Irigaray's ideas on a placental economy, I make plaster molds of a human placenta. The rich red blood of the placenta leaches into the wet plaster chemically fixing its image as a fresco. The network of blood vessels and translucent folds of skin translate through casting into complex ravines that could appear as the face of a landscape. It is as though each mold expresses the singularity of a mediation between two living beings in the form of a rotund opacity of folds, clots and the traces of damage from the birthing process (Presa, email to Burchill, November 26, 2024).

We thank Mimesis Edizioni for permission to reproduce in English translation chapter 10, "Intertwinements of Pictorial Research and Speculative

Effort: The Noetic Dance Between Barbara and Luce." This translation is based on the following chapters of *Quando il futurismo è donna. Barbara dei colori* (2009) by Francesca Brezzi, published by Mimesis Edizioni (an imprint of MIM Edizioni srl):

- *Il corpo magico della donna: le pitture placentarie* (pp. 63–72)

- *Un granda danza noetic tra Barbara e luce, un danza infinita* (pp. 63–72; including the images)

An earlier version of chapter 13, "Performing the Icon and Other Maternal Gestures," appeared in Rebekah Pryor's monograph, *Motherly: Reimagining the Maternal Body in Feminist Theology and Contemporary Art* (London: SCM Press, 2022).

Louise Burchill, Rebecca Hill, and James Sares

List of Abbreviations
(Works by Irigaray)

Books

BEW   *Between East and West: From Singularity to Community*. Translated by Stephen Pluháček. Columbia University Press, 2001. (Originally published as *Entre Orient et Occident. De la singularité à la communauté*. Grasset, 1999.)

C   *Conversations* with S. Pluháček and H. Bostic, J. Still, M. Stone, A. Wheeler, G. Howie, M. R. Miles and L. M. Harrington, H. A. Fielding, E. Grosz, M. Worton, and B. H. Midttun. Continuum, 2008.

CAC   *Le corps-à-corps avec la mère*. Les éditions de la pleine lune. Conference and interviews, 1981.

CFN   *Challenging a Fictitious Neutrality. Heidegger in Question*. Edited by Irigaray. Palgrave Macmillan, 2022.

DB   *Democracy Begins Between Two*. Translated by Kirsteen Anderson. Routledge, 2000. (Originally published as *La democrazia comincia a due*, Bollati-Boringhieri, 1994.)

EP   *Elemental Passions*. Translated by Joanne Collie and Judith Still. Routledge, 1992. (Originally published as *Passions élémentaires*, Minuit, 1982.)

ESD   *An Ethics of Sexual Difference*. Translated by Carolyn Burke and Gillian C. Gill. Cornell University Press, 1993. (Originally published as *Éthique de la différence sexuelle*, Minuit, 1984.)

FA   *The Forgetting of Air in Martin Heidegger*. Translated by Mary Beth Mader. University of Texas Press, 1999. (Originally published as *L'oubli de l'air. Chez Martin Heidegger*, Minuit, 1983.)

IB   *In the Beginning, She Was*. Bloomsbury, 2013.

ILTY   *I Love to You: Sketch of a Possible Felicity in History*. Translated by Alison Martin. Routledge, 1996. (Originally published as *J'aime à toi. Esquisse d'une félicité dans l'Histoire*, Grasset, 1992.)

IR   *The Irigaray Reader*. Edited by Margaret Whitford. Basil Blackwell, 1991.

JTN   *Je, tu, nous: Toward a Culture of Difference*. Translated by Alison Martin. Routledge, 1993. (Originally published as *Je, tu, nous: Pour une culture de la différence*, Grasset, 1990.)

KW   *Luce Irigaray: Key Writings*. Continuum, 2004.

ML   *Marine Lover of Friedrich Nietzsche*. Translated by Gillian C. Gill. Columbia University Press, 1991. (Originally published as *Amante marine: De Friedrich Nietzsche*, Editions de Minuit, 1980.)

NCE   *A New Culture of Energy: Beyond East and West*. Translated by Stephen Seely, Stephen Pluháček, and Antonia Pont. Columbia University Press, 2021.

PP   *Le Partage de la parole*, special lecture series 4, European Humanities Research Centre. University of Oxford/Legenda, 2001.

S   *Speculum of the Other Woman*. Translated by Gillian C. Gill. Cornell University Press, 1985. (Originally published as *Speculum. De l'autre femme*, Editions de Minuit, 1974.)

SA   *Speculum. De l'autre femme*. Editions de Minuit, 1974.

SG   *Sexes and Genealogies*. Translated by Gillian C. Gill. Columbia University Press, 1993. (Originally published as *Sexes et parentés*, Editions de Minuit, 1987.)

SN   *To Speak Is Never Neutral*. Translated by Gail Schwab. Continuum, 2002. (Originally published as *Parler n'est jamais neutre*, Editions de Minuit, 1985.)

SW   *Sharing the World*. Continuum, 2008.

TBB   *To Be Born: Genesis of a New Human Being*. Palgrave Macmillan, 2017.

TBT   *To Be Two*. Translated by Monique M. Rhodes and Marco F. Cocito-Monoc. Routledge, 2001. (Originally published as *Être Deux*, Grasset, 1997.)

TD   *Thinking the Difference: For a Peaceful Revolution*. Translated by Karin Montin. Continuum-Routledge, 1994. (Originally published as *Le Temps de la différence: Pour une révolution pacifique*, Libraire Générale française, Livre de poche, 1989.)

TS   *This Sex Which Is Not One*. Translated by Catherine Porter with Carolyn Burke. Cornell University Press, 1985. (Originally published as *Ce sexe qui n'en est pas un*, Minuit, 1977.)

TVB   Irigaray and Michael Marder. *Through Vegetal Being: Two Philosophical Perspectives*. Columbia University Press, 2016.

WL   *The Way of Love*. Translated by Heidi Bostic and Stephen Pluháček. Continuum, 2002. (Also published as *La Voie de l'amour*, Éditions Mimésis, 2016.)

Articles and Chapters

AB   "The Age of the Breath." In *Luce Irigaray: Key Writings*, translated by Katja van de Rakt, Staci von Boeckman, and Luce Irigaray. (Originally published as *Le temps du soufflé*, Christel Göttert Verlag, 1999.)

BTI   "Beyond Totem and Idol, the Sexuate Other." Translated by Karen I. Burke. *Continental Philosophy Review* 40, no. 4 (2007): 353–364.

CLB   "Interview: Cultivating a Living Belonging." Interview with Emily Anne Parker. *Journal of the British Society for Phenomenology* 46 no. 2: 109–116.

EST   "Entering a Space and a Time in the Feminine." In *La dona, metamorfosi de la modernita*, exhibition catalogue, Fundació Joan Miró, Barcelona, edited by Gladys Fabre. 2004.

HCA "How Could We Achieve Women's Liberation?" In *Thinking Life with Luce Irigaray: Language, Origin, Art, Love*, edited by Gail Schwab. State University of New York Press, 2020.

HM "How to Make Feminine Self-Affection Appear." In *Two or Three or Something: Maria Lassnig and Liz Larner*, exhibition catalogue. Kunsthaus Graz am Landesmuseum Joanneum, 2006.

JLI " 'Je—Luce Irigaray': A Meeting with Luce Irigaray." Interview with Elizabeth Hirsh and Gary A. Olson. *Hypatia: A Journal of Feminist Philosophy* 10, no. 2 (1995): 93–114.

NL "A Natal Lacuna." Translated by Margaret Whitford. *Women's Art Magazine* 58 (1994): 11–13. (Originally published as "Une lacune natale." *Le Nouveau Commerce* 62–63 [1985]: 39–47.)

PI "To Paint the Invisible." Translated by and interview with Helen Fielding. *Continental Philosophy Review* 37 (2004): 389–405.

TR "The Return." In *Rewriting Difference: Luce Irigaray and "the Greeks,"* edited by Athena Athanasiou and Elena Tzelepis. State University New York Press, 2010.

TSI "Towards the Sharing of an Invisible Touch." In *Charlie Murphy, the Anatomy of Desire*, edited by Violet McClean and Laura Fennell. Text+Work, 2010.

WDM "What Does It Mean to be Living?" Interview with Stephen D. Seely. *philoSOPHIA* 8, no. 2 (2018): 1–12.

WE "Women's Exile." Interview with Diana Adlam and Couze Venn. Translated by Couze Venn. *Ideology and Consciousness* 1 (1977): 62–76.

Introduction

Louise Burchill and Rebecca Hill

In one of her rare pieces of writing on the work of specific women artists, "How to Make Feminine Self-Affection Appear?" Luce Irigaray declares the basic question informing the endeavor of the sculptor-installation artist Liz Larner to be that of "How can I come and be in space?" Our culture, Irigaray adds, has systematically confounded space with body, in particular the maternal or feminine body. Hence, the question then becomes: "How could I"—a woman—"reappropriate space instead of being appropriated to the subjective spatial requirements of the other?" Of course, the rethinking of space in its multiple senses is central to Irigaray's philosophical project of articulating the ontology of sexual difference, as Irigaray scholars have long recognized. Yet, the reconfigured structuration of space—which is to say, the *topology*—Irigaray promulgates throughout her oeuvre, as well as the manifest implications such a reconceptualization holds for not only philosophy but other disciplines and practices as well, has remained insufficiently explored and elaborated. *Topologies of Sexual Difference: Space in Philosophy and Visual Art After Irigaray* focuses, for its part, on the transvaluation of space in the affirmation of sexual difference. The collection thematizes Irigarayan space as porous, fluid, continuous, and self-differentiating in contrast to conceptions of space as inert container or as homogeneous extension. Its aim is to demonstrate the importance of space's transvaluation for a recalibration of philosophy—one eschewing the coordinates of a metaphysics privileging the demonstrable, the bounded, the circumscribable, and the countable—and for new fashionings in the visual arts, to which Irigaray has attributed a crucial role in deconstructing the Western tradition's logic of calculation and containment, as well as, and above all, in elaborating a possible future for Western culture.

To our knowledge, this is the first edited volume to thematize Irigaray's ontology of space as such and to consider issues such as Irigaray's understanding of the relationship between space and matter. It is equally the first to focus on Irigaray's thinking on space in relation to the visual arts and to ponder Irigarayan space at work in the process of artistic creation. While several of its chapters have been composed specifically for this volume, the majority are based on papers first presented at meetings of the Luce Irigaray Circle, especially the meeting cohosted by RMIT University and the University of Melbourne in 2014, which was organized under the eponymous theme "Topologies of Sexual Difference." An important feature of this meeting was the exhibition of the work of eighteen women artists organized in parallel with the academic conference.[1] Three of the artist-researchers from the exhibition have contributed chapters to this volume and another, Elizabeth Presa, is the creator of the work that is depicted on the cover of this book.

Topologies of Sexual Difference is organized into four parts: (1) Differential Space; (2) Of Sensibility and the Elemental; (3) Feminine Genealogies; and (4) Sexuate Art in the Making. The chapters gathered under these headings address the conceptualization of space and topological relations in Irigaray's philosophy from multiple perspectives. They include original readings in the philosophy of sexual difference that consider Irigaray in relation to Simone de Beauvoir, Gilles Deleuze and Felix Guattari, Martin Heidegger, Friedrich Nietzsche, Plato, Gilbert Simondon, Sophocles' *Antigone*, and psychoanalysis. Their theoretical foci include the concept of topology, research into the origins of life, affect, the relation between the feminine and difference, the aesthetics of the maternal and placental, and a reading of Irigarayan morphology that accounts for trans embodiment. The final part of our volume is an especially novel contribution to Irigaray scholarship in which artist-researchers theorize their creative practice in relationship to the framework of sexuate difference. To these themes and foci, we would add that Irigaray's critical rethinking of space also suggests ways for thinkers and artists subjectified by the norms and concepts of Western metaphysics to become otherwise and to learn to perceive and to think in relation to other traditions, traditions that articulate different space-worlds irreducible to the violent totalizing projections of Western homogenous space.

Our volume's attention to philosophy and the visual arts as sites of Irigarayan space's operativity is testimony to the inseparability of Irigaray's "aesthetics" from her thinking of sexual difference. Just as sexual difference is, for Irigaray, the question that philosophy in our age must think through, and which, if accomplished, would bring about a new age in which sexuate humanity can cultivate care for our shared life (ESD, 9; SG, 187), so too "sexuate belonging" is "the most crucial dimension that art has to work out" (KW, 98). Irigaray contends that it is art's task "to create another reality by transforming the real that we are, that we live" (KW, 98). Accordingly, her calls for a new era of creativity in art punctuate her philosophical expositions of the conditions required for the recognition and cultivation of sexual difference. A compelling dramatization of the discursive interweaving of art and philosophy is found in the introduction of *In the Beginning, She Was*. Here, Irigaray first examines Pre-Socratic Greek philosophy's substitution of "man's house of language" (IB, 4) for a relationship between a thinker and a generative feminine other. Irigaray contends that the development of Ancient Greek thought leads to the construction of a closed world at Western man's disposal. In this closed universe, the feminine is reduced to a resource for man, and the vital creativity of her contribution is occluded from the system of representation. For Irigaray, the Ancient Greek constitution of world determines the evolution of Western metaphysics and social relations. To engender an open and shared world today, it is necessary for Western philosophy to take up the problem of sexual difference and to consider the cultivation of relational sexuate identity as a decisive stage of becoming human, of becoming woman or man. In this task, philosophy can be guided by art. Here, Irigaray conceives of art as a generalized and continuous practice that can "maintain and cultivate the between-us." Art is crucial for developing a sexuate philosophy "more appropriate for humanity as formed by beings-in-relation" (IB, 22).

Irigaray has also composed texts that take the question of art as a primary field of problematization. These essays extol the role of art in the transfiguration of reality and the new perspectives for artistic creation opened by the consideration of sexuate subjectivity.[2] Some of her art-focused texts engage with the work of specific women artists.[3] Among the works on women artists, her essay on Unica Zürn, "A Natal Lacuna," is the only text to have received sustained critical attention; her other essays on women artists are rarely referenced.[4] Arguably, the attention devoted to "A Natal Lacuna" is due to the vehemence of Irigaray's appraisal of both Zürn and of her work.[5] In this essay, Irigaray reads the fragmented and distorted forms characteristic of Zürn's paintings and drawings as a manifestation of Zürn's incapacity to detach herself from the phallocentric system of representation that is fundamental to Western culture (NL, 12). For Irigaray, Zürn remains trapped in a masculine imaginary in which women can only experience themselves in bits and pieces (NL, 12–13). Zürn fails to give expression to an imaginary in the feminine and fails, as a woman, to "enter into a [woman's] morphology" (NL, 13).

Of the critical responses to Irigaray's analysis of Zürn, the most influential has undoubtedly been Margaret Whitford's contention that Irigaray ascribes to women artists the task of creating beauty through the expression of a harmonious and whole feminine identity, a divine feminine, and a world of relations between women as well as the world of the sexuate couple (Whitford 1994, 15). In contrast, the creations of Zürn, and other modern women artists deploying fragmentation and distortion, are "ugly" figurations (JTN, 107–108; Whitford 1994, 15). While these figurations speak to the suffering and dismemberment of women in patriarchy, they fail to express a specifically feminine subjectivity, divine women and relations between women (JTN, 107–108; Whitford 1994, 15–16). For Whitford, Irigaray's framing of art as a means to express sexual difference valorizes figurative representation over abstraction on the grounds that only representational art can portray an "ideal" wholeness of woman's identity or auto-affection in the feminine (15). In this light, Whitford characterizes Irigaray's aesthetics as prescriptively conservative (16).

While we agree with Whitford's contention that Irigaray conceives of the task of art in terms of the project of articulating sexuate difference (1994, 16), we think that Irigaray's position on nonfigurative art is less prescriptively conservative than Whitford suggests. Indeed, when revisiting Whitford's reading of Irigaray's aesthetics in the 2010s, Elaine Miller and Linda Daley argue that Irigaray can be read to favor abstraction rather than any logic of representation (Miller 2010, 2011, 2016; Daley 2014, 2015). Not only does Irigaray emphasize color as opposed to form in a number of her art-focused texts but she equally pays particular attention to the role of invisible forces, such as light and sound waves, in producing the perceptual field. One passage from "How Can We Create Our Beauty?" is of especial interest to Miller and Daley given that it highlights the intrinsic connection between color and flesh and resonates with Irigaray's critique of Zürn's failure to wrest herself from "the morphology man reflects back to her" (NL, 12). Stating that women must break out of the forms in which patriarchal culture has imprisoned them if they are to exist, Irigaray cautions that this act of liberation is double-edged. On the one hand, the dissolution of forms created in the making of art can lead to women's own destruction instead of "inducing a second birth" (JTN, 109; trans. modified).[6] On the other hand, art making potentially enables us to "discover what flesh we have left." Color ". . . is what's left of life beyond forms [. . .]. When all meaning is taken away from us, there remains color, colors, in particular those corresponding to our sex" (JTN, 109). For Miller, these claims reveal something about transformative art. "In dissolving reified forms, a process that would include fragmentation, even the fragmentation of the body, new possibilities open up for reconfiguring them" (2011, 49). Miller continues, "[a] kind of abstract expressionism, an art of pure color without form . . . does have an important place in [Irigaray's] aesthetic theory, as a precondition for a new morphology of the sexualized body" (49). Daley, for her part, highlights the role Irigaray attributes to color in painting as that which renders visible the nonvisible forces (material, physical forces as well as "inner" and relational ones) that affect subjectivity's becoming. Daley focuses predominantly on "Flesh Colors" (KW), a text in which Irigaray notably proposes the adoption of the practice of painting in psychoanalytic treatment as a means of rectifying the "perceptual imbalance" occasioned by analysis' privileging of speech and hearing and the analysand's supine, "blind," position vis-à-vis the analyst (KW, 113). Crucially for our concerns here, Irigaray argues painting can remedy this imbalance because its objective (as Klee proclaimed) is "to *spatialize perception* and render *time simultaneous*" (KW, 114). The projection of past and future into the present is given expression in a spatial field, formed of/by color, and this process of painting helps the analysand to represent her or his perceptions and to form a perspective in space-time. A balance between hearing, sight and touch, sound and light can then be found, and this takes place through colors (KW, 114). What Daley retains from Irigaray's text (as well as from Irigaray's critical dialogues with Merleau-Ponty) is less, however, the intrinsic connection between space and color than Irigaray's attention to "the painter's task to think through the materiality of their medium" (Daley 2014, 377). It is this form of embodied thinking, "a making considered as a work carried out *inside* subjectivity," and not "representations of women *in* art," that is the concern of Irigaray's aesthetic of sexual difference (Daley 2014, 392; citing Irigaray, WL, 115).

Materiality and abstraction, color and spatialization, subjective becoming in the making of art and new configurations of the sexualized body: all these components of an Irigarayan aesthetic irreducible to the representations of an "ideal self" are elaborated and explored in the chapters of this volume on the visual arts, as we shall shortly see. Here, though, a final argument for abstract or nonrepresentational art as an appropriate style for the expression of women's sexual specificity needs to be noted—especially as, in this instance, it comes from Irigaray herself. We have already mentioned that in "How to Make Feminine Self-Affection Appear"—one of Irigaray's rare texts concerning the work of specific women artists—one of the artists she considers is the nonrepresentational sculptor-installation artist Liz Larner. In striking contrast to her appraisal of Unica Zürn's art, Irigaray deems many characteristics of Larner's work to "express self-affection in the feminine," characteristics that pertain, crucially, to the artist's investigation of space. Judging Larner's "basic question" to be that of "[h]ow can I come and be in space?" Irigaray notes that the artist "seems to be in search of a spatial architecture which could be appropriated to feminine subjectivity, even in its intimate dimensions" (HM, 58). Irigaray describes the logic and properties that Larner mobilizes in this endeavor as "a volume without mass, an expansion without weight, a density without gravity, a presence without visible form(s), and also [. . .] fluidity, malleability, instability, transformation, evanescence, etc." (HM, 57). What is remarkable is the resemblance these properties and logic, so described, bear to the properties and logic attributed to woman's morphology in Irigaray's crucial chapter "Volume Without Contour" from *Speculum.* Compare, for example, "a form which is in(de)finitely transformed without closing up on her appropriation" (IR, 56); "metamorphoses where no totality ever consists" (IR, 59); and an "expansion that she is not, never will be at any moment, as a definable universe" (IR, 59). All of these properties characterize what Irigaray names "an other topo-(logy) of jouissance" (IR, 56). This topology is a transposition of the phallocentric framing of woman's body as lack and abyss into an affirmative figuration of unbounded, ever-transformative volume. In short, in appraising Larner's search for auto-affection, Irigaray is led back, via the relation to space that is inherent to the work of the sculptor/installation artist, to her early reflections on the redeployment of space as the necessary condition for the expression of feminine sexual specificity.

The properties of space Irigaray describes in the passages that we have just quoted from "Volume Without Contour" are what express this space's topology. This is the topology of feminine jouissance that is irreducible to the topology of "the Subject," defined in isomorphism with masculine auto-affection (S, 133). In *An Ethics of Sexual Difference*, Irigaray explicitly designates the properties characterizing this other topology as "the 'half-open' and fluid sets, as well as anything articulating the problem of edges, of the passage between things, or the fluctuations taking place between different thresholds" (ESD, 123; trans. modified). Other properties mobilized by Irigaray include continuity, folding, overlap, the passage between inside and outside, or porosity, overflow, nonclosure, connectedness, retouch, self-touching, indeterminate expansion, and continuous transformation or self-differentiation. All such properties—or qualitative relations—must be understood to be properly topological, as distinguished from quantitative properties such as lengths, angles, and areas that depend on the specific measurement and exact shapes of objects, which form the domain of geometry. Unlike geometry, the mathematical discipline of topology disregards measurement and scale and deals only with the structure of space qua space and with the essential shape of figures. What makes topological properties so crucial in understanding shapes and spaces is that they pertain to characteristics that remain invariant under continuous deformations, such as stretching or bending, but not tearing or gluing. In the classic example, a coffee cup and a donut are considered the same (homeomorphic) because one can be deformed into the other without cutting or attaching new parts. In other words, they are topologically equivalent spaces because both have one hole and the number of holes is a topological property preserved under continuous one-to-one mappings. These qualitative relations are fundamental for Irigaray's thought because they are fluid concepts that can give sense to the becomings of sexual difference.

～

The four chapters of this volume's first part, "Differential Space," precisely focus on the topological properties of Irigarayan space, preeminently as differentiated and self-differentiating, to explore what these properties permit to come into being and what they allow to be thought. The first two chapters—Kristin Sampson's "*Chôra* Reconsidered in View of a Topology of Sexual Difference" and Louise Burchill's " 'Putting the Accent Back on Space': Irigaray's Topology, *Chôra*, and Feminine Jouissance"—attend to the topology of feminine auto-affection that Irigaray delineates in *Specu-*

lum of the Other Woman, as well as her other early works. Sampson and Burchill draw, in this context, on the concept of space (chôra / χώρα in Greek) formulated by Plato in the *Timaeus*, with both contributors highlighting the quality of self-differentiation that Plato attributes to chôra in its originary "unordered," "non-homogenised" state. Sampson offers an original reading of one of Plato's images of chôra, that of a winnowing basket. Succinctly stated, Plato likens chôra to a winnowing basket because of its being full of disparate potencies (qua beings in becoming) that cause it to shake and sway, just as chôra then shakes these potencies in turn. It is, precisely, through this *unordered* shaking and swaying that chôra imparts an *order* to the potencies, which, by virtue of this motion, are grouped in constellations according to their various sizes and weights. The question Sampson's chapter raises is what rethinking this image of the winnowing basket might proffer for a reconsideration of the concept of space. Taking Irigaray's reflections on space as an interval of difference as a point of departure, Sampson examines what an incorporation of the interval—volatile, unordered movement—might contribute to such a reconceptualization of space.

Burchill's chapter argues that Irigaray's reading of chôra is problematic insofar as Irigaray positions chôra as paradigmatic of both metaphysical determinations of space and phallogocentrically determined femininity. For Burchill, this gesture occults Plato's preliminary characterizations of chôra as a differential, ever-changing manifold that is isomorphic with the very space that Irigaray herself seeks to recover. Burchill's broader concern, however, is to establish that the reconceptualization of time and space Irigaray sees as necessary for sexual difference consists primarily in a redeployment of *space* such that space is no longer subordinated to time nor reducible to undifferentiated, homogeneous extension. To these traditional determinations of space, as well as, more specifically, to Lacan's elaboration of the topology of the subject, Irigaray precisely opposes what she names "an other topology" (IR, 56). And she does so not only discursively, Burchill underlines, but also schematically: Irigaray's famed morphological models being, *by definition*, equally topological ones. Within this framework, Burchill focuses her analyses on three pivotal aspects of Irigaray's topological refashioning of space. The first is that, as seen, of Irigaray's resistance to recognizing Plato's chôra as a feminine space displaying two very distinct topologies. The second consists in the prognosis Irigaray was to deliver of Lacan's psychoanalytic refashioning of women's traditional association with space: "Putting the accent back on space was—perhaps—to restore some chance for the jouissance of the other—woman" (TS, 98). And thirdly, the final aspect of Irigaray's refashioning of space examined by Burchill consists of the philosophical underpinnings of Irigaray's choice of topology as the formal organon most suited for her description of female sexuate specificity.

The third chapter in part 1 is by Annu Dahiya, "The Deepest and Most Initial Vital Structure Is Topological": A Feminist Philosophy of the Origins of Cellular Life with Irigaray and Simondon." Dahiya reads Irigaray with mid-twentieth-century French philosopher Gilbert Simondon as a way into thinking about the origins of cellular life. Both address the question of life in their respective works, Irigaray most notably in *An Ethics of Sexual Difference* and Simondon in *Individuation in Light of Notions of Form and Information*. Simondon pays specific attention to the critical importance of cellular membranes, which engender a specific kind of topological space that is unique to life. Irigaray calls attention, for her part, as Dahiya underlines, to how the biological sciences have been slow to study the permeability of membranes, something Irigaray argues has an affinity with the "feminine universe" (C, 6). For Dahiya, the attention Irigaray places on embodiment, gestation, and birth can powerfully frame and guide new research into origins. Simondon makes an allied claim, arguing that scientists attempting to understand the condition of life by trying to create life from inert matter are doomed to fail because they forget that the topological condition of life is primordial "in the living being qua living being" ([1964] 2020, 250). In fact, the essence of the living being—its particular topology—fundamentally "cannot be known based on the physics and chemistry that typically use Euclidean space" (250). Dahiya argues that Simondon complicates Irigaray's claim by focusing on the concept of space that life requires, writing in detail about the importance of the polarity of the living membrane. Both French philosophers understand the nature of life decades before contemporary origins of life research begins to grapple with these ideas. For Dahiya, thinking Irigaray with Simondon can thus give us the tools to understand one of the most enduring philosophical questions: how life first began.

In the final chapter of part 1, "Carnal Being-with: Irigaray in Dialogue with Heidegger," Jennifer Carter argues that a differential space is generated in the dynamic meeting between two ontologically different subjects. Carter traces Irigaray's thinking of space through her engagements with Heidegger in *The Forgetting of Air, To Be Two* and her recent work, *Challenging a Fictitious Neutrality*. Carter's chapter attends to Irigaray's deployment of the concepts of threshold, air, interval, and passage as ways of reconceiving spacing with others. Touch is a focus of Carter's reading. Through relations of touch, Carter maintains, Irigaray opens a spatial dynamism at the meeting place between irreducible subjects. This locus is a threshold where subjects form an affective exchange that returns a subject to themselves and propels a transcending of self in relation with others. The space between ontologically different subjects is a differentiated space that necessitates new modes of speaking and thinking of spacing. For Carter, these Irigarayan intersubjective modes of spacing are more comprehensive than Heideggerian modes of spatialization, which remain solipsistic.

In part 2 "Of Sensibility and the Elemental," Ellen Mortensen and Rebecca Hill consider Irigaray's theorization of space as the instantiation of the four elements—air, earth, fire, and water—in three extraordinary books that Irigaray composed between 1980 and 1983, namely *Marine Lover: Of Friedrich Nietzsche, Elemental Passions,* and *The Forgetting of Air in Martin Heidegger.* Mortensen's chapter develops a reading of Irigaray as a philosopher of "affective poiesis." In Mortensen's argument, affective poiesis is a sensuous mode of thinking that is marked by sexual difference, as this is articulated in Irigaray's musings on the elemental and, above all, on the element of earth, which she understands, together with the other three elements, as the condition of possibility for human existence and love between and among the sexes. Mortensen's chapter focuses primarily on Irigaray's intervention into Heidegger's poetic meditations on the onto-logical conditions for human dwelling on earth. The chapter then shows how Irigaray's elemental meditation, as a projection of affective poiesis, might find nourishment in and shed light on the ethico-aesthetic project of Deleuze and Guattari. In "To Speak of Immemorial Waters: Irigaray with Nietzsche," Hill argues that *phusis,* for Irigaray, is a sexuate giving of life and precedes and exceeds the logic and language of Western metaphysics. Hill contends that there are many concepts that express *phusis* in Irigaray. They include woman, nature, the feminine, the envelope, and immemorial waters. These concepts are often interpreted by Irigaray's readers in ontic terms to designate actual beings, especially cis women. Yet, while these concepts are related to women in Irigaray's corpus, they designate in a fundamental sense the very giving of life. Hill's chapter focuses on the saying of immemorial waters from *Marine Lover of Friedrich Nietzsche.* She relates Irigaray's saying of immemorial waters to Zarathustra's teaching of fidelity to the earth in Nietzsche. Hill argues that while Irigaray is critical of the elision of the maternal and the feminine in Nietzsche, Irigaray's saying of immemorial waters is also a tribute to Nietzsche.

The final chapter in part 2 is Athena Colman's "'A *Morphé* in Continual Gestation': The Sensible Transcendental, Gesture, and Morphology in Irigaray." As Colman explains, Irigaray's account of morphology is given through her concept of the sensible transcendental, in terms of which the transcendence of one human subject to another is always also sensible or immanent, and what is sensible is always transcendent. By attending to Irigarayan morphology as distinct from the teleology of anatomy, Colman can specify a concretization of the sensible transcendental in Irigaray's thinking of gesture. This argument is established through reading Irigaray's engagement with Sigmund Freud's fort/da game (SG, 91–104). Colman posits sensible transcendental gesture as a thinking of the future anterior of sexual difference. She argues that this approach offers resources for thinking trans subjectivities and embodiment, thereby actualizing the manifold meaning of Irigaray's claim that nature and sexual difference is "at *least* two."

The contributors to part 3 "Feminine Genealogies" engage with Irigaray's spatial thought as a topology of relations between women as creators of thought and of politics, or, again, of art as this intersects with philosophy. In chapter 8 "Simone de Beauvoir and Luce Irigaray: A Genealogy Reconsidered," Gail Schwab reveals underappreciated resonances between Beauvoir and Irigaray. Schwab argues that while neither Beauvoir nor Irigaray ever fully recognized the importance of their intellectual kinship, there are significant resonances between them. This chapter looks closely at those texts where Irigaray discusses Beauvoir and her active contributions to feminism and to philosophy, as well as texts where their respective thinking seems to exhibit certain similarities or affinities, particularly as it concerns sexual difference, woman as other, and becoming. In "Luce Irigaray and the Fate of Antigone: Respect for Sexuate Identity" Marguerite La Caze elaborates on the evolution and tensions in Irigaray's many engagements with Sophocles' Antigone. In "Between Myth and History: The Tragedy of Antigone," a chapter of Irigaray's *In the Beginning, She Was* from 2012, Irigaray identifies with Antigone's exclusion and asserts the brother-sister relationship as the basis for conceptualizing sexuate identity and difference. La Caze suggests that this is oddly dissonant with Irigaray's earlier readings of Antigone in *Speculum of the Other Woman* and *An Ethics of Sexual Difference*, which affirm neither an identification with Antigone nor the brother-sister relationship as representative of sexuate identity and difference. La Caze's chapter explores the distinct possibilities for sexuate identity presented by Irigaray's more recent reading of *Antigone* and asks what it means to valorize Antigone today.

The final chapter in part 3, "Intertwinements of Pictorial Research and Speculative Effort: The Noetic Dance Between Barbara and Luce," is written by Francesca Brezzi, a prominent Italian feminist philosopher. Brezzi develops a comparative reading of several texts by Irigaray and two series of paintings executed in the 1970s and 1980s by the Italian artist known as Barbara (a pseudonym adopted by Olga Biglieri) to demonstrate that Irigaray's theses about sexual difference find a transposition, in color and signs, in Barbara's paintings. Barbara is unique in having written extensively about her artistic practice in relation to Irigaray's thought in the last decades of the twentieth century. The painter chronicles what she characterizes as the "mysterious harmony" between Irigaray's "words-thought-life" and her own "painting-thought-life" in her autobiography, *Barbara dei colori* (Biglieri Scurto, 1998). Drawing on Barbara's autobiography, Brezzi presents Barbara's own comprehension of her work's relation to Irigaray's philosophy and a careful analysis of Irigarayan tenets that would find a reverberation in Barbara's art. Presented here as a single unified chapter, Brezzi's analyses comprise, in fact, two distinct sections of the monograph she published on Barbara in 2009 (Brezzi). The translation of these sections, by Edoardo Bellando and Tamara Lee (revised by Caroline Petricola and, subsequently, by Louise Burchill), was commissioned specifically for this volume. By way of contextualization of certain aspects of Brezzi's argument, we have provided an introduction to her chapter in situ; here we would simply underline the astonishment Barbara relates having felt on first reading Irigaray and discovering that the fluid, manifold, and infinitely open expansion that she was seeking to express in her painting was likewise, for Irigaray, the space characterizing women's corporeal and subjective specificity.

The authors of the chapters comprising this volume's fourth and final part, "Sexuate Art in the Making," are practicing artists engaged in thinking with Irigaray through the materiality of their respective media. We think that the insights and inflexions they offer on Irigaray's aesthetics are all the more interesting and generative for being composed in relation to the differences and specificities of each woman's art practice. Following Irigaray and Daley, we could say that making/thinking takes place inside subjectivity and outside subjectivity (KW, 114; Daley 2014, 377). Making/

thinking is a matter of, and a relation to, other-than-human forces. This topological torsion of inside and outside, this reverberation of speculative effort and material/spatial endeavor, is an engagement with Irigaray's thought of a kind that has rarely been explicated by practicing artists. To our knowledge, the only other artist to write about the relationship between their practice and the aspects of Irigaray's thought of interest to them is Barbara, the painter that Brezzi discusses in chapter 10.

With Jacqueline Taylor's "Painterly Poetics and Difference in the Making," we return to the question of abstraction in relation to the production of sexuate art considered earlier in this introduction. Taylor proposes a new perspective in which the expression of sexual difference is located in the very materiality and the process of making of abstract painting once abstract painting is itself rethought in the manner of Irigaray's refashioning of space-time. Taylor's argument is multilayered: she begins with a recapitulation of the fraught relationship between women and abstraction as this has played itself out in the context of modernist and postmodernist art practice. Suffice it to recall here that modernism's anointment of abstract painting as the dominant paradigm of twentieth-century art was accompanied by a discursive encoding of both the artwork and the artists as quintessentially masculine. Many feminist artists in the 1970s accordingly rejected abstract painting for its perceived phallocratic values and conventions. For the women who did continue to engage with abstract painting and the articulation of sexual difference, the aspects of Irigaray's work of most interest tended to be her poetic deployment of language along with her schematization of the feminine in terms of qualities such as heterogeneity, fluidity, plurality, and amorphousness. To translate qualities such as these into abstract painting, women artists adopted what Taylor calls "a painterly language and aesthetic that utilizes flux, flow, fluidity and tactility in its form and materiality." Yet the feminine aesthetic so developed, Taylor argues, remains defined by visual and formal characteristics that *represent* the feminine and sexual difference, even if these characteristics are themselves abstract in nature (such as swirls, curvilinear or spherical shapes, and the properties of paint). In contrast, Taylor proposes to rethink the very entity of abstract painting in terms resonant with Irigaray's topological refashioning of classical geometric space as a multidimensional and indefinitely shifting space. Abstract painting then takes the form of a continuous spatiality that is characterized by mobility and flux in its internal structure. The unfolding and enfolding of subjective forces and singularities that take place through the process of making is the locus of difference. For Taylor, sexual difference is but one type of difference among others that is manifested through this becoming.

In "Irigaray and the Baroque: Exploring Sexual Difference Through Creative Practice," Danielle Hamilton thinks Irigarayan difference with Deleuze's concept of the baroque fold and links this to her own art making (Deleuze, 1993). Hamilton attends to Irigaray's famous argument that sexual difference should be conceived as an ongoing, creative project between the sexes. As part of that project, Hamilton considers Irigaray's account of language in terms of full-bodied communication practices untethered from the primacy of speech. According to Irigaray, we are positioned in the realm of embodied language—a language constituted through our bodies to express our needs and desires and to enable us to live. Irigaray discusses how women might explore and materialize morphologies appropriate to their own bodily becoming in these terms (NL). Hamilton explains that this offered her a tantalizing possibility of reinhabiting and reinventing her bodily becoming through art practice. This dynamic capacity for becoming, central to Deleuze's and Irigaray's thought, inspired Hamilton's making of "Entanglement," an art installation consisting of large-scale gestural paintings on plexiglass sheets that shift and transform according to proximity. "Entanglement" was also a response to a performance by a musician friend, whom Hamilton then invited to compose a flute piece in response to her own emerging artwork. The new forms of language that emerged contemporaneously in Hamilton's and her friend's respective works are, therefore, the expression of a double creation, anchored in a woman-to-woman relationship. This is the invention of a language between women enabled by the cultivation and respect of a space of shared but never appropriative sensation.

The final chapter in this volume is Rebekah Pryor's "The Icon and the Absent Other." Like Hamilton and Taylor, Pryor is invested in the invention of a new creative language. Unlike her co-contributors in part 4, however, Pryor's artistic and theoretical concern is with representational art and particularly the Christian iconography of Mary. In distinction from the "idol of motherhood" generated by the Christian church's fixation on Mary as virgin mother, Pryor sets out to represent the motherly body as sexuate, constantly animated, multiple, and relational. In this sense, her endeavor aligns closely with the task of reappropriating space that Irigaray sees as vital for women. Pryor's work *Performing the Icon* consists of a series of twelve photographic collages, each depicting a single gesturing figure, whose maternal relation to a child is suggested only by her posture or gestures, extended toward or enfolding an absent other. *Performing the Icon* constitutes a new iconographic language *and* subverts the traditional representation of the female body by having the maternal body move with such autonomy that "she eludes objectivation in making space for relation." It is by virtue of this space that the woman and child maintain their uniqueness in respect of each other, as Pryor emphasizes in her chapter by recalling that the third space of the Irigarayan interval safeguards the difference between two subjects. All in all, Pryor's project can be understood as an exploration—in thought and in embodied gesture—of not only how to represent such a space for relation but also how to vitally realize it.

What has emerged over the course of this introduction is undeniably the polysemic nature of Irigarayan space. Many of our contributors draw on Irigaray's reconceptualization of space as a multidimensional multiplicity, ever changing and uncircumscribable, as first formulated in *Speculum*. Some of these contributors equally stress though, along with others in this volume, Irigaray's various formulations of a space of relationality: a gathering-together of relations, to oneself, to the other, and to others (both human and nonhuman). To this nexus of relationality, Rebekah Pryor adds the relation to the divine. Whatever be, however, the specific topologies examined in the chapters in this volume, that which is axiomatic is the importance Irigaray's transvaluation of space holds for the articulation of sexual difference in a reconfigured thought and new era of creativity in art, which is to say, for a transformation of the real that we are, for the real that we live.

Notes

1. The exhibition took place at the Georges Paton Gallery. The exhibiting artists were Cherelyn Brearley, Janet Burchill, Virginia Fraser, Helen Johnson, Marina Kassianidou, Danielle Hamilton, Joanne Makas, Alex Martinis Roe, Caroline Phillips, Kerrie Poliness, Elizabeth Presa, Julieanna Preston, Grace Pundyk, Utako Shindo Kanai, Tania Smith, Jacqueline Taylor, Terry Taylor, and Alison Thomson.

2. These include "To Paint the Invisible" (PI); "The Fecundity of a Sexuate Art" (KW); "Flesh Colours" (SG); and "How Can We Create Our Beauty?" (JTN).

3. These include "A Natal Lacuna" (NL), on the German surrealist artist and writer Unica Zürn; "Entering a Space and Time in the Feminine" (EST), a catalogue essay for an exhibition on representations of women in modern art,

including work by Georgia O'Keeffe, Niki de Saint Phalle, Tarsila do Amaral, Picasso, Matisse, and Klee; and "How to Make Feminine Self-Affection Appear" (HM), a text that focuses on the work of the painter Maria Lassnig and the sculptor-installation artist Liz Larner. Irigaray has also written on the work of the contemporary woman artist Charlie Murphy: "Towards the Sharing of an Invisible Touch" (TSI).

4. The exception here is Elaine Miller's commentary on "Entering a Space and Time in the Feminine" in her "Beyond the Madonna: Revisiting Luce Irigaray's Aesthetics," 51–52.

5. Chronology also plays a large part in this reception: up until 2005, Irigaray's text on Zürn constituted her unique piece of critical writing on a specific corpus of artwork and was read, on its publication in English translation in 1994, as a paradigmatic expression of Irigaray's aesthetics.

6. It is pertinent to note in this context that Unica Zürn committed suicide in 1970, at the age of 54.

References

Biglieri Scurto, Olga ("Barbara"). 1998. *Barbara dei colori*. Centro Internazionale Antinoo per l'Arte.

Brezzi, Francesca. 2009. *Quando il futurismo è donna. Barbara dei colori.* MIMESIS, Saggi e narrazioni di estetica e filosofia.

Daley, Linda. 2014. "Luce Irigaray's Aesthetic." *Multidisciplinary Journal of Gender Studies* 3 no. 1: 373–395.

Daley, Linda. 2015. "Rendering Visible: Painting and Sexuate Subjectivity." *Educational Philosophy and Theory* 47 no. 6: 608–621.

Deleuze, Gilles. (1988) 1993. *The Fold: Leibniz and the Baroque.* Translated by Tom Conley. University of Minnesota Press.

Miller, Elaine. 2010. "Reconsidering Irigaray's Aesthetics." In *Returning to Irigaray*, edited by Elaine Miller and Maria Cimitile. SUNY Press.

Miller, Elaine. 2011. "Beyond the Madonna: Revisiting Luce Irigaray's Aesthetics." In *Thinking with Irigaray*, edited by Sabrina L. Hom, Serena J. Khader, and Mary C. Rawlinson. SUNY Press.

Miller, Elaine. 2016. "Irigaray and Kristeva on Anguish in Art" In *Engaging the World: Thinking After Irigaray*, edited by Mary Rawlinson. SUNY Press.

Simondon, Gilbert. (1964) 2020. *Individuation in Light of Notions of Form and Information.* Translated by Taylor Adkins. University of Minnesota Press.

Whitford, Margaret. 1994. Woman with Attitude. *Women's Art Magazine* 60: 15–17.

Part One

Differential Space

Chapter One

Chôra Reconsidered in
View of a Topology of Sexual Difference

KRISTIN SAMPSON

The two most common classical Greek words for place are *topos* and *chôra*.[1] In Plato's *Timaeus*, however, the "place" or "space" perhaps most commonly known as *chôra*—which is connoted as feminine—famously receives a multitude of names. It is called not merely "ever-existing place" but equally "mother," "necessity," "all-embracing," "receptacle," "nurse," "mixing-bowl," and "moulding-stuff," to mention just a few of its many designations. Over the past decades, *chôra* has received a lot of attention, not least from a feminist perspective. In addition to Luce Irigaray, others who have reflected on *chôra* and the imagery of the *Timaeus* include Jacques Derrida, Elizabeth Grosz, Julia Kristeva, and John Sallis. The present chapter considers an aspect of *chôra* that has received comparatively little attention, namely the image of the winnowing basket. This image is introduced at a point in Plato's text where *chôra* emerges as a kind of unordered receptacle of potentialities. It is filled with potential power but sways in an uneven and unbalanced manner by virtue of being affected by unordered shaking. The question this chapter raises is what rethinking this image of the winnowing basket might proffer for a reconsideration of the concept of space. Taking Irigaray's reflections on space as an interval of difference as my point of departure, I wish to examine, in other words, what an incorporation of volatile, unordered movement might contribute to a reconceptualization of space.

Before turning to Irigaray, I will first take a closer look at *chôra* in Plato's *Timaeus*, with special attention to the image of the winnowing basket. I will then say something briefly about Irigaray's reading of *chôra* and Plato's myth of the cave before taking up her suggestion that the Western tradition's conception of space and time could—or should—be reconsidered, which I propose to do here precisely in light of the image of the winnowing basket.

The Feminine Figure *Chôra*

In the *Timaeus* we are presented with the famous description of the generation of cosmos as a birth involving two parents, both a mother and a father. As Plato writes at *Timaeus* 50c–d: "[W]e must conceive of three kinds (*genê tritta*),—the Becoming (*to gignomenon*), that 'Wherein' it becomes (*to en hô gignetai*), and the source 'Wherefrom' (*to hothen*) the becoming is copied and produced (*phuetai*). Moreover, it is proper to liken the Recipient to the Mother, the Source to the Father, and what is engendered between these two to the Offspring." This passage brings, for the first time, a mother into the picture. Timaeus had previously tried to formulate a cosmology merely with two principles: that which becomes and its source. At this point, however, he realizes that he has forgotten about the third necessary principle, namely "that wherein it becomes:" the receptacle or mother. This receiving principle is also called *chôra* and, through this depiction as a mother, *chôra* emerges as a feminine-maternal figure. The term *chôra* is explicitly used for this maternal, receiving principle a little later in the text: "[. . .] a third Kind (*triton genos on*) is ever-existing Place (*to tês chôras aei*), which admits not of destruction, and provides room for all things that have birth, itself being apprehensible by a kind of bastard reasoning by the aid of non-sensation, barely an object of belief; for when we regard this we dimly dream and affirm that it is somehow necessary that all that exists should exist in some spot (*en tini topô*) and occupying some place (*chôran*) [. . .]" (*Timaeus* 52b–c). While rendered as "place" in the translation of this passage, the word *chôra* can be translated in several ways. The two main categories of translation are, firstly, that of "space," "room," or "place" and, secondly, that of "land" or "country" (Liddell and Scott 1994). However, none of the terms involved here apply perfectly to *chôra* in the *Timaeus*. Both "space" and "place," for instance, have other, more common, words in Greek: *to kenon* is used for space, that is, empty space, and *topos* is the customary word for place. That said, at this point in the *Timaeus* the word *topos* is used synonymously with *chôra*, as can be seen in the use of *en tini topô* ("in some spot") in the quote from *Timaeus* 52c above. It is, though, impossible for *chôra* to be *a* place, in the sense of any specific place. It—or, rather, "she," and in the following I will refer to *chôra* by the feminine pronoun to underline the feminine-maternal connotation inherent to this notion in Plato's *Timaeus*—has been named as all-embracing and qualified as a necessary condition for the procreation of the existing beings of sense perception. *Chôra* is thus rather the place of all places. She is the soil in which all transient beings of the world of sense perception are sown, but she cannot herself be, as such, a specific place or ground perceivable by the senses. *Chôra* is the eternal ever-existing Place: *to tês chôras aei*. And, since she is depicted as the place of everything that comes into existence, she is without a place herself. Attempting to read *chôra* as akin to *topos* carries thereby the risk of assimilating the chorology of Plato to the topology of Aristotle, which is something against which John Sallis (1999, 115), along with other commentators, have warned.[2]

Nor for that matter can *chôra* be understood as mere space, in the sense of an empty space that receives everything within itself. This becomes evident through some of the other images deployed in the *Timaeus*. As mentioned above, the third necessary kind Plato introduces to account for "wherein" all things become is given a number of different names, of which "necessity" (*anagkê*), "receptacle" (*hupodochê*), "nurse" (*tithênê*), and *chôra* (*Timaeus* 48a, 49a, 52b–c) are just a few. Timaeus also refers to her as the "bowl" (*kratêra*) in which the Demiurge blended and mixed the soul of cosmos (*Timaeus* 41d), as well as the "moulding-stuff" (*ekmageion*) for everything, comparing her in this respect to gold that is molded into many forms and figures (*Timaeus* 50b–c)—which is a point Jacques Derrida takes up in his interpretation.[3] Likened to gold, *chôra* can hardly be space, at least not an empty space. Through this image, *chôra* seems to be infused with a certain materiality. If the gold itself was not substantial—relatively solid, hard, and resistant—it would be unable to display the figures imprinted in it. Yet, to receive the generated imprints, the gold needs to be liquid as well as solid, since a complete lack of liquidity would make it too adamant to receive imprints of any kind, just as a complete lack of solidity would make the imprinting akin to writing on water. Portrayed as gold, *chôra* is therefore clearly *something* and not nothing or some form of empty space.

This granted, let me now turn to the image of *chôra* as a winnowing basket.

The Image of the Winnowing Basket

The image of the winnowing basket (*Timaeus* 52e) is introduced in a passage where *chôra* appears as a kind of unordered container of potentialities. Filled with potential power, she is not evenly balanced but "sways unevenly," "shaken" by the forms she receives. Plato quite explicitly describes *chôra* as filled with forces. He writes: "but owing to being filled with potencies that are neither similar nor balanced, in no part of herself is she equally balanced, but sways unevenly in every part, and is herself shaken by these forms and shakes them in turn as she is moved" (*Timaeus* 52e). Presented as this uncontrolled, powerful force, *chôra* seems irrational and dangerous. This is the point at which the image of the winnowing basket is introduced to explain the function and nature of *chôra* as the container of all the potencies:

> [T]he forms, as they are moved, fly continually in various directions and are dissipated; just as the particles that are shaken and winnowed by the sieves (*hôsper ta upo tôn plokanôn*) and other instruments used for the cleansing of corn fall in one place if they are solid and heavy, but fly off and settle elsewhere if they are spongy and light. [. . .] Before that time, in truth, all these things were in a state devoid of reason or measure [. . .]. (*Timaeus* 52e–53a)

Curiously, this description of mother *chôra* through the image of the winnowing basket brings out the characteristic of *chôra* as an entity or instance that functions as an ordering principle. By means of her unordered shaking—her unbalanced and uneven swaying—the winnowing basket sorts the various elements contained within, that is, the becoming beings. Through this image of the winnowing basket *chôra* appears double, both unordered and ordering. Moreover, it is through the unordered shaking and swaying that the ordering occurs. In other words, the cosmos, which literally means the organized and ordered universe, emerges through the disorganized motions of *chôra*.

Furthermore, in her likeness to a winnowing basket, *chôra* is obviously not simply a passive recipient. It is through her shaking and swaying that the becoming beings are ordered, and this shaking and movement is not something that is being done to the winnowing basket. There is no mention or any hint of anyone doing the shaking of *chôra* in Plato's text. Neither is *chôra* herself portrayed as the agent of this unordered swaying and shaking. The unordered motion is rather portrayed as inherent to *chôra* herself. In a sense, this complicates the very opposition of activity and passivity as well. The image of *chôra* as a winnowing basket thus emerges as inherently ambiguous, both in terms of order and disorder and in terms of the active-passive dualism.

One of the other names attributed to *chôra* shows a similar ambiguity with respect to passivity and activity. *Ekmageion* is used by Plato in several different, and apparently conflicting, senses. It can signify a model, an impression or imprint, but also that on or in which an impression is made. Another of its senses is that of an entity that wipes something off, like a napkin.[4] As such, *ekmageion*, as Emanuela Bianchi points out, "holds together at once, and indeterminately, the mutually contradictory meanings of mark receiving, mark giving, and mark removing" (2006, 128).[5] *Chôra* is not, therefore, the only inherently ambiguous image or name used by Plato in the *Timaeus* in respect of this third necessary principle.

To summarize, *chôra* is something, not nothing, which sways and shakes in an unordered motion by means of which the order of the cosmos is created. As embodying this volatile motion, *chôra* cannot be conceived as either causal, or mechanical, or as instilling cosmos with a deterministic structure. Instead, as unevenly shaking and swaying, she inscribes the world with a certain unpredictability and openness. I would argue that she thereby also infuses cosmos with difference, in the sense that the very unorderliness of her motion operates as a differentiating function.[6] The fact that this differentiating principle is also portrayed as a feminine-maternal figure brings us to Irigaray and her thinking of sexual difference.

Irigaray's *Chôra*

On Irigaray's reading, Plato's expositions of space—*chôra*—in the *Timaeus* establish the feminine as a place solely for the constitution of the masculine.[7] As she writes in *Speculum of the Other Woman*: "She is always a clean slate ready for the father's impressions, which she forgets as they are made. Unstable, inconsistent, fickle, unfaithful, she seems ready to receive all beings into herself. Keeping no trace of them. Without memory. She herself is without figure or proper form" (S, 307). This conception of *chôra* as an almost forgotten and ungraspable maternal principle is, of course, something Irigaray criticizes. Femininity and space need to be rethought and created in new and different ways.

What I hope to bring out in my reading of Plato's *Timaeus* is that his portrayal of *chôra* is more ambiguous and offers more resources for such a reconceptualization than many feminist interpretations have allowed for. The forgetting of the feminine is explicitly thematized and commented on in Plato's dialogue, as are the difficulties of getting a grip on *chôra* by the use of reason and concepts. In the *Timaeus*, *chôra* is brought into the picture by necessity. The dialogue's whole argument comes to a halt and must be started anew because she is—at first—missing or has been forgotten. *Chôra* is not nonexistent, nor is she completely ungraspable. As Plato explicitly states in the *Timaeus* (52b), she is "apprehensible by a kind of bastard reasoning." Although this feminine-maternal principle emerges as troublesome, she is not completely ignored and overlooked in the depiction of the generation of the cosmos. Instead, Plato portrays her as precisely a troubling factor that has to be taken into consideration. The reasoning applied is of a bastard kind, but it is a reasoning nonetheless. Irigaray does not disregard this.

Moreover, I would like to emphasize that Irigaray recognizes the potential that resides in Plato's descriptions of the feminine.[8] This holds for both *chôra* and the figure of the cave in the *Republic*. In her wonderful readings in *Speculum*, Irigaray brings out these figures' ambiguities. On the one hand, these feminine figures have been forgotten, at least in the tradition of Platonic interpretation, such that they have constituted blind spots for centuries; these blind spots, especially the figure of the cave, and in particular the materiality of the wall of the cave, are rendered visible through Irigaray's readings. On the other hand, the cave and *chôra* are both there, present in the Platonic texts and, in the case of *chôra*, even explicitly commented on by Plato in respect of its problematic aspects. These figures are, as such, visible in Plato's text, with this being, of course, what allows Irigaray to subject them to her singularly perspicacious scrutiny.

The figure of the feminine in Plato that Irigaray explores at greatest length and most thoroughly is, by far, the cave.[9] Indeed, Irigaray's remarks concerning *chôra* quoted above are found in the section of *Speculum*,

"Plato's Hystera," devoted to the myth of the cave. In her reading of this myth, Irigaray shows how Plato portrays the feminine as something ideally without characteristics of her own. The fact that Plato's portrayal of the feminine attests to a way of thinking that does not allow for real difference is brought out by Irigaray in a speculative way—which is to say, Irigaray's reading functions in the fashion of a speculum, in a manner that is both illuminating and deflectively twisted or warped. Focusing on how Plato, through the myth of the cave, gives a depiction of the feminine that is distorted in specific ways, Irigaray emphasizes and highlights these distortions in her own reading by directing a speculum of her own, as it were, toward Plato's text. By doing this, Irigaray achieves several things, one of which is to show how the myth itself functions as a speculum in relation to the feminine. She also opens up thereby a place where the feminine may emerge in a different way, that is, as a radically different other. One could argue that this strategy of reading proffers a consciously warped reflection (Irigaray's) of a more unconsciously warped reflection (Plato's) of something feminine. The fact remains, however, that the cave is *there* in Plato's myth. Described in the *Republic* as both unavoidable and as something that it is necessary to transcend, the cave of Plato's myth shares with *chôra* the status of something that is problematic but at the same time necessary and ineluctable.

There is both a problem and a possibility embedded here. From Irigaray's perspective, it is Plato's attempt to reinscribe the feminine in a reductive manner that is problematic. For Plato, it is rather the necessary and unavoidable existence of *chôra* and the cave that poses a problem—whereas, for Irigaray, this is precisely where the possibility resides: the feminine is always already there. As such, that which Irigaray views as a problem, appears, from a Platonic perspective, to be a solution, namely, to reduce and negate the specifically feminine as much as possible, thereby no less reducing and negating difference.

What I wish to argue is that the figurations of *chôra* in the *Timaeus* can be drawn on to reconceptualize space as self-differentiating, although Plato genders this figuration in ways that specifically attempt to diminish *chôra's* self-differentiation. The disordered motion and volatility by which differentiation is engendered emerge as problematic in Plato, as does the figure of the feminine itself. For a project seeking to reconceptualize space—and the feminine—both the self-differentiating aspect and the femininity of *chôra* need to be rethought as representing possibilities instead of problems.

Irigaray's notion of sexual difference represents—in my view—a way of reconceptualizing not only femininity but also the world itself. I agree with Elizabeth Grosz when she writes, in *Becoming Undone: Darwinian Reflections on Life, Politics, and Art*, that "Irigaray's project is nothing short of the elaboration of a new understanding of the real, a new conception of the dynamic forces of the universe itself, half of which have been hidden and covered over by the other half" (2011, 100). I also agree with Grosz' reading of Irigaray's concept of sexual difference as "the very machinery, the engine, of living difference, the mechanism of variation, the generator of the new" (101). However, Grosz draws a distinction between life and the world itself when she writes: "If difference is the engine of the world itself—as Derrida and Deleuze seem to argue—then sexual difference is the engine of life, of nature, of all that lives" (103). Here, Irigaray's sexual difference is tied to life and all that lives, while difference for thinkers such as Derrida and Deleuze is connected to the world itself. This is the point where I would shift the formulation slightly. Let me try to explain.

In Plato's figuration of the generation of cosmos he uses the image of birth, that is, an image of sexual reproduction that connects the world itself to sexual difference. By rereading this image to bring out the feminine, Irigaray thus proffers a description of cosmos—and *phusis*—as something that, by its very nature, is alive. By virtue of the receiving principle that is named *chôra*—and which is also depicted as a maternal principle—cosmos is infused with differentiation, not least through the volatile movements attested to by the image of the winnowing basket. Differentiation itself is thereby sexed/gendered as feminine by virtue of this image. In my view, this is an aspect that Irigaray takes up and runs with in several of her texts, such as "This Sex Which Is Not One" and "When Our Lips Speak Together." Both of these latter texts are written in highly poetical, creative language by which Irigaray attempts to invent other and different—fluid, nonstable, nonunitary[10]—figurations of femininity, which, embedded in sexual difference, allow for a new thinking of difference.

The sexual difference that Irigaray has consistently emphasized the importance of thinking through and of creating in new ways is, as such, a difference that goes beyond life and living existence. This is particularly evident in *An Ethics of Sexual Difference* when Irigaray states that "[i]n order to make possible to think through, and live, this difference, we must reconsider the whole problematic of *space* and *time*" (ESD, 7). In order to think through the radical difference that sexual difference is, in other words, it is necessary for even vital ontological concepts related to cosmos, such as those of space and time, to be rethought. Aspects such as fluidity, unordered movement, and differentiation are figured as feminine in our history, culture, and tradition in the West and are indeed aspects attributed even to cosmos and *phusis* by some of the founding fathers of this tradition. This being the case, I would contend that Irigaray's conception of sexual difference extends beyond what has to do with life and living nature and encompasses cosmos: the world itself.

Self-Differentiating Space

One might argue that Plato's cosmology—or rather, cosmogony—has little relevance for modern notions about the universe and space. But is this really the case? If we think of space as a passive, three-dimensional extended entity—in line with the Cartesian and Newtonian conceptions introduced within the framework of modernity— then Plato's image in the *Timaeus* does indeed seem strange. It is probably no coincidence that interest in the *Timaeus*—which was one of the most read and commented-on of Plato's dialogues from Aristotle through the Middle Ages—radically declined during the Renaissance, with the emergence of the new natural sciences. However, if we turn to modern physics, and in particular the theories of the Danish physicist Niels Bohr, a different picture emerges.

Bohr's physics represents a challenge to both Cartesian and Newtonian conceptions of space. While I have neither the intention nor the competency to elaborate here on Bohr's theories of atomic physics and quantum mechanics, it is clear, if one looks, for instance, at Bohr's debate with Albert Einstein from 1949 onward, that at the heart of the matter is the question of determinism.[11] Bohr's notion of indeterminacy is related to the unpredictability of quantum mechanics,[12] and this unpredictability gives a character of openness to the universe of Bohr's physics. Hence, in respect at least of this aspect of indeterminacy and openness, there is a resonance between modern theories of physics, such as Bohr's, and Plato's image of *chôra* as unordered—and unpredictable—movement. They both inscribe a form of openness at the core of cosmos/*phusis*.[13] Still, it is striking how Plato, through the image of the winnowing basket, weaves together order and disorder and infuses the cosmos with an element of chaos. Furthermore, it is remarkable how, through this image, the unordered motion itself is depicted as an inherent element of the ordering, thus connecting the order of the universe to chaos in an integral way.

It has been claimed that Plato's *chôra* in the *Timaeus* anticipates Deleuze and Guattari's conception of a smooth space.[14] There is a connection here to the discussion between Einstein and Bohr concerning determinism. In their chapter "1440: The Smooth and the Striated" in *A Thousand Plateaus*, Deleuze and Guattari refer to a debate between Einstein and the philosopher Henri Bergson in 1922.[15] This dispute shares similarities with the exchange between the physicists Bohr and Einstein. As Jimena Canales points out in *The Physicist and the Philosopher. Einstein, Bergson, and the Debate That Changed Our Understanding of Time*, "Einstein obsessively searched for unity in the universe believing that science could reveal its immutable laws and describe them in the simplest possible way. Bergson, in contrast, claimed that the ultimate mark of the universe was just the opposite: never-ending change. [. . .] While Einstein searched for consistency and simplicity, Bergson focused on inconsistencies and complexities" (2015, 21). And indeed, in *Duration and Simultaneity: With Reference to Einstein's Theory*, Bergson was to argue that the problem with Einstein's theory of time is that it prevents us from recognizing that "the future is really open, unforeseen, indeterminate" ([1922] 1965, 145). Both the debate between Einstein and Bergson and the one between Einstein and Bohr are thus deeply connected to the question of indeterminacy.

Deleuze and Guattari's "1440: The Smooth and the Striated" is a text in which they equally contrast the classical natural sciences, which rely on Euclidian geometry, with more recent conceptions of space, such as those found in non-Euclidian geometries. They specifically reference in this respect Riemannian spaces, ametric geometry and Mandelbrot's fractals ([1980] 2004, 535, 537). This is the context into which they envelop the notion of smooth space, which, as mentioned, has been compared to *chôra*. Smooth space can be understood as a modality, or force of space, rooted in chaos, the unordered and unpredictable. Striated space is a modality or force of space that functions around order and the structurally defined and organized. These two types of spaces do not really delimit a distinction between chaos and order, however, for, as Grosz points out by way of underlining Bergson's influence on Deleuze, "each of Deleuze's and Bergson's pairs are always a *mixture* of both" (2003, 83).[16] And indeed, on the very first page of "1440: The Smooth and the Striated," Deleuze and Guattari set down that these two spaces "in fact exist only in mixture: smooth space is constantly being translated, transversed into a striated space; striated space is constantly being reversed, returned to a smooth space" ([1980] 2004, 524). They no less emphasize this same point, moreover, about the interconnection between the smooth and the striated at the end of this chapter.[17] *Chôra* similarly displays a mixture of order and disorder. However, it is through her unordered, volatile motion that order is created. One might argue that this constitutes something more than a mere mixture of two different aspects, in that the disorderly motion is an intrinsic element of the ordering itself. This complicates the distinction between chaos and cosmos in a vital way. Furthermore, both the disorder and the ordering come to pass through motion. This resonates with an image of the world as somewhat vibrant and alive, at least in the sense that it does not consist of motionless matter. There seems to be some accordance here with Irigaray's depiction of the world as alive.

For Irigaray, the understanding of the world we inhabit as a living entity is deeply connected to sexual difference. For Plato as well, in the *Timaeus*, the depiction of *chora*, including the image of the winnowing basket, is introduced first after the cosmos has received not only a father but a mother as well. Even in Plato, it seems, the depiction of cosmos as imbued with this unorderly ordering motion is dependent on some form of sexual difference, where cosmos is compared to a living being—a child—with two sexually different parents. The unpredictability that the element of disorder brings with it, unfolds the world as open and, at least to some degree, arbitrary. Space, understood through the inherently ambiguous, feminine-maternal figure of *chôra*, weaves together order and disorder—through vibrant movement—in a way that inscribes sexual difference within the very core of the world and gives it an openness toward the future as unknown and unpredictable. Furthermore, as vibrating and alive with motion, *chôra* unfolds the world as anything but controllable lifeless matter.

What, then, is the possible relevance for us today of taking *chôra* as an entity swaying with unordered motion into consideration? One of the vital issues of our age is the question of how we are to relate to the world we inhabit in a way that does not lead to ecological destruction. And if, as for example Jane Bennett argues in *Vibrant Matter: A Political Ecology of Things*, "an image of inert matter helps animate our current practice of aggressively wasteful and planet-endangering consumption, then a materiality experienced as a lively force [. . .] could animate a more ecologically sustainable public" (2010, 51). I sympathize with this view that connects man's aggressive and destructive practices toward the world we inhabit—and are fundamentally part of—with a certain conception of the materiality of this cosmos as nonliving matter. If this is indeed the case, we need to think differently about the spatial materiality of the world. We need to conceive of it as living and also something that defies our attempts at control. Part of such a project could be to envisage something that complicates the oppositions between active and passive and order and disorder. Considered in light of Irigaray's philosophy of sexual difference, Plato's *chôra* offers, as we have seen, complications of these notions. The spatial materiality of the world as depicted through the figuration of *chôra* is rather revealed as infused with indefiniteness and volatility and as swaying beyond the range of human control. Our salvation may well be dependent on our recognition of this revelation.

Notes

1. An early draft of this article was presented at the conference Topologies of Sexual Difference at RMIT University, Melbourne, December 10–12, 2014, and I would like to thank the audience for helpful comments and questions. I also owe a debt of gratitude to Stein A. Hevrøy and Louise Burchill, as well as an anonymous reader, for useful and valuable comments to previous versions of the chapter.

2. Commentators who equally point out the distinction between Plato's *chôra* and Aristotelian *topos* include D. Rita Alfonso, "Space and Irigaray's Theory of Sexual Difference," (101), and Elaine Miller, "Beyond the Madonna." Alfonso also refers to Aristotle's own remarks on how he differs from Plato on this point in the fourth book of the *Physics*, while Judith Butler comments on the differences between Plato's *chôra* and Aristotle's notion of *hyle*. Butler, "Bodies That Matter" (170, especially note 21). For more on Irigaray and Aristotle's topology, see Rebecca Hill's illuminating and original book *The Interval: Relation and Becoming in Irigaray, Aristotle, and Bergson.*

3. See Jacques Derrida, *On the Name.* And, as David Farrell Krell writes: "Now the discourse requires a third kind for which it is difficult to find words. Timaeus calls it 'the receptacle and a sort of nurse of all generation'" (49a 5–6). Krell, "Female Parts in *Timaeus*," 412.

4. At both *Laws* 800b and *Laws* 801d, Plato uses *ekmageion* in the sense of "typical case," while in the *Theaetetus*, at 194d and 194e, *ekmageion* has the meaning of "mold." In *Theaetetus* we also find instances of *ekmageion* where it signifies that on, or in, which an impression is made, as, for example, at 191c and, again, at 196a, where it means a "lump" of wax to be imprinted on. In the *Timaeus* 72c, we even find *ekmageion* used in the simple sense of a "napkin" that is laid beside a mirror always ready to wipe it clean.

5. Bianchi continues on the same page: "It signifies, then, a capacity to be marked, a passive undergoing, moved and inscribed by Being, but also an indeterminate agentic capacity for inscription and erasure." Bianchi, "Receptacle/Chôra: Figuring the Errant Feminine in Plato's *Timaeus*."

6. Here I have some support from Bianchi, who writes that *chôra* "effects through self-motion a sort of self-differentiation." Bianchi, "Receptacle/Chôra," 135.

7. See for instance, Irigaray's "Une Mère de Glace" (S, 168–180).

8. According to Athena Athanasiou and Elena Tzelepis: "Reading the figurations, or dis-figurations, of the disavowed feminine through the *chora* (the receptacle, *hypodoche*) in Plato's *Timaeus*, in her well-known essay 'Platos Hystera,' Irigarays resists the conflation of the *chora* and the maternal; she is, rather, interested in how the discursive articulation of this reduction performs a certain figuration of the feminine as perennial outside." Athanasiou and Tzelepis, "Thinking Difference as Different Thinking," 4.

9. The five or six pages over which the myth of the cave extends in Plato's dialogue is expanded to an exposition of approximately 150 pages in Irigaray's reading of Plato's myth in the section of *Speculum* entitled "Plato's Hystera."

10. See, for example, the following quotes from "This Sex Which Is Not One" and "When Our Lips Speak Together": "One would have to listen with another ear, as if hearing *an 'other meaning' always in the process of weaving itself, of embracing itself with words, but also getting rid of words in order not to become fixed, congealed in them*" (TS, 29). "Neither one nor two. I've never known how to count. Up to you. In their calculations, we make two. Really, two? Doesn't that make you laugh? An odd sort of two. And yet not one. Especially not one. Let's leave *one* to them: their oneness, with its prerogatives, its domination, its solipsism: like the sun's" (TS, 207; emphasis in original).

11. See, for example, Bohr, "Diskusjon med Einstein om erkjennelsesteoretiske problemer i atomfysikken" and "Atomene og den menneskelige erkjennelse" in *Atomfysikk og menneskelig erkjennelse*.

12. For a posthumanist reading of Bohr, see for example, Karen Barad's article "Posthumanist Performativity."

13. In this they share a certain opposition to thinkers such as René Descartes and Isaac Newton.

14. Edward S. Casey claims this, although he also points to the order that *chôra* imposes through her "violent thrashing motions." Casey, "Smooth Spaces and Rough-Edged Places," 271.

15. As Deleuze and Guattari write: "On April 6, 1922, in Paris, Albert Einstein and Henri Bergson publicly debated the nature of time. Einstein considered Bergson's theory of time to be a soft, psychological notion, irreconcilable with the quantitative realities of physics. Bergson, who gained fame as a philosopher by arguing that time should not be understood exclusively through the lens of

science, criticized Einstein's theory of time for being a metaphysics grafted on to science, one that ignored the intuitive aspects of time." Deleuze and Guattari, *A Thousand Plateaus*, 534. Deleuze and Guattari also explicitly refer to Bergson on pages 533 and 534 in the same book.

16. Flora Lysen and Patricia Pisters also point this out in their introduction to the special edition of *Deleuze Studies* named *The Smooth and the Striated*. Lysen and Pisters, "Introduction," 1. It is important to not interpret the concepts of Deleuze and Guattari in a dualistic or dichotomous way. As Grosz maintains, Deleuze and Guattari are, along with for instance Irigaray, "among a few major contemporary philosophers to insist on the impossibility of dualistic and dichotomous distinctions that rely on an either/or model." Grosz, *The Incorporeal*, 131.

17. As they write on the last page of this chapter: "What interests us in operations of striation and smoothing are precisely the passages of combinations: how the forces at work within space continually striate it, and how in the course of its striation it develops other forces and emits new smooth spaces." Deleuze and Guattari, *A Thousand Plateaus*, 551.

References

Alfonso, D. Rita. 2011. "Space and Irigaray's Theory of Sexual Difference." In *Thinking with Irigaray*, edited by Mary C. Rawlinson, Sabrina L. Hom, and Serene J. Khader. State University of New York Press.

Athanasiou, Athena, and Elena Tzelepis. 2010. "Thinking Difference as Different Thinking in Luce Irigaray's Deconstructive Genealogies." In *Rewriting Difference: Luce Irigaray and "the Greeks,"* edited by Elena Tzelepis and Athena Athanasiou. State University of New York Press.

Barad, Karen. 2003. "Posthumanist Performativity: Toward an Understanding of How Matter Comes to Matter." *Signs. Gender and Science: New Issues* 28, no. 3: 801–831.

Bennett, Jane. 2010. *Vibrant Matter: A Political Ecology of Things*. Duke University Press.

Bergson, Henri. (1922) 1965. *Duration and Simultaneity: With Reference to Einstein's Theory*. Translated by L. Jacobson. Bobbs-Merrill.

Bianchi, Emanuela. 2006. "Receptacle/Chôra: Figuring the Errant Feminine in Plato's *Timaeus*." *Hypatia* 21, no. 4: 124–146.

Bohr, Niels. (1957) 1967. *Atomfysikk og menneskelig erkjennelse*. Translated by H. Wergeland. J. W. Cappelens Forlag.

Butler, Judith. 1994. "Bodies that Matter." In *Engaging with Irigaray*, edited by C. Burke, N. Schor, and M. Whitford. Columbia University Press.

Canales, Jimena. 2015. *The Physicist and the Philosopher: Einstein, Bergson, and the Debate that Changed Our Understanding of Time*. Princeton University Press.

Casey, Edward S. 1997. "Smooth Spaces and Rough-Edged Places: The Hidden History of Place." *Review of Metaphysics* 51, no. 2: 267–296.

Deleuze, Gilles, and Félix Guattari. (1980) 2004. *A Thousand Plateaus: Capitalism and Schizophrenia*. Translated by Brian Massumi. Continuum.

Derrida, Jacques. (1993) 1995. *On the Name*. Translated by D. Wood, J. P. Leavey, Jr., and I. McLeod. Stanford University Press.

Grosz, Elizabeth. 2003. "Deleuze, Theory, and Space." *Log* 1: 77–86.

Grosz, Elizabeth. 2011. *Becoming Undone: Darwinian Reflections on Life, Politics, and Art*. Duke University Press.

Grosz, Elizabeth. 2017. *The Incorporeal: Ontology, Ethics, and the Limits of Materialism*. Columbia University Press.

Hill, Rebecca. 2012. *The Interval. Relation and Becoming in Irigaray, Aristotle, and Bergson*. Fordham University Press.

Krell, David Farrell. 1975. "Female Parts in *Timaeus*." *Arion: A Quarterly Journal of Classical Culture* 2, no. 3: 400–422.

Liddell, Henry George, and Robert Scott. 1994. *A Greek-English Lexicon*. Oxford University Press.

Lysen, Flora, and Patricia Pisters. 2012. "Introduction: The Smooth and the Striated." *Deleuze Studies* 6, no. 1: 1–5.

Miller, Elaine. 2011. "Beyond the Madonna." In *Thinking with Irigaray*, edited by Mary C. Rawlinson, Sabrina L. Hom, and Serene J. Khader. State University of New York Press.

Plato. (1921) 1987. *Theaetetus*. In *The Loeb Classical Library*, vol. VII: *Theaetetus. Sophist*, translated by H. N. Fowler. Harvard University Press.

Plato. (1929) 1989. *Timaeus*. In *The Loeb Classical Library*, vol. IX: *Timaeus, Critias, Cleitophon, Menexenus, Epistles*, translated by R. G. Bury. Harvard University Press.

Plato. (1926) 1994. *Laws*. In *The Loeb Classical Library*, vol. X: *Laws, Volume I: Books 1–6*, translated by R. G. Bury. Harvard University Press.

Plato. (1926) 1994. *Laws*. In *The Loeb Classical Library*, vol. XI: *Laws, Volume II; Books 7–12*, translated by R. G. Bury. Harvard University Press.

Sallis, John. 1999. *Chorology. On Beginning in Plato's Timaeus*. Indiana University Press.

Chapter Two

"Putting the Accent Back on Space"

Irigaray's Topology, *Chôra*, and Feminine Jouissance

L O U I S E B U R C H I L L

Isn't all jouissance a matter of space?

—ESD, 52; trans. modified

Of the conditions requisite for the thought and realization of sexual difference that Luce Irigaray sets out in the great ground-laying texts of the
first phase of her work—that consisting in the critique of the monocen-
trism of the Western (male) subject, a world constructed and interpreted
from a single sexuate perspective—the most preeminent is indubitably
the necessity to rethink space. Nowhere is this requisite more incisively
set down than in the proto-programmatic pronouncement of the opening
chapter of *An Ethics of Sexual Difference*: "Perhaps we are passing through
an epoch in which *time must redeploy space*. [. . .] A recasting of immanence and transcendence, notably by that *threshold* which has never been
examined as such: the female sex" (ESD, 18; emphasis in original; trans.
modified). That such a redeployment of space would entail revoking the
priority granted throughout the Western tradition to time—be it by its
identification with (a) God or the interiority of the subject or, indeed, the
meaning of Being—is clear as much from the succinct historical overview
of the problematic of time and space that Irigaray gives earlier in the same

35

chapter of *Ethics* as it is from certain of her later works, most notably *The Forgetting of Air* in which, after positioning the "transcendental priority" Heidegger attributes to time as contingent on a prior operation of time's incorporation of space, she discerns the "unthought" of the Western tradition to consist not of the meaning of Being qua ecstatic temporality but, rather, a "spatial necessity that has been forgotten in the economy of time" (FA, 152). And yet, as clear as such diagnoses are of the necessity to redeploy a space or spatiality that has been subordinated to, or supplanted by, time, Irigaray's injunction of a radical reconsideration of the tradition's whole problematic of time and space has nonetheless tended to be interpreted not only—quite rightly—as challenging the metaphysical and scientific determinations of space that make of it a pure extension, characterized by an isotropic or homogeneous relationality of "*partes extra partes*" with universal applicability to all things that exist, but equally—with far less validity—as confirming space to be, in Irigaray's view, irretrievably unsalvageable from such metaphysical-scientific determinations. Given that the latter have equally throughout the tradition been predicated, *mutatis mutandis*, of "feminine being," conceived in consequence as a neutral, formless, passive and undifferentiated "receptacle" capable of serving as the support for the impression, or reflection, of masculine projections, space finds itself not only reduced to its geometrico-metaphysical determinations but impugned for its paradigmatization of the attributes associated with a phallogocentrically determined femininity. In terms of this line of interpretation, the redeployment of space Irigaray advocates would consist, in fact, in jettisoning metaphysics' construction of "universal, undifferentiated *space*" in favor of an attention to "bodily-sexually specific *place*"[1] or something of the order of localized, fluid, dynamic sets of relations, qua intertwined complexes of "space-time," that would permit of a sexual modelization more affine with the female corporeal/subjective specificity Irigaray seeks to give expression to. The problem with such an interpretation is not only that it curiously elides—or indeed, in some instances, resolutely inverts[2]—Irigaray's reiterated insistence on the subordination of space to time in our tradition but that it concomitantly ignores her prescription of a necessary "recovery" or "reappropriation" of space. "How can I [a woman] recover space in a culture that privileges time?" is a query orienting Irigaray's 2006 text "How to Make Feminine Self-Affection Appear" (HM, 55) just as some thirty years earlier, in "Cosi Fan Tutti," she was to set down, in respect of Lacan's contemporary retake on the tradition's association of women and space, that "putting the accent back on space was perhaps to restore some chance for the jouissance of the other—woman" (TS, 98; trans. modified). It is "space" that must be recovered—or redeployed—according to Irigaray, not "place" or "space-time," whatever the exigency for the latter to equally be reconceived and perceived differently for sexual difference to be realized. The space in question here is obviously not that metaphysically determined as an undifferentiated, homogenous extension, which shares the predicates of formlessness and passivity with the maternal feminine as framed within the Western tradition. To this determination of space—the template of which is, for her, indubitably the Platonic *chôra*—Irigaray precisely opposes a different ordering or structure of space, which is to say, a different topology. And she does so not only discursively but also schematically: her famed "morphological models" being, *by definition*, equally topological ones. Which is to say that in her own writing Irigaray puts the accent back on space twice over—a redoubled accentuation, as it were, that, as I hope to show in this essay, resonates with the "reduplication," or topological parallelism, characterizing women's auto-affection.

Why it is that space's retrieval or reappropriation restores some chance, for Irigaray, to a jouissance that is more in harmony with women's sexual identity than that obeying the phallic order is the question from which we will start. Why topology is the "formal organon" most suited for Irigaray's description of female sexuate specificity can then be elaborated. This will lead us finally to query the strange spatial equivocity that characterizes Irigaray's various references to the Platonic chôra: a "space" she consistently positions as paradigmatically metaphysical despite Plato's having equally endowed it with an alternative, very different, topology that is not only isomorphic with the space she herself seeks to recover but that is described by Plato—again just like Irigaray herself—as subject to a "covering-over" by homogeneous extension in conformity with the geometrico-metaphysical determinations of a paternal logos. Why not acknowledge—we must query of Irigaray—that her characterization of feminine being as an uncircumscribable and immeasurable volume that would be repressed, occulted or covered-over by measurable, masterable, and undifferentiated extension finds a precedent in Plato's account of the chôra as a "feminine space" displaying two very distinct topologies? In this sense, to put the accent back on space, both with Irigaray and on our own account, is to interrogate not only the manifest operations of her topology but also that which—in a manner not all that dissimilar to the monocentric manipulations of Lacan that Irigaray denounces—she thereby forecloses.

An Other Topo-(logy) of Jouissance

"Cosi Fan Tutti"—Irigaray's critical gloss of Lacan's (1972–1973) *Encore* seminar—takes as its overarching premise that the psychoanalytical discourse on female sexuality is the discourse of truth, which is to say the discourse that tells the truth about the logic of truth: namely, that "the feminine only takes place therein within models and laws devised by male subjects" (TS, 86; trans. modified). This truth, this logic of truth, is that governing the entire Western (philosophical) tradition. Psychoanalysis' specificity for Irigaray is that in repeating this tradition (to some extent unwittingly) it brings this truth of woman's position qua construct of male models and laws—as man's symptom—to light and does so, this time, in respect of the definition of sexual difference. Interweaving *Encore*'s discursive claims within a running commentary that relativizes their monologic projections by opening up another perspective, Irigaray's critical dialogue with Lacan focuses on two main thematic threads of Seminar XX. First, woman is inscribed in discourse but as a lack, fault, or flaw: "If what I am suggesting is true, namely that woman is not-all, there is always something in her that escapes discourse" (Lacan, cited by Irigaray, TS, 89). That is to say—Irigaray glosses—that woman is in a position of exclusion *internal* to the order of male discourse, which sets down the logical requirement that language determines the definition of sexual difference. This discourse, however, is "perhaps not all there is" (TS, 88). Second, women cannot speak about the jouissance that is proper to them: "about this jouissance, woman knows nothing" as shown by the fact that "women analysts haven't made the slightest progress on female sexuality;" "they tell us . . . not all": "not a word" (Lacan 1998, 57, 75; trans. modified). To which Irigaray objects: "the question whether, in his logic, [women] can say anything at all, whether they can be heard, is not even raised. For raising it would mean granting that there may be some other logic and one that upsets his own" (TS, 90).

Underlying both these thematic threads, raveling and unraveling as they do the logic governing psychoanalytic discourse and its determination of woman as not-all at the place of phallic jouissance, is the postulate, designated by Lacan as the very basis of psychoanalysis, of the impossibility of the sexual relation (1998, 9). This is a postulate Irigaray completely concurs with . . . declaring it tantamount to an admission that the discourse of truth, the discourse of "de-monstration," cannot incorporate the relation between the two sexes within the economy of its logic (TS, 99). As such, before turning to her characterization of space as that which could potentially allow something of female jouissance to be expressed—which is to say, something of an other sex—it is necessary to recall what Lacan understands by the absence of sexual relation. This is not a denial that relations between the sexes exist; the axiom "there is no sexual relation" sets down, rather, the lack of any reciprocity or complementarity—any common being—between them. Why this is the case follows from the sexuate positions' being governed by a symbolic order that is fundamentally asymmetrical insofar as it instates the phallus as the sole signifier determining sexuation. Sexual difference is defined, that is, regardless of any biological criterion, in terms of what Lacan designates as "the phallic function," understood as the "universal quantifier" that divides the sexes on either side of a unary trait: having or being the phallus. There is, then, no sexual relation because any interaction between the sexes is mediated by the phallic signifier, equally specified as the "cause of jouissance": "jouissance, as sexual, is phallic, which is to say that it does not relate to the Other ["to a sex as Other"] as such" (Lacan 1998, 9; 1975, 14). Indeed, phallic jouissance "is the obstacle owing to which man does not manage [. . .] to enjoy [*jouir de*] woman's body, precisely because what he enjoys [*jouit*] is the jouissance of the organ" (Lacan 1998, 7; trans. modified). This failure of the sexual relation is "supplemented," as regards the masculine position, by the object *a*—a body part, for example—that takes the place of the missing partner, with this being played out in the order of phantasm. Yet, while phallic jouissance is always jouissance of an object borne by the body (viz. the object *a*) and neither the other's body nor, even less, "the other" as such, all those who occupy the feminine sexuate position have, in Lacan's terms, access to a "supplementary jouissance"—a jouissance "beyond the phallus"—at the basis of which "something other than the object *a* is involved in the attempt to supplement the sexual relation that doesn't exist" (Lacan 1998, 63; 1975, 59). "Not-all" under the phallic function or, in other words, not wholly within the economy of the object, the feminine position escapes the "finitude" of phallic jouissance and renders problematic the function's universality. Not that woman is *not* under the phallic function; simply, she has access to a jouissance that goes beyond this function—a jouissance that, *infinite* in nature, is a "plus" and not a negation or restriction, or, again, a measurable quantity or extension.

It is in order to formalize this differential relation of the sexes to "the space of jouissance" that Lacan first turns in his *Encore* seminar to topology, which he defines as discourse about place. Given that the place Lacan wishes to examine is the "place of the Other," of "a sex as Other," the topological notion most appropriate to this end, he states, is that of compactness—for "nothing is more compact than a fault" (Lacan 1998, 9). Now, the "fault" or "gap" referred to here is equally a "limit" in accordance with general topology's attributing to a compact space the inclusion of all its points' limiting values, which is to say that it has no "punctures" or missing endpoints but potentially contains an infinite number of sets or elements within a bounded and closed space. Leaving the technical details of Lacan's demonstration aside,[3] the result he reaches by the "hypothetical application" of the property of compactness to the space of jouissance is that phallic jouissance *covers* this space, as composed of an infinite sequence of ("feminine") open or nonbounded sets (excluding any limiting values), with a *finite* number of bounded sets. In other words, what makes the property of compactness interesting is that it formalizes the move from the infinite to the finite, from which it follows that the "demonstrable finity of open spaces" can then be counted or "be taken one by one"—as is illustrated, less technically, by the *mille et tre* of the list of Don Juan's conquests (10).

Irigaray, when referring to this demonstration by Lacan, foregoes any mention of compactness to focus rather on the resultant covering (over) of woman's fault or gap in the operation of discourse, which she underscores (quoting Lacan, who is subject thereby to discursive destabilization) as "phallicism's compensation" for its inability to relate to the Other as such—for its failing, in other words, the sexual relation. "To woman's not-all in the order of the expressible in discourse there is a corresponding necessity of having them all, at least potentially, all of them, in order to make them bear the fault of the unsayable. [. . .] The ek-stasy of the Other with respect of pronounceable language [. . .] is moderated, measured, mastered in the counting up of women" (TS, 98). She immediately adds, however, that there is an additional way that this fault in discourse is covered over, namely, by recourse to that substance Descartes baptized extension, the "substance" that for modern science is pure space. Crucially though, the passage from *Encore* that Irigaray cites as textual justification for this claim does not strictly support her gloss. Certainly, Lacan refers here to the Cartesian dyad of thinking and extended substance and qualifies the *res extensa* as "modern space—the substance of pure space, like we say 'pure spirit'" (Lacan 1998, 23). He does so, moreover, in the context of opposing to extended substance so defined his conception of a third substance, "the substance of the body, on the condition that it is defined only as that which enjoys itself [*se jouit*]" (23), which he puts in correlation with feminine jouissance or "jouissance of the Other." Nothing in this passage indicates, however, that by specifying this "enjoying substance" (*la substance jouissante*) to entail "something other than the *partes extra partes* of extended substance" (23), Lacan is pointing thereby to a covering-over of the first substance by the second. He is not, that is, replicating a *demonstration* of the kind he conducted by recourse to topological compactness: in no way is he positing, as Irigaray's gloss would seem to suggest, that pure space covers over the gap in discourse that woman as not-all symbolizes. This is to say that it is Irigaray, not Lacan, who makes this claim, citing *Encore* solely by way of recuperating the reference to space. And indeed, as Irigaray's elaboration of this claim immediately makes clear, her "gloss" of Lacan's text in this instance pertains not to its argument (unlike her remarks on compactness qua "phallic compensation": professed by Lacan himself) but to its operativity or what it itself does: it is through his very mobilization of the science of topology that Lacan (unwittingly . . . to a certain extent) excludes from expression—*covers over*—the space of woman's jouissance.

Irigaray's argument, after citing *Encore*'s reference to pure space, is as follows:

> The place of the Other, the body of the Other, will then be spelled out in topo-logy. At the point nearest to the coalescence of discourse and fantasy, in the truth of an ortho-graphy of space, the possibility of the sexual relation is going to be missed.
>
> For to put the accent back on space was—perhaps—to restore some chance for the jouissance of the other—woman. But to once again make a science of it amounts to bringing it back inside the logic of subject. To an over-and-beyond back over to the same. To reducing the other to the Other of the Same (TS, 98–99).

By his thematization and demonstration of a "space of jouissance" through recourse to the science of topology, Lacan would once again (*encore!*) inscribe feminine jouissance/auto-affection as *excluded within* the economy of truth determined by the male subject. This is a tenet of Irigaray's philosophy of sexual difference from which she has never wavered: a discourse of knowledge "privileging the demonstrable, the thematizable, the formalizable" (TS, 99) is a logos in the service of male auto-affection, a logos or reason whose characteristics—the principle of identity, the principle of noncontradiction, binarism—all display an "isomorphism with man's sexual imaginary" (ESD, 122). And yet, that which is nonetheless underscored by Lacan's mobilization of topology—not restricted, moreover, to the concept of compactness: *Encore* notoriously proposes the Borromean knot as a model of the subject's spatiality and the advent of subjectivity through the linking of signifiers (Cutrofello 2002, 162–163)—is the singular importance Lacan accords to space when attempting to "bring out something new regarding feminine sexuality" (Lacan 1998, 57): viz. "space of jouissance," "enjoying substance/expanse," "space as forming part of the unconscious." Putting, in this way, "the accent on space," Lacan would have touched on, in Irigaray's view, the condition for the expression of feminine jouissance and, more largely, of a feminine specificity articulated in accordance with a "logic" different to that—phallic—privileging the demonstrable, the bounded, the circumscribable, the countable. . . . This other logic—this "feminine logic" (HM, 57)—would, Irigaray elaborates elsewhere, reject all closure or circularity in discourse, privilege the "near" rather than the "proper" of the philosophical tradition, entail a different relation to unity and self-identity, and retraverse "differently" the dyads of matter/form, potentiality/act, and so on (TS, 153–154). To this other logic there necessarily corresponds, for Irigaray, an other "topo-(logy)" (S, 230): not the topo-logy, as wielded by Lacan, that closes and covers the space of feminine jouissance, making of it a substratum that serves as the support for phallic auto-affection, but a topology pertaining to properties such as the "half-open," and the passage-between or porosity, as well as to rims or edges and fluid sets (ESD, 123). How extensively Irigaray deploys this "other" topology throughout her early work is perhaps most immediately gauged by her equating the two terms *topology* and *morphology* (ESD, 105): her renowned "morphological model" of the "two lips," for example, is equally her topological modeling of a space irreducible to Euclidean geometry and Descartes' *partes extra partes* extension. But it is, of course, in the "core" chapter of *Speculum*, "The Uncircumscribable Volume," that her topology of the feminine subject finds its most concentrated exposition, this chapter being, not incidentally, the first iteration of the argumentation Irigaray develops three years later in "Cosi Fan Tutti."

Before turning to this core chapter, a number of final points concerning Irigaray's references to space in her critical gloss of *Encore* need to be noted. First, by designating space the condition for feminine jouissance, Irigaray is proposing her version, as it were, of the millennia-old association of woman and space. This association does, that is, indeed exist for Irigaray but must be salvaged from a metaphysics isomorphic with the male imaginary and recast, or reappropriated, from the perspective of the sexuate subject "woman." Such a recasting or reappropriation necessarily draws—in keeping with Irigaray's definition of sexual difference (KW, x; BEW, 129)—on both psychoanalytic and morphological tenets, which, while obviously mobilized in "Cosi Fan Tutti," are most clearly referenced in this respect in a key section of *Ethics* dealing with the different ordering of space and time characterizing the two sexes (ESD, 64–65). Here Irigaray gives us to understand that "if woman can occupy the place of spatiality," if, in her jouissance, "she extends infinitely in space," this is first of all because she retains a connection to the mother/maternal body, qua "first space," that is denied the man, whose separation from the maternal body at birth is experienced (and reiterated later in his development) as "being cut off from/in *space*," leaving him in perpetual pursuit of regaining access to, indeed, mastery over, a space he henceforth objectifies as a Whole (ESD, 64; trans. modified). But feminine jouissance's taking the form of "an expanse extending on and on forever" is equally contingent on woman's morphology in relation to the sexual act: woman's jouissance is not regulated, that is, as is the man's (at least in a phallic economy), by the "rhythm of detumescence;" for her, "thresholds do not necessarily mark a limit, the end of an act," she can find pleasure indefinitely, in principle, in touching; her jouissance "a horizon forever open" (ESD, 65). In short, "putting the accent back on space" is indeed to underline the conditions of feminine jouissance . . .

Second, Irigaray's gloss of *Encore* is remarkable for her focusing, in its final section, on Plato's notion of chôra, it being rare for her to *explicitly* reference the latter. Arguably, the first concept in the Western tradition of space in general, as distinct from the space occupied by any particular thing, chôra functions in the Platonic onto-cosmogonic system as a necessary "third kind" (or intermediary) that complements the dualist framework of intelligible model (the ontological sphere of the Forms or Ideas) and phenomenal copy (the empirical sphere of becoming, or the sensible) by serving as the "medium" or "place" in which the genesis of the sensible through the mimetic impression of intelligible form can occur.

To fulfill this role of receiving the forms of the intelligible and of assuring their faithful reproduction in the phenomenal world, chôra (often designated by Plato "the receptacle") must have no features or characteristics of its own. What is required of it is absolute morphological neutrality. It must be deprived—which is precisely what Irigaray picks up on—of any power of "self-shaping" or, let's say, of "auto-affection," and can for this reason, Irigaray argues, be said to be without any expression or knowledge of itself. What Irigaray does not mention, however, is that much of Plato's characterization of chôra in the *Timaeus* precisely pertains to the mathematical and topological operations by which chôra is transformed from a self-shaping space in constant metamorphosis, without measure or reason, into the "passified," stable, and homogeneous container—measurable, masterable, and morphologically neutral—required for, and by, his metaphysical system. Indeed, Irigaray focuses exclusively on the "passified" chôra that results from these operations of "commensuration" and closure, arguing that its properties or characteristics stand in an analogical relation to Lacan's determination of woman as Other insofar as Lacan reproduces the traditional—that is, Platonic—division between the intelligible and the sensible. Both chôra and the Other are subordinated, Irigaray underlines, to an intelligible order that gives them form: both are subject to the inscription of forms without their knowledge. No form-giving activity of their own—no "auto-affection"—is possible since it is only on this condition of passive formlessness that they can serve as the place of inscription ensuring the reproduction of the prevailing order. Accordingly, just as chôra is described by Plato as a matrix/womb for "paternal" forms, so the Other, states Irigaray, "serves as matrix/womb for the subject's signifiers." "The impossible 'auto-affection' of the Other by itself—of the other by herself?—would be the condition making it possible for any subject to form his desires" for "were there some other—without that leap, necessarily ek-static, of the capital letter—the entire autoerotic, auto-positional, auto-reflexive economy . . . of the subject, or the 'subject,' would find itself disturbed" (TS, 101; trans. modified).

From Irigaray's analogy of chôra and woman as Other, let us retain the following two crucial points. First, chôra is paradigmatic, for Irigaray, not just of the sensible as determined within the metaphysical binary subordinating it to the intelligible but, equally, by virtue of its ("passified") amorphousness and lack of (self) identity, of the phallic construct of woman as the support or precondition of the masculine. Space and femininity are thereby conjoined in the figure of an impassive, ever-receptive, ever-penetrable container-recipient. Second, for this container-recipient to give form to itself (or expression to its own form/s), a different spatial structuration—which is to say, topology—is necessary: such a structuration consisting, as it were, in a self-shaping of the space, a generation of its own topological properties. "Woman," Irigaray states elsewhere (and precisely in "The Uncircumscribable Volume") "remains the whole of the place that cannot be gathered into a space because it is no more than a receptacle for the (re)productions of the same" (IR, 66). For woman to no longer be a receptacle subjected to the inscription of forms—in accordance with the traditional hylomorphic model conjoining the dyads form/matter and intelligible/sensible—but a self-structuring space, that which is therefore required is a "gathering into a space."

Let us now turn, then, to the chapter that Irigaray places at the core of *Speculum*—a position signaling that in these pages the means of representation of sexual difference is to undergo involution.

Gathering into a Space of Auto-Affection

It is best to begin with a remark, or two, on translation. Referring to the title she gave to the central chapter of *Speculum*, "L'incontournable volume," Irigaray was to specify in an interview conducted in 1994 that what she meant by this was "simply a volume that can't be circumscribed because it's open. Thus, it didn't mean either 'volume fluidity' [the title found in the English translation of *Speculum* by Gillian Gill] or 'volume without contours' [the translation proposed by David Macey in *The Irigaray Reader*]. It's an allusion to the morphology of the female body, and I say that this morphology is an open volume, one that can't be circumscribed. A closed volume can be circumscribed; an open volume can't be circumscribed" (JLI, 346). That the most appropriate translation of this chapter's title is, therefore, "The Uncircumscribable Volume" seems straightforward,[4] but the "errors of translation" Irigaray is concerned with here—and which she attributes, in part, to the fact of her opening up a new field of thought—have contributed imperceptibly, for readers of this chapter in English, to the obscuration of Irigaray's mobilization of topological terminology.

Not having the space here to demonstrate such obscuration in any great detail—and in immediately noting that this is in no way to denigrate the immense, ground-laying effort of the translators—let us simply set side by side the two versions in English translation of a sentence taken from a passage presenting what Irigaray names "an other topo-(logy) of jouissance"—a topology transposing the female body's traditional alignment with both lack and excess into a positive figuration of unbounded volume in "in(de)finite transformation."

"Lips of the same form—but of a form that is never simply defined—ripple outwards as they touch and send one another on a course that is never fixed into a single configuration." (S, 230; translation Gillian Gill)	"Lips of the same form—yet never simply defined—overlap by retouching one another, referring one (to) the other for a perimeter that nothing arrests in one configuration." (IR, 56; translation David Macey)

As can be seen, one version employs a vocabulary indebted to physics ("ripple outwards," "send . . . on a course"), while the other is more faithful to the topological schematization Irigaray deploys here by rendering *se débordant* and *pourtour* as "overlap" and "perimeter."[5] It is, indeed, an "error of the interpretative imagination"—as Irigaray again puts it in the 1994 interview—to translate terms that strictly refer to spatial relations alone into the idiom of physical processes or properties; the dynamism of "rippling outwards" and being "sent on a course" is simply not present in the original French: Irigaray is not describing (directly at least) intensities or physical fluxes but, to reiterate, spatial relations. That these relations may correspond or correlate to the distribution of intensities or fluctuations in matter (or what Irigaray, in borrowing the term from Merleau-Ponty, names "flesh") is a quite separate question to that of their abstract, formal articulation, even if, as we shall elaborate later, one of the reasons topological thinking is so apt for Irigaray's purpose of "schematizing" an other, "feminine," auto-affection is undoubtedly its status as the rigorous abstract structure closest to the realm of the aesthetic/sensible. Now, relations such as those of overlap and perimeter, as well as continuity, disjunction, and conjunction, passage between inside and outside (porosity), neighborhood, rim (or lip), and edge, are precisely—to reiterate—the purview of topology, which, unlike geometry (the domain of which is exact measurement), disregards measurement and scale and deals only with the structure of space qua space and with the essential shapes of figures. Topology treats figures, in other words, as manifolds—spaces whose coordinates are not extrinsic, as with a line embedded within a Cartesian grid, but rather intrinsic to the surface itself—and focuses on what aspects of a figure remain invariant when the surface is folded, stretched, squeezed, or rotated, but not cut or torn. The fact that topology is concerned with questions "of the half-open, of fluid sets, of anything articulating the problem of edges, of the passage between things, of the fluctuations taking place between one threshold and the other of defined sets"—to cite Irigaray's analysis in *Ethics* of the "sexuate logic" of the sciences (ESD, 123; trans. modified)—is precisely what sets *this* science apart, for her, from the mathematics characterized by a logic isomorphic with male auto-affection: topology deals, that is, with relations ignored, or "repressed," by the (male) "subject of science." Which is to say that topology could well potentially "restore some chance for feminine jouissance," albeit, Irigaray cautions, as parametrized in the prevailing discursive order, topological science would "put the accent more on that which closes up than on that which remains without possible circularity" (ESD; trans. modified). Just as Lacan was to do, of course, in his recourse to topology: his formalization of uncircumscribable volume ("without any possible circularity") effectively rendering it bounded, closed, and computable. Irigaray's topology is other than this: it is the "other" topology, the one concerned with spatial relations such as the half-open, the passage between inside and outside, the re-touch . . . The topology of an auto-affection other than that of the male subject.

It is, as such, imperative that the "figures" of the sexuate specificity of women Irigaray proffers—the most famous being, of course, "the two lips"—are recognized as *topological* figures and not, as has variously been proposed, as of the order of metaphor, strategic (essentialist) representation, deconstructive concepts, or, indeed, literal anatomical mapping.[6] Whatever the arguments adduced in support of these readings, they all fail to rigorously analyze the function of these figures in Irigaray's texts as a *schematism* of the concepts she is attempting to elaborate. The term *schematism* is—as, we shall see, Irigaray specifies—to be understood here in its strict Kantian sense as the procedure through which a concept or category is given an "image," or "sensible transposition" (that is, in intuition), and presented accordingly in its spatio-temporal determination. While Kant defined the schemata of pure concepts as "transcendental determinations of *time*" (qua the form of pure inner intuition, or inner sense), he was adamant that space alone, qua pure outer intuition and that which uniquely testifies to a veritable alterity—that is, to something other than the subject—furnishes the schemata with "objective reality," without which they remain empty: "simple chimeras." Moreover, in the case of pure *sensible* concepts, such as concepts of geometric figures or of abstract forms, Kant subtracts, as it were, time's transcendental priority: the corresponding schemata for such concepts are quasi "im-mediate" determinations of spatial intuition, "rules of synthesis of the imagination, in respect to pure figures in space" ([1781/1787] 1985, 182). Irigaray directly references Kantian schematism when elucidating, in the same interview as that addressing the errors of translation, the manner in which she composes her texts: "At the philosophical level [. . .] there is in my composition a counterpoint between [. . .] that which concerns the order of schematism and that which concerns the order of discourse. [. . .] Above all, translate my words literally. [. . .] When I speak of "schematism" I'm alluding to Kant's word. If you use some other word, what I said no longer makes sense" (JLI, 349). What we are to understand, therefore, is that the concepts Irigaray elaborates relating to woman's sexuate specificity are *schematized*, or given a sensible transposition, in the "images"—or motifs—of female morphology she presents. Morphology being a question of form and structure, these images necessarily privilege spatial, and not spatio-temporal or dynamic, relations: they are well and truly transpositions of a topological order. And indeed, Irigaray renders this equivalence between morphology and topology explicit when, in reference to "the symbolisation of the feminine," she speaks of "a topology or morphology that must remain open" (ESD, 105).

Irigaray's deployment of Kantian schematism inflects the latter in one crucial aspect. For Kant, the concept has the function of guiding the schematizing process consisting in a synthesis of sensible diversity; he mobilizes as such the hylomorphic opposition between form-giving mind (the synthesis of imagination in the service of the unification represented by the concept) and "passive" matter/sensible diversity (as given in outer intuition). This is not the case for Irigaray. The sensible given can, for her, play an active role—one of auto-synthesis, in a sense—in the formation of concepts. Schematism is not then reducible to a movement from the intelligible to the sensible (as with Kant's transcendental concepts); the sensible equally has agency in orienting the conceptual alignment.[7] It is precisely this form of sensible/conceptual alignment that Husserl forefronts, for his part, in his characterization of *morphological concepts*. As concepts pertaining to "vague configurational types which are directly seized on the basis of sensuous intuition," morphological concepts would, Husserl specifies, be fixed in just as vague (or indeterminate) a fashion as the intuitable types of forms themselves, but "the *vagueness* of such concepts"—which is to say, their anexact nature, as contrasted with the exact concepts of geometry—does not make them defective. On the contrary, morphological concepts such as "roundness," "notched," "lens-shaped," and "umbelliform" are the most appropriate conceptual expressions by which to describe what is given in sensible intuition in a "fluid" form (Husserl [1913] 1983, 166). That we find here further corroboration of the complicity between morphology and topology is shown by the morphological idealities of "round," "notched," and so forth, finding a topological translation (to cite Michel Serres' illuminating analyses in *Hermes I: Communication*) in "Jordan curves, Riemann surfaces, spheres equipped with cross-caps, and so on"—all topological notions formulated at the very time Husserl was writing (Serres [1967] 2023, 86). Both morphology and topology qualify, in fact, in Serres' terms, as the "rigorous structures closest to the aesthetic;" they are "geometries" having freed themselves from quantity and measurement that thereby constitute the most appropriate "formal organon" to use "when we wish to describe phenomena eluding by nature any prior measurement, when we wish to grasp the rigour of a pure form, of a continuous and nonquantifiable variation" (Serres 2023 [1968], 174–175). Given Irigaray's project of bringing to articulation a form without determinable limits that "neither open nor closed" is uncircumscribable and in "continuous becoming," the most appropriate formal organon at her disposition is indeed the compendium of topological concepts.

Her adoption of this conceptual corpus, of this formal organon, is motivated, however, by yet one other, final, factor—which is, in fact, the first and most patent of reasons why her morphological figures are rigorously to be understood as topological ones. Namely, it is the dialogue with Lacan—her main interlocutor (though rarely identified as such) throughout her early work—that frames her configuration of feminine sexuality/subjectivity, with this being counterposed to, or com-plicating, "the topology of the subject" expounded in *Encore*. Just as she does in "Cosi Fan Tutti" and *Speculum*'s "Uncircumscribable Volume," so too in *Ethics* Irigaray criticizes Lacan—to complete the quote given earlier—for "making an enclosure of a topology or morphology that must remain open" (ESD, 105); the subject of Lacan's topology indeed "represses" this open structure/volume and transforms it into a substrate such that it is no longer "full of its own becoming." To this, Irigaray's response can but be, in a sense, to elaborate or "uncover" that open topology corresponding to the "other" corporeality/jouissance repressed/silenced in the Lacanian (and traditional) order of discourse. The topological properties Irigaray draws on to this end—qua the appropriate description of "what is given in sensible intuition in a fluid form"—include, as we know, those of continuity, porosity, passage between inside and outside, folding, the half-open, overlap, overflow, nonclosure, connectedness, re-touch, self-touching, expanse, opening, rim, edge, and perimeter. In "The Uncircumscribable Volume," Irigaray privileges the properties of continuity and nonclosure, indeterminable expansion, and continuous variation:

> Woman is neither closed nor open. Indefinite, in-finite, *form is never complete in her.* [. . .] This incompleteness of her form, of her morphology, allows her to become something else at any moment, which is not to say that she is (n)ever univocally anything. [. . .] But becoming the expansion that she is not, never will be at any moment, as a definable universe. [I]n the self-touching of the/a woman, a whole touches itself because it is in-finite, unable or unwilling to close up or to swell definitively to the extension of an infinite. This (self-)touching giving woman a form which is in(de)finitely transformed without closing up on her appropriation. Metamorphoses where no totality ever consists, where the systematicity of the One never insists.[8]

Elsewhere, in *This Sex* and *Ethics*, the "other topo-(logy)" of feminine jouissance—as well, importantly, as that of the "carnal exchange of lovers" (viz. the "sexual relation" foreclosed in the economy of male auto-affection)—is configured by Irigaray predominantly in terms of porosity, re-touch, folding and self-unfolding, the passage between inside and outside, and the half-open. Whatever the properties convoked by Irigaray, however, her topological schematizations of woman's morphology/feminine jouissance quasi-invariably take shape, as it were, through constant contrast or counterpoint with the position and properties attributed to woman by the male subject, whose topology and discursive order privilege, or indeed enforce, enclosure, discontinuity, bound form, the one and unity. There is not simply the contrast of two topologies, however; Irigaray equally delineates the topological transformation necessary to "pass" from one topology of auto-affection (the male) to the "other."

A "gathering into a space"—this, as signaled earlier—is the topological operation that is required for the transformation of the "place of the Other" into a "space of sexuate specificity." The first indications of what this entails are given at the very start of "The Uncircumscribable Volume": Woman must "appropriate herself as such," "gathering together" that which (of her) has been "dispersed into x places" and which remain the support for the discursive order's reproduction. Woman must, that is, create a place—or more properly, a space—of her own. A space of "auto-affection" that is, of course, structurally excluded in/by the topology consecrated by the tradition and reprised by Lacan, in which woman—like the chôra—can be "no more than a receptacle for the re-production of the same." It is, though, *An Ethics of Sexual Difference*—a veritable refrain of topological transformation—that sets out most precisely how the topology of the receptacle is transformed into one of auto-affection. Here the operations comprised by "the gathering into a space" are preeminently those of folding back around, redoubling and re-enveloping, and the tracing of limits such that the perimeter so created is ever in constant variation . . . "[Woman] lacks a 'proper' place. She would have to re-envelop herself with herself, and do so at least twice: as a woman and as a mother" (ESD, 11). She must attain "the power to fold back around her the dwelling she is" (ESD, 65). "If desire is to subsist, a double place is necessary, a double envelope" (ESD, 48). By means of such a redoubling or re-enveloping—or, let's say, topological parallelism—of the space or place that she is, woman can "create a space for herself" and no longer serve as receptacle for the re-production of the same.

Of the Spatial Equivocity (of Irigaray's Reading/s) of the Platonic Chôra

Let us look though more closely at the topology Irigaray attributes to the receptacle . . . as this is configured in Plato's *Timaeus*. There are, in fact, very few places in her work where she refers *explicitly* to Plato's text, although implicit, indirect references to chôra abound. One reference, in "Place, Interval," singularly stands out for Irigaray's suggesting that Plato's *receptacle* (unfortunately rendered as "container" in the English translation) "would in some way be 'the nature' of matter and form, the habitat where the one marries with the other, never-endingly and in their extension"—just as "would be the case for both masculine and feminine if the schize between them . . . were surmounted" (ESD, 37; trans. modified). Chôra would here be endowed with a certain self-shaping, a self-giving of form—which, as we are shortly to see, is exactly a property Plato grants to this space in its "original" form. Everywhere elsewhere in her work, however, Irigaray characterizes chôra as an impassive, ever-receptive, ever-penetrable container-recipient, refusing it any isomorphism with the topology she associates with feminine auto-affection.

The chapter in *Speculum* that deals with chôra is particularly eloquent in this respect. Comprised entirely of quotations from Plotinus's commentary in the Sixth Tractate of the *Enneads* (thus miming Plotinus' own "imitation"—as the French edition of the *Enneads* puts it—of Plato's *Timaeus*), this chapter exemplifies her intractability to any reading of the chôra as a precursor of her elaboration of a feminine space. By filtering Plato through Plotinus, who upholds an absolute transcendence of the intelligible vis-à-vis the sensible sphere far more trenchantly than does Plato himself, Irigaray is indeed better able to denounce Plato's association of chôra and "the feminine" (chôra being described as "mother" and "nurse") as resolutely metaphysical on the grounds that, enframed as they are by the binary oppositions of intelligible/sensible and form/matter, both "the feminine" and the chôra are understood in terms of a purely receptive matter-support—without any identity, essence, or productivity of its own—awaiting the virile impression of the forms. She equally consecrates thereby Plotinus' identification of chôra with Aristotle's "matter" (*hulé*)[9]—despite Plato himself never using the latter term in relation to the chôra, and the rare occurrences of *hulé* elsewhere in his work always having the sense of a building material such as wood. On Irigaray's reading then, Plato would have identified "the feminine" with a passive spatio-material support in such trenchant, unambiguous terms that no possibility remains of even envisaging the existence of something in excess of his phallogocentric economy pretending to systematic closure.

And yet . . . , if we turn to the *Timaeus*, we find that Plato accords *two* very distinct topologies to the chôra. Simply stated, the description of chôra as amorphous, with neither shape nor attributes of its own, pertains to the state in which "the nurse of all becoming" exists as a *result* of the creation of the cosmos—which is to say, an ordered whole—out of, or on the basis of, a preexisting state of a disordered universe. Before the cosmos came into being, chôra yielded a very different configuration of space (and the feminine), destined to be "covered over" through the cosmos-constructing operations of ordering, stabilization, and commensuration that the *Timaeus* describes in technical (mathematical and geometric) detail.

As characterized in paragraph 52d4–53a7 of the *Timaeus*, this "pre-cosmic" chôra manifests an active movement in a reciprocal mobilization of itself and the elements—or fleeting traces—found within it. Because these traces—pre-cosmic prefigurations of the four elements, fire, air, earth and water, qua building blocks of the universe—are heterogeneous "forces" of unequal weight, chôra lacks all equilibrium. It is in a state of complete and continuous (self-)differentiation. Shaken by the elements it contains—"full of its own becoming"—chôra shakes these in turn. This "reciprocal dynamism," whereby the space and the forces or elements within it impart movement and form one to the other such that all distinction between activity and passivity is effaced, is, though, to be passified within the circumstructure of cosmic order. Such, indeed, is the task of the Demiurge—the divine "crafts worker" Plato portrays as an architect deploying mathematics and measurement as the means by which to *construct* the four elements in accordance with the values of rationality and proportion that preside over beauty and virtue. By rendering the heterogeneous traces commensurate and stereometric, the Demiurge equally stabilizes chôra such that it meets the criteria of homogeneity and isotropy requisite for it to fulfill its (metaphysical) role as the matrix of a sensible world that is as true a likeness as possible of the intelligible Forms.

Chôra remains, nonetheless—on Plato's own admission—refractory to order, reason and measure even after the intervention by the Demiurge, thus thwarting the tentative to subordinate it completely to the categories structuring Platonic metaphysics. This is the reason why, moreover, many of Irigaray's philosophical peers—most notably, Jacques Derrida, Gilles Deleuze, Julia Kristeva and Jean-François Lyotard—were to hail this notion as a precursor of their own notions of "difference" or "differance," "multiplicity," and "heterogeneity."[10] All sought to reclaim, or to recover, the infinitely repeatable divisibility and ever-changing configuration that characterizes chôra as it exists in its pre-cosmic state, before Plato's attempts to render it amorphous. Indeed, for these philosophers, the *Timaeus* narrates nothing less than metaphysics' inaugural repression of difference: Plato would, indeed, have constructed a geometrically homogeneous space-support out of an infinitely diversified space and thus transformed a moving, differential multiplicity into a container or receptacle. Surely, Irigaray could equally have recognized Plato's account of chôra in the *Timaeus* as a founding tale of metaphysics' repression of a feminine, self-shaping space. . . .

Contrary to her contemporaries, Irigaray disregards, however, Plato's characterization of the pre-cosmic chôra as a differential, ever-changing manifold—despite the latter's displaying a topology she endorses elsewhere as feminine. Indeed, by reading Plato through Plotinus, and thus reinforcing the opposition of matter and form, the intelligible and the sensible, Irigaray *forecloses* any ascription of chôra as a space refractory to metaphysical determinations of a homogeneous "passive" or "inert" extension. She would seem unable to countenance chôra to be a notion that would not only testify to but quite radically expose the operations by which metaphysics appropriates its originary support and transforms an uncircumscribable, transformative, spatiality into a receptacle for the reproduction of the same.

It is undoubtedly (in part at least) Plato's status as a founding father of philosophy that precludes Irigaray from recognizing his having "touched upon" something of the feminine—albeit to suppress it. Philosophy is, after all, exemplary for Irigaray of masculine modes of thought ceaselessly driven to obliterate the debt they owe to that most primordial of all spaces, the maternal space. To recognize Plato's pre-cosmic chôra as a precursor of her elaboration of "uncircumscribable volume" would call into question, that is, a basic tenet of her philosophy of sexual difference: no veritable conception of a/the feminine-other is to be found in the Western tradition. This is a tenet she emphasizes repeatedly: even those (male) philosophers to whom she recognizes a certain attention to alterity (or to carnality) are judged ultimately incapable of thinking otherwise than in a solipsistic or monocentric manner.[11] For a feminine-other to be conceived, what is required is a thought that is itself of a "feminine character" (TBT, 17 passim.), which is to say, put succinctly, that of a woman-philosopher.

And yet—to reiterate—she could well have argued Plato's topological transformation of pre-cosmic chôra into a measurable and masterable extension to be paradigmatic of such an obliteration of the feminine-maternal. She was, after all, to recognize Lacan as having touched on something of feminine jouissance with his accentuation of space even though he too—just like Plato—immediately inscribes this space, via operations of topological "conformation," within the logic of metaphysics. Why recognize in Lacan what she forecloses in Plato? Especially given that Lacan is here "reproducing"—as Irigaray herself puts it—the schemas bequeathed by the (Platonic) tradition.

That granted, Irigaray's foreclusion of another topology to Plato's chôra could equally be motivated by more specific considerations. The notion of chôra—in its original "pre-cosmic" state—was elaborated by Plato on the basis, or appropriation, of prior, pre-metaphysical, notions of a "primordial spatiality" connoted as feminine (as found, for example, in the Orphic cosmogonies). For this reason, if chôra can be attributed a precursor of Irigaray's feminine space, it is not, in fact, Plato to whom credit for having endowed this space with an "other" topology is due. Remember Irigaray's injunction to "recover" or "reappropriate" space: by her foreclusion of an ever-changing chôra as it exists in its original state, Irigaray is perhaps indicating that reappropriation can in no way credit the perpetrator of an originary *v(i)ol* (theft/rape). The resources to recover space are to be found elsewhere: the early cosmogonies them-selves precisely, as well as various Pre-Socratic texts, but above all—as Irigaray's texts preponderantly attest—by a certain mobilization of modern topology.

Notes

1. Casey, *The Fate of Place*, 330. My emphasis.

2. Elizabeth Grosz, in *Space, Time and Perversion*, maintains that in the history of scientific, mathematical and philosophical conceptions of space and time "representations of space have always had [. . .] a priority over representations of time." While this position echoes Bergson's critique of the tendency to con-fuse—necessarily spatial—*representations* of time with time itself, Grosz implies that Irigaray equally condemns the "domination of time by space" by referring in this context to Irigaray's "genealogy of space-time" in *Ethics of Sexual Difference*. See *Space, Time and Perversion*, 97–99.

3. There are, in fact, not only a number of imprecisions in Lacan's presen-tation of the theorem of compactness but additionally several important errors in the transcription (which is to say, publication) of this part of his seminar. It is, as such, "difficult to give a limpid reading of this application of topology to the space of jouissance"—to cite Adam Price's conclusion to his overview of this section of *Encore*. See Price, "Je pars de la limite," footnote 9. Otherwise, for a general commentary in English, see Geneviève Morel, "The Hypothesis of Compactness."

4. Rebecca Hill, the co-editor of this volume, is also of this opinion.

5. The passage in which this sentence figures in the French is as follows: "Ce qui suppose un excès à toute identification à/de soi. Mais cet excès (n')est rien: la vacance de la forme, la faille de la forme, le renvoi à un autre bord où elle se re-touche sans/grâce à rien. Les lèvres de la même forme—mais jamais simplement définie—se débordant en se retouchant et se renvoyant l'une (à) l'autre pour un pourtour que rien n'arrête dans *une* configuration." *Speculum: de l'Autre Femme*, 285.

6. Margaret Whitford, in *Luce Irigaray: Philosophy in the Feminine*, gives an overview of the different readings that have been proposed of the "two lips," 170–173.

7. Rachel Jones equally points out this specificity of "Irigaray's mode of post-Kantianism" in the context of reading Irigaray's "figure of the two lips"

56 | Louise Burchill

along the same lines as myself, as a schema. See *Irigaray: Towards a Sexuate Philosophy*, 173.

I have argued that "the category of the feminine" functions as a schema (in the strictly Kantian sense) for the French philosophers (Deleuze, Kristeva, Derrida, Lyotard, most notably, in addition to Irigaray) having recourse to this category in the last decades of the twentieth century in Burchill, "Re-situating 'the feminine' in Contemporary French Philosophy."

8. These passages are predominantly drawn from Macey's translation (56, 59), but I have, at times, modified them in accordance with Gill's (*Speculum*, 229, 233) or with a rendering of my own.

9. As does Judith Butler in *Bodies That Matter*.

10. I elaborate this in more detail in "Reconsidering *Chôra*, Architecture and 'Woman.'"

11. Irigaray criticizes, for example, the "labyrinthine solipsism" of Merleau-Ponty's notion of the flesh of the world—a reading that David Farrell Krell has queried for its "highly selective analysis." See Krell, *Archeticture*, 164–167.

References

Burchill, Louise. 2006. "Re-Situating 'the Feminine' in Contemporary French Philosophy." In *Belief, Bodies and Being*, edited by Deborah Orr. Rowman & Littlefield.

Burchill, Louise. 2017. "Reconsidering *Chôra*, Architecture and 'Woman.'" *Field* 7, no. 1. www.field-journal.org. https://doi.org/10.62471/field.77.

Butler, Judith. 1993. *Bodies That Matter*. Routledge.

Casey, Edward S. 1998. *The Fate of Place. A Philosophical History*. University of California.

Cutrofello, Andrew. 2002. "The Ontological Status of Lacan's Mathematical Paradigms." In *Reading Seminar XX: Lacan's Major Work on Love, Knowledge, and Feminine Sexuality*, edited by Suzanne Barnard and Bruce Fink. State University of New York Press.

Grosz, Elizabeth. 1995. *Space, Time and Perversion*. Routledge.

Hill, Rebecca. 2012. *The Interval: Relation and Becoming in Irigaray, Aristotle, and Bergson*. Fordham University Press.

Husserl, Edmund. (1913) 1983. *Ideas Pertaining to a Pure Phenomenology and to a Phenomenological Philosophy. First Book: General Introduction to a Pure Phenomenology*. Translated by F. Kersten. Martinus Nijhoff, 1983.

Jones, Rachel. 2011. *Irigaray: Towards a Sexuate Philosophy*. Polity Press.

Kant, Immanuel. (1781, 1787) 1985. *The Critique of Pure Reason*. Translated by Norman Kemp Smith. MacMillan.

Krell, David Farrell. 1997. *Archeticture. Esctasies of Space, Time, and the Human Body.* State University of New York.

Lacan, Jacques. (1975) 1988. *On Feminine Sexuality: The Limits of Love and Knowledge, the Seminar of Jacques Lacan, Book XX, Encore.* Translated by Bruce Fink. Norton, 1998.

Morel, Geneviève. 1995. "The Hypothesis of Compactness in Chapter One of Encore." *Journal of the Centre for Freudian Analysis and Research* 5. https://www.google.com/url?sa=t&source=web&rct=j&opi=89978449&url=https://jcfar.org.uk/wp-content/uploads/2016/03/The-Hypothesis-of-Compactness-Genevieve-Morel.pdf&ved=2ahUKEwjRgt2jhcOFAxVoUqQEHfj0CiwQFnoECBIQAQ&usg=AOvVaw0OYWGvTjLlw7UtB0hQnAYe

Plato. *Timaeus.* 1977. Translated by Desmond Lee. Penguin Classics.

Price, Adam. 2013. "Je pars de la limite—Sur le premier chapitre du Séminaire XX, Encore." https://nls-quebec.org/publications/14-je-pars-de-la-limite-sur-le-premier-chapitre-du-s%C3%A9minaire-xx-encore

Serres, Michel. (1968) 2023. *Hermes I: Communication.* Translated by Louise Burchill. University of Minnesota Press.

Whitford, Margaret. 1991. *Luce Irigaray: Philosophy in the Feminine.* Routledge.

Chapter Three

"The Deepest and Most Initial Vital Structure Is Topological"

A Feminist Philosophy of the Origins of Cellular Life with Irigaray and Simondon

Annu Dahiya

Introduction: Thinking Life Beyond a Framework of Death

Life, in Western philosophy at least, has too often been theorized through a framework of death. Thinking with Irigaray, one could say that "certain properties of the 'vital' have been deadened into the 'constancy' required to give" the theoretical machinery of Western philosophy its form (TS, 115). As a result, this theoretical machine and its accompanying logic fundamentally misunderstand and misrepresent life. This tacit understanding of life through death also occurs in a cultural and scientific sense, the most lucid example being Shelley's *Frankenstein* (1818) in which metaphors of light and electricity providing the "spark" of life abound. Frankenstein himself notes that in order "to examine the causes of life, we must first have recourse to death" (2003, 46). The boundary between life and death is porous and impermanent for Victor Frankenstein, one that he seeks to fully control:

> Life and death appeared to me as ideal bounds, which I should
> first break through, and pour a torrent of light into our dark
> world. A new species would bless me as its creator and source;

> many happy and excellent natures would owe their being to me.
> No father could claim the gratitude of his child so completely
> as I should deserve theirs . . . if I could bestow animation upon
> lifeless matter I might in process of time (although I now found
> it impossible) renew life where death had apparently devoted
> the body to corruption. (2003, 48)

Frankenstein brings about life by suturing together different parts of corpses in a piecemeal-like way. His masculine scientific desire to pursue nature in her "hiding places" (2003, 42; 44) reminds me of how in *An Ethics of Sexual Difference*, Irigaray argues that "it is apparent in many ways that the subject of science is not neuter or neutral. Particularly in the way certain things are not discovered at a given period as well as in the research goals that science sets, or fails to set, for itself" (ESD, 112). If Frankenstein were to try to understand life, *especially* its *origins*, his attempts would all fail. Thinking about life *through life*, rather than death and control, is a difficult task that seems insurmountable if we remain within dominant Western scientific and philosophical paradigms.

In this chapter, I argue that Irigaray provides us with a radically different conceptualization of life, one so profound that it can also help us reimagine the origins of cellular life itself. To further flesh Irigaray's ideas, I put her in conversation with Gilbert Simondon, whose work also has the potential to fundamentally reframe how we understand life through his philosophy of individuation. This is because the question of *where* philosophy begins (and in a sense *we begin*) is critically important for both thinkers. For Irigaray, philosophy needs to begin anew by acknowledging and always remembering its maternal conditions of emergence, instead of treating it as its covered-over "origin" that it then systematically appropriates and extracts from to (re)produce itself. For Simondon, philosophy has misguidedly taken the individual as its starting point when it should begin with the individuation *process* of which the individual is an effect. Philosophy should begin anew to fully elaborate a theory of ontogenesis.

I am not the first to think Irigaray and Simondon together. According to Elizabeth Grosz, feminist theorists can use Simondon to "reorient some of the central questions of feminist thought," including (but not limited to) fundamental questions about reality, nature, and life (2012, 52). Stephen Seely has also explored the significance of Irigaray and Simondon for queer-feminist theory and politics by generating a novel understanding of the origins of sex, and its further individuations in living beings, arguing that Simondon's work "provides the elements for a profound reconceptualization of sexuality" (2021, 25) and that his "theory of individuation is of immense importance in conceptualizing an ontology, or rather an ontogenesis, of sexual difference" (2016, 113). Indeed, Irigaray herself engages with Simondon's theory of sexuation in her most recent text, *The Mediation of Touch* (which I will not address here). My focus here, instead, is the striking moments of resonance about life in Irigaray and Simondon around the question of the *topological* space that life ceaselessly creates for itself.

I contend that Irigaray and Simondon grasp the nature of life decades before contemporary origins research began to grapple with these ideas. I do not present a holistic overview of origins research, instead focusing on *certain* strands of research that are thinking life through an Irigarayan–Simondonian logic. The origin of cellular life from matter on Earth is thought to have occurred somewhere between 3.8 and 4.2 billion years ago, but such research is inherently speculative in nature[1] as there are no direct "fossils" from this period on Earth, making this an impossible question in an empirical sense. But this also makes the origins of cellular life such a rich philosophical question. How matter and life are conceptually conceived have a profound influence on how we approach this question.

Irigaray and Simondon refuse a binary relation between matter and life. They address the question of life in their respective works, Irigaray most notably in *An Ethics of Sexual Difference* and Simondon in *Individuation in Light of Notions of Form and Information*, paying specific attention to the critical importance of cellular membranes, which engender a specific kind of topological space unique to cellular life. More specifically, Irigaray calls attention to how the biological sciences have been slow to study the *permeability* of membranes, something she argues has an affinity with "the feminine universe" (C, 6). The attention Irigaray places on embodiment, gestation, and birth can powerfully frame and guide novel origins research (Dahiya 2022, 67). Simondon makes an allied claim, arguing that scientists attempting to understand the condition of life by trying to create life from inert matter are doomed to fail because they forget that the *topological* condition of life is primordial "in the living being qua living being" ([1964] 2020, 250). In fact, according to Simondon, the essence of the living being—its particular topology—fundamentally "cannot be known based on the physics and chemistry that typically use Euclidean space" (250). Simondon further complexifies Irigaray's claim by focusing on the specific kind of space life requires, writing in detail about the importance of the *polarity* of the living membrane, something of considerable interest in recent origins research.

A phallocentric theory of the origin of life posits a hierarchy between life and matter and understands them as fundamentally opposite to each other. In such a framework, life and matter are always external to one another, and matter is denigrated at the expense of life. In creating a division between matter and life, phallocentric approaches to the origins of life create a dilemma for themselves because they need to pinpoint exactly when life emerges; in other words, they need to answer and explain exactly when "inanimate" matter is animated or penetrated with a logos of life. A feminist philosophical approach to life's cellular origins challenges and refuses a binary (and hierarchical) relation between matter and life therefore bringing us closer to understanding this "impossible" question of how cellular life first emerged. Irigaray and Simondon together move us closer to this goal.

An Individuating Logic that Is Not One: The Living Being as "a Theatre of Individuation"

For Irigaray, thinking life necessitates a logic that does not organize itself around the privileging, dominion, and sameness of the "One," which is precisely the "language of man" that lies at the core of Western metaphysics, which "is built on a binarism that has never been radically scrutinized" (SN, 230). Irigaray argues that, because of a deep adherence to the logic of the One, the philosophical and scientific framework we have inherited is ill-suited to understanding the concept of life. In "The Mechanics of Fluids," Irigaray writes that there is a "powerlessness of logic to incorporate in writing all the characteristic features of nature" (TS, 107). The physical reality that resists symbolization here is outside the logic of the one and a logic of solids. Such a logic cannot be counted through whole numbers; it is between one and two. Moreover, any theory of difference gendered through the mechanics of solids would be one where difference is molded through exteriority. A difference that differs *within* and from itself is impossible to conceive in a logic of solids.

Furthermore, when such a logic theorizes difference, it understands difference as binary and as a hierarchical ordering between two pairs (one marked as "lack" and inferior so that the other term can be elevated and marked a superior), resulting in an inadequate theory of difference. A logic of *at least two* would challenge the primacy and privileging of the principles of self-identity and noncontradiction (two of the three major tenets of Aristotelian logic), and in doing so, would move us toward an altogether different logic, one that would be a logic of *contiguity* that generates difference in itself rather than through oppositions (Jones 2011, 85). Instead of a principle of contradiction that focuses on the mutual exclusiveness between two terms, Irigaray cultivates a logic of difference, one that is fundamentally fluid and therefore at odds with the principle of identity and the principle of noncontradiction (Hass 2022, 80).

A logic of solids, what we could also call the logic of the One, can never capture the nature of life because it deadens the properties of the vital. The language of the subject is rooted in and made possible by a certain formulation of logic, one that not only separates subject and object but also operates through freezing reality, one molded on the logic of solids (and by extension, a rigid sense of being)—all of which is incapable of attuning itself to the study of life. Irigaray argues:

> Occidental logic appeals to and is based on the mechanics of solids. Fluids always overflow reason, the ratio, exceed the measure, plunge back into undifferentiation: they are the universe of myths and magic, of darkness resistant to the light of the philosophers who approach it only to enclose it within the confines of their thought. Forgetting that, without fluid, there would be no unity, since fluid always remains *between* solid substances in order to join them together, to reunite them . . . Have the sciences, in their own way, not interpreted the end of philosophy as the end of the predominance of the logic of solids? Have they not discovered or rediscovered the properties of a dynamics of flux to which discourse remains resistant, constraining us in obedience to a world of outdated reason, even though we are actually living in a universe where the power of fluids is increasingly dominant? (SN, 233; emphasis in original)

Irigaray draws attention to fluids because they embody an alternative window on how to conceive of reality and consequently another way to practice logic. The properties of fluids that the sciences are (re)discovering exemplify that fluids correspond with the real; solids are "cut" from fluids—a solid is a staticized block of what was once first fluid. A fluid logic would be an expression of the logic of nature, the *real* real, bringing forth a feminist philosophy of life.

Simondon also moves us toward a feminist philosophy of life through his philosophy of ontogenesis. Individuation lies at the heart of Simondon's philosophy of difference. Instead of centering ontology, his central philosophical aim is generating a theory of *ontogenesis* grounded in individuation. He argues that (Western) philosophy has taken the *individual* as its starting point, which it then uses as its frame of reference to conceptualize individuation. Philosophy consistently beginning with the individual is an error because starting with the individual will never disclose a principle of individuation. Beginning with the individual thinks in the form of a term already given and does not begin with life—in fact, "[i]ndividuality can only appear with the death of beings; death is the correlate of individuality" (Simondon [1964] 2020, 181). Simondon states: "If, on the contrary, we supposed that individuation doesn't just produce the individual, we would not seek to pass quickly through the stage of individuation to arrive at this ultimate reality that the individual is: we would try to grasp ontogenesis in the whole unfolding of its reality and *to know the individual through individuation rather than individuation starting from the individual*" (3; emphasis in original). Individuation is a becoming that is never at rest, its inherent movement and ontogenesis of becoming bring us closer to articulating the forces of nature itself. This maneuver cannot be thought—indeed is not possible—through the logic of the One. *Neither* individuation—nor the living being—can be understood through or as *unity*. The individual is a *relative* reality, a "certain phase of being which supposes a preindividual reality prior to it and which, even after individuation, does not fully exist all by itself, for individuation does not exhaust in a single stroke the potentials of preindividual reality" (3). The pre-individual is an inexhaustible source of potential energy. To know individuation through the individual renders the individual as something that can auto-institute itself—in other words, something that can birth *itself*. In contrast, to know the individual through *individuation* is to stress its conditions of emergence—the pre-individual—in all its further complexifications. No one concept can explain pre-individual reality, and Simondon notes that there is "the quantic and the metastable complementary (the more than unity), which is the true pre-individual" (6). For Simondon, the pre-individual is pre-physical because it is "as unphased and unstructured" the conditions of emergence of microphysics itself (Simondon 2013, 327; cited in Seely 2021, 42).

The living being is "a theatre of individuation," keeping alive the original *charge* of the pre-individual in all of its activities (Simondon [1964] 2020, 7). This theater of individuation is an expression of an Irigarayan logic that is not one. Vital individuation, at its origin, is a difference of degree rather than a difference in kind from physical individuation. On this, Grosz writes: "Life remains indebted to the pre-individual to the extent that the resources for all its becomings, all its future individuations, self-actualizations, must be drawn from these singularities which its own must incorporate. [. . .] Life does not emerge as a self-driven force; rather, it is possible only to the extent that it perpetuates but also finds a further form of elaboration and development of the pre-individual and of physical individuality" (2012, 49). This idea fundamentally recasts the relationship between matter and life thereby opening itself up to a feminist philosophy of life that thinks outside a hierarchically binary logic. The emphasis on the process of individuation *above* the individual for Simondon organically moves us outside of autologic(al) closure of masculinist paradigms of becoming.

"The Deepest and Most Initial Vital Structure Is Topological"

Irigaray makes almost prophetic predictions of areas of science that are *under*theorized in dominant paradigms of research that are crucial for us to examine (WDM, 2–3). Regarding the biological sciences, she writes: "*The biological sciences* have been very slow to take on certain problems. The constitution of the placental tissue, the permeability of membranes, for example. Are these not questions directly correlated to the female and maternal sexual imaginary?" (ESD, 123)

Ethics was originally published in French in 1984. Irigaray foreshadows what origins of life research begins to grapple with almost three decades later (Martin and Russell 2003, 59–60). The disequilibrium that living systems "convert into a specific cascade of usable internal disequilibria" (Branscomb and Russell 2018a) requires a specific kind of topological space: a membrane that is semipermeable, which allows for critically vital reactions to take place—the specific sorts of thermodynamic processes that occur across membranes are deeply complex and therefore could not have been *initially* sustained by the first living systems trying to emerge. They therefore needed to rely on a milieu that initially provided these far-from-equilibrium semipermeable conditions.[2] In short, cellular life needed primordial wombs for its birth. I have explored this through Irigaray's work and contemporary origins research in-depth elsewhere (Dahyia 2022, 67–71). Here, I will focus on the specific kind of *topology* these primordial wombs provided, that life, since then, has sustained. An Irigarayan attention to the permeability of membranes, combined with Simondon's theory of ontogenesis and his understanding of the specific topology (as well as chronology) of living being, already begins to put in practice a logic of at least two.

It might be surprising to learn that attention to the *space* in which cellular life first began is often not considered in research at all. On this forgetting, three scientists write:

> What has been largely missing from experimental work on the origin of life over the last 70 years is much insight from life itself. . . . Prebiotic chemistry has been approached from the intellectual tradition of synthetic chemistry, and the apotheosis is the "one-pot synthesis." . . . But cells are not simply a pot of chemicals; they have a structure in space. Biochemistry is vectorial . . . meaning that reactions have a direction in space, frequently in relation to structures such as membranes. (Sojo et al. 2016, 182)

The overwhelming focus in much of origins research on synthesizing the "molecules of life" understands life as a process that is just "chemistry in a bag" (Branscomb and Russell 2018a) because the researchers fail to consider the far-from-equilibrium conditions or milieu that the birth of cellular life required (thereby misunderstanding a fundamental irreducible feature of life). For life, "equilibrium is death" (Sojo et al. 2014). Furthermore, the reaction pathways and reacting agents that so much of origins research focuses on seem to not use insight from life at all in that no known living organism uses the chemical compounds and pathways being studied (Sojo et al. 2016, 182). This can especially be the case with "soup theories" that model themselves after Stanley Miller's 1952 experiment in which the biochemical building blocks for nucleic acids were synthesized within a laboratory using electrical discharge (which, interestingly enough, shares striking parallels to Frankenstein's experiment) (Branscomb and Russell 2018a). Before Miller's experiment, the idea of the precursors to life being created in vitro was not believed possible. In sum, a vast amount of attention has focused on the molecules of life at the expense of thinking about *where* cellular life began. Attending to this second question can reframe the origins of life's biochemistry itself. What particular, specific *place* was crucial for life? How might life have begun from a nonspecified ancient oceanic milieu? I will return to this question below.

A particular strand of origins of life research, however, *is* deeply *place*-based and follows an Irigarayan–Simondonian logic. This research focuses on a specific type of deep-sea vents called alkaline vents (discovered in 2000 near the Mid-Atlantic Ridge in the depths of the Atlantic Ocean [Hines 2008]) as the possible site of cellular life's origins. In these ancient geochemical sites, microscopic pores naturally and spontaneously were created that miraculously parallel the membrane topology of the two most ancient domains of life (archaea and bacteria). While Irigaray foreshadows the *semipermeability* of these microscopic pores, Simondon portends the significance of their specific topology for life.

In *Individuation in Light of Notions of Form and Information*, Simondon argues that it is the *membrane* that constitutes the living being qua living. Simondon's ideas on the polarity of the membrane prefigure the focus on the crucial role of "semipermeable compartmentation" in life's cellular emergence in geologically and geochemically rooted research (that is, hydrothermal vent theories). Both stress how vital the membrane, or "semipermeable compartmentation," is to life for/in the particular topology of life. The laboratory synthesis of urea in 1828 by Wöhler is often regarded as the experiment that shattered the doctrine of vitalism (the idea that there is an immaterial force that fundamentally differentiates life from matter). By synthesizing a chemical associated with biological processes, this proved that living matter is not different in composition from inert matter and that the chemical components of life can be created in vitro. This focus on the "fabrication of living matter from inert matter" continues to motivate how we understand the relation between matter and life. The synthesis of urea does not address the qualities most central to life and its difference from matter. Boldly put, and like Irigaray, Simondon is calling attention to the tendency and desire to (try to) understand life through death, writing:

> There is still quite a gap between the production of substances utilized by life and the production of the living being [. . .] [To get] closer to life, we would need to produce the *topology* of the living being, its particular type of space, the relation between a milieu of interiority and a milieu of exteriority. The

> bodies of organic chemistry do not bring with them a different topology than that of the usual physical and energetic relations. However, perhaps the *topological* condition is *primordial* in the *living* being qua living being [. . .] perhaps the essence of the living being is a certain topological arrangement that cannot be known based on the physics and chemistry that typically use Euclidean space. (2020, 250)

Euclidean space is a homogeneous space "whose infinite divisibility makes possible the point-like localization of material particles" (Čapek 1969, 306). The infinite divisibility and homogeneity of Euclidean space suggest that a spatial point exists in an external relation to another spatial point in this kind of space. Simondon's incisive point here of the significance of the membrane finds a theoretical ally in the origins of life research that argues the specific kind of *topology* was crucial for the origins of cellular life. This is the complete opposite of the "one-pot synthesis" approach to the origin of life because there is a fundamental understanding that "cells are not simply a pot of chemicals; they have a structure in space" (Sojo et al. 2016, 182; emphasis added). Furthermore, the simplest organism

> is the one that does not possess a mediate interior milieu but merely an absolute interior and an absolute exterior. For the organism, the characteristic polarity of life is at the level of the membrane; it is here that life essentially exists as an aspect of a dynamic topology which itself maintains the metastability by which it exists. Life is self-maintaining metastability, but a metastability that requires a topological condition: structure and function are linked, because the most primitive and deepest vital structure is topological. (Simondon [1964] 2020, 252)

This deepest vital structure carries within it a specific topology and chronology, both of which have the pre-individual as their source, and together form "the first dimensionality of the living being" (Simondon [1964] 2020, 254). The mutual presence of topology and chronology differs from Euclidean space, where "space and physical time cannot coincide" (255). Furthermore, "the fact of being within the interior of the selective polarized membrane means that this substance has been held in the condensed past" (254). Within the membrane that allows living individuation to emerge, the interiority of its milieu is in touch with itself, as there is "no distance in topology" (254, 255); the past then begins to serve a purpose in living individuation, becoming a memory that living individuation carries within itself that it further elaborates.

If its polarized, semipermeable membrane keeps the living being alive at every moment, what are the origins of life's ability to repolarize membranes? Origins research and Simondon address this question in different but intertwined ways. For the former, one of "the great unsolved problems in biology" is that the membrane *bioenergetics* of the two most ancient domains of life (archaea and bacteria) are universal but that their membrane *compositions* are quite different (Sojo et al. 2014). Bacterial and archaeal membranes are *polarized* in the same way in terms of the concentration of ions on one side of their membrane (which creates a disequilibrium that these cells harness to perform chemical reactions), but the membranes themselves chemically differ. This problem also finds a solution in deep-sea alkaline vents because "vent pores and [modern] autotrophic cells have analogous topology" (Sojo et al. 2016, 183). Before cellular life would have been able to re(create) this chemical disequilibrium at their membranes themselves (using membrane pumps to move H+ ions outside their membranes), these steep electrochemical pH gradients would have been sustained in the vents through "continuous hydrothermal flow and ocean convection" (183). Because "biochemistry is fundamentally vectorial, all autotrophic cells draw on electrochemical differences in ion concentration across membranes" (192) to convert carbon dioxide (CO_2) into organic compounds. This leads to the question of what sort of chemiosmotic membrane LUCA—the "last universal common ancestor" before the ancient divergence of the two oldest domains of life—may have had. Current research suggests that LUCA was born in and subsequently harnessed "geochemically sustained proton [H+] gradients" within in these far-from-equilibrium deep-sea alkaline vents, first as "leaky" or "semipermeable" protocells that, over time, were able to sustain this semipermeability themselves (Sojo et al. 2014).

Like origins research, Simondon thinks about polarity in an electrochemical sense, but he also provides a deeper ontological framework of what kind of topological space the polarity and permeability of the membrane create, a specific kind of topology that living individuation amplifies and ceaselessly maintains. Following Simondon, one could say that living individuation, in its first phase of individuation, originates *within* physical individuation. On polarity and individuation, Simondon writes:

> There is a preparation of individuality every time that a polarity is created, every time that an asymmetrical qualification, an orientation, and an order appear; the condition of individuation resides in this existence of potentials that allow matter to be polarized, whether living or not . . . an entire theory of polarization is to be made that would no doubt further clarify the rapports of what we call living matter (or organized matter) and inert or inorganic matter; it indeed seems that non-living matter is already organizable and that this organization precedes any passage to functional life, as if organization were a sort of intermediate static life between inorganic reality and functional life properly speaking. The latter would be that in which a being reproduces itself, whereas in non-living matter the individual indeed produces effects on other individuals but does not generally produce individuals similar to it. ([1964] 2020, 223)

If one of the distinguishing differences between physical individuation and vital individuation is the dynamic topology of the living—something noted by Simondon and contemporary origins researchers—it is in these pores (or, to use more Irigarayan terminology, within these wombs) that the ontogenesis of vital individuation can begin. Though vital processes are seen to be more complex than nonvital physiochemical processes,

> vital individuation does not come after physicochemical individuation but during this individuation and before its fulfillment, by suspending it at the moment when it has not reached its stable equilibrium and by making it capable of expanding and propagating before the iteration of the perfect structure merely able to repeat itself, which would conserve in the living individual a bit of pre-individual tension, of active communication, in the form of internal resonance between extreme orders of magnitude . . . vital individuation would come to be inserted in physical individuation by suspending its course, by slowing it down and by making it capable of propagating in the inchoate state. The living individual would be, in some sense and on its most initial levels, a crystal in the nascent state that is amplified without stabilizing. (Simondon [1964] 2020, 163–164)

In this remarkable passage, vital individuation, at its origin, is not a difference in kind from physical individuation. In vital individuation, the metastability (still rife with potential) that is necessary for the propagation is maintained, slowed down (in the sense of not going to stable equilibrium) and somehow even amplified. This "amplification without stabilization" of vital individuation is possible when and where the metastability of the system that will individuate into a living being is rife with potential but also in continual movement. Indeed, the living being has "the effect of deferring and delaying physical reality by expanding the initial phase of its constitution; it would necessitate more precise and more complex conditions of initial tension and metastability capable of 'neotenizing' physical individuation," thereby keeping it within its initial tense, metastable regime (Simondon [1964] 2020, 164).

Returning to place-based origins research focused on alkaline sea vents, it is in these sites that an opening in physical individuation can engender living individuation. Moreover, the specific kind of space, semi permeable compartmentation generated from the hydrothermal exhalation of metallic and sulfide-rich waters, could provide the conditions for cellular membranes to emerge (Martin and Russell 2003, 65). If living individuation is not different in kind from physical individuation, the topology of a hydrothermal vent closes the gap for this new order of individuation to come into being. Thus, microscopic iron sulphide pores, as well as the continuous laminar flow of alkaline vent water creating a gradient with acidic cooler ocean water, are the theoretical, chemical, and physical seeds for vital individuation to "insert itself" into physical individuation thereby sustaining the dynamic topology that marks cellular membranes. The resolution of the physical individuation is kept open, amplified without stabilizing, thereby unfolding vital individuation.

If "the living being is characterized by the fact that it discovers in its field of reality structural conditions that allow it to resolve its own incompatibilities," it can then have "the capacity for the autogenesis of structures" (Simondon [1964] 2020, 162–163). This capacity to make itself, ontologically made possible by the pre-individual (which is prephysical and prevital), needs a specific physical milieu to unfold. It is this crucial attention to the specific *milieu* that origins research stresses. Simondon gives us a radical way to understand self-organization through the ontogenesis of individuation. Because his philosophical project is an incorporeal materialism, centering "the subsistence of the [pre-individual] ideal *in* the material or corporeal" (Grosz 2017a, 5), his work not only foreshadows place-based geochemical origins research; it also speaks about the relation between physical and living individuation that scientific research, rooted in empiricism, cannot address because ontogenesis is the condition of emergence of what science studies.

Coda: A Lived Ethics

Though they may not be as directly urgent as projects focusing on lives that are in immediate peril, feminist philosophies of life must also include questions about the most abstract metaphysical and ontological aspects of life. For Hasana Sharp and Chloë Taylor, to craft a feminist philosophy of life, "it is not enough to expose the tendency of discourses to normalize and exclude racialized, feminized, differently abled, and gender nonconforming people, although such a task remains central to feminist theory. . . . It is also necessary to ask what life is. What are the conditions under which life on Earth is possible? To what extent do we share the struggles and needs of other living beings?" (2016, 1–2). Allied with contemporary struggles for life, feminist philosophies of life must make space for more abstract questions regarding life and its relation to matter and the Earth because it is here that conceptual displacement of the human can generate a new onto-ethics—in other words, "an ethics of life lived in a world of difference" (Grosz 2017b, 16).

A central aim in Irigaray's political commitment is to bring about a lived ethics that would reinvent our relationship with ourselves, with each other, and our living milieu. Rejecting a binary between the biological and the social and political, this lived ethics can be engendered by starting from ourselves as living beings. Our language would then be alive, embodying change, and cultivating the capacity for genuine dialogue between subjects.

"The living," for Irigaray, "is that which continues to grow, to become" (C, 7). This growth is never simply an increase of the same, but, at the same time, the new is not ushered in a way that would destroy what currently exists. A living being continues to become by carefully and endlessly modulating itself. It invents new ways to live but in a manner that does not exterminate itself (because to do so would mean it would cease to live). Irigaray gives us a philosophy of *relation* that rejects and works outside the logic of oneness because it "contests the cleavages sensible/intelligible, concrete/abstract, matter/form, living/dead" and "refuses the opposition between being and becoming. As such, it is always metastable, becoming (C, 12).

Irigaray and Simondon bring attention to intimately allied arguments about the ontological nature of life, but it is Irigaray who explicitly demonstrates how a rethinking of the living can be brought about by closely examining and disrupting how philosophy, as well as science, has marked and treated the "maternal" or "feminine," both through the denigration of these two concepts and ignoring and covering over their critical importance. A feminist philosophy of life would rethink how we conceive of our origins and, in doing so, perhaps push us to consider who or what we would like to become.

Notes

1. The gap between the inorganic world and the cell seems insurmountable because the cell is a clearly bounded autonomous individual that can reproduce itself.

2. On what the complex thermodynamics processes that occur across cell membranes tell us about the required milieu for life's cellular emergence, see Martin et al. (2014), Lane and Martin (2012), and Branscomb and Russell (2018b).

References

Branscomb, Elbert, and Michael J. Russell. 2018a. "Frankenstein or a Submarine Alkaline Vent: Who Is Responsible for Abiogenesis? Part 1: What Is Life—That It Might Create Itself?" *Bioessays* 40, no. 8: 1700179.

Branscomb, Elbert, and Michael J. Russell. 2018b. "Frankenstein or a Submarine Alkaline Vent: Who Is Responsible for Abiogenesis? Part 2: As Life Is Now, So It Must Have Been in the Beginning." *Bioessays* 40, no. 8: 1700182.

Čapek, Milič. 1969. "Bergson's Theory of Matter and Modern Physics." In *Bergson and the Evolution of Physics*, edited by P. A. Y. Gunter. University of Tennessee Press.

Dahiya, Annu. 2020. "The Conditions of Emergence: Towards a Feminist Philosophy of the Origins of Life." PhD diss., Duke University.

Dahiya, Annu. 2022. "The Conditions of Emergence: Irigaray, Primordial Wombs, and the Origins of Cellular Life." In *Horizons of Difference: Rethinking Space, Place, and Identity with Irigaray*, edited by Ruthanne Crapo, Yvette Russell, and Brenda Sharp. State University of New York Press.

Grosz, Elizabeth. 2012. "Identity and Individuation: Some Feminist Reflections." In *Gilbert Simondon: Being and Technology*, edited by Arne De Boever, Alex Murray, Jon Roffe, and Ashley Woodward. Edinburgh University Press.

Grosz, Elizabeth. 2017a. *The Incorporeal: Ontology, Ethics, and the Limits of Materialism*. Duke University Press.

Grosz, Elizabeth. 2017b. "Irigaray, the Untimely, and the Constitution of an Onto-Ethics." *Australian Feminist Law Journal* 43, no. 1: 15–24.

Hass, Marjorie. 2022. "Fluid Thinking: Irigaray's Critique of Formal Logic." In *Representing Reason: Feminist Theory and Formal Logic*, edited by Marjorie Hass and Rachel Joffe. Rowman and Littlefield.

Hines, Sandra. 2008. "Lost City Pumps Life-Essential Chemicals at Rates Unseen at Typical Black Smokers." *University of Washington News*, January 31. https://www.washington.edu/news/2008/02/07/lost-city-pumps-life-essential-chemicals-at-rates-unseen-at-typical-black-smokers-2/

Jones, Rachel. 2011. *Irigaray: Towards a Sexuate Philosophy*. Polity Press.

Lane, Nick, and William Martin. 2012. "The Origin of Membrane Bioenergetics." *Cell* 151: 1406–1416.

Martin, William, and Michael J. Russell. 2003. "On the Origins of Cells: A Hypothesis for the Evolutionary Transitions from Abiotic Geochemistry to Chemoautotrophic Prokaryotes, and from Prokaryotes to Nucleated Cells." *Philosophical Transactions of the Royal Society of London B* 358, no. 1429: 59–85.

Martin, William F., Filipa L. Sousa, and Nick Lane. 2014. "Energy at Life's Origin." *Science* 344: 1092–1093.

Russell, Michael J., Roy. M. Daniel, Allan J. Hall, and John A. Sherringham. 1994. "A Hydrothermally Precipitated Catalytic Iron Sulphide Membrane as a First Step Toward Life." *Journal of Molecular Evolution* 39, no. 3: 231–243. doi:10.1007/ BF00160147.

Seely, Stephen D. 2016. "Does Life Have (a) Sex? Thinking Ontology and Sexual Difference with Irigaray and Simondon." In *Feminist Philosophies of Life*, edited by Hasana Sharp and Chloë Taylor. McGill-Queens University Press.

Seely, Stephen D. 2021. "Individuation, Sexuation, Technicity." *Theory, Culture, & Society* 38, no. 4: 23–45.

Sharp, Hasana, and Chloë Taylor. 2016. "Introduction." In *Feminist Philosophies of Life*, edited by Hasana Sharp and Chloë Taylor. McGill-Queen's University Press.

Shelley, Mary. 2003. *Frankenstein*. Barnes and Nobles Classics.

Simondon, Gilbert. (2013). L'individuation à la lumière des notions de forme et d'information, 2nd ed. Éditions Jérôme Millon.

Simondon, Gilbert. (1964) 2020. *Individuation in Light of Notions of Form and Information*. Translated by Taylor Adkins. University of Minnesota Press.

Sojo, Victor, Andrew Pomiankowski, and Nick Lane. 2014. "A Bioenergetic Basis for Membrane Divergence in Archaea and Bacteria." *PLOS Biology* 12, no. 8: 1–12.

Sojo, Victor, Barry Herschy, Alexandra Whicher, Eloi Camprubi, and Nick Lane. 2016. "The Origin of Life in Alkaline Hydrothermal Vents." *Astrobiology* 16, no. 2: 181–197.

Yong, Ed. 2012. "How Life Emerged from Deep-Sea Rocks." *Nature*, December 20. doi.org/10.1038/nature.2012.12109.

Chapter Four

Carnal Being-with

Irigaray in Dialogue with Heidegger

Jennifer Carter

In *Being and Time*, Martin Heidegger writes that human existence, "[. . .] Dasein is essentially being-with [. . .]" ([1927] 2010, 117). He contends human existence is not an objective presence like other things we encounter but a special mode of existing he characterizes as being-in: being-in-the-world. His comments about being-with are significant because he affirms that being-with, or being with others, is just as primordial to human existence as being-in-the-world. However, this co-being, according to Heidegger, typically takes place inauthentically, in a way that does not reveal its underlying truth.

Irigaray suggests that there are obstacles to being in communion with another human being but nonetheless that being-with is fundamental to human existence. Irigaray diverges from Heidegger in what she considers being-with to be. Heidegger understands being-with first as caring about what we encounter and do together. That is, we *are* with each other when, and insofar as, we care about the same things ([1927] 2010, 114–117). In contrast, Irigaray says that Heidegger's overall understanding of care does not encompass the whole context and quality of being with an other. She thinks, moreover, that to care is not sufficient for being-with, even when it means caring with or caring about another. For Irigaray, caring on its own lacks the potential for subjectifying one and another as truly "co-," even though we may both care—and about the same things. Despite that we certainly do co-care, Irigaray suggests that we only do so as being-with "authentically" when we are truly ourselves and being for and with one another as ourselves. To be with another is difficult, suggests Irigaray, because we are likely to be confronted with subjective or cultural barriers to genuinely appreciating who the other really is in their difference from us and to being with them in a truly sensitive way. Even if one is able to care together in an authentic way according to Heidegger's understanding, Irigaray remains skeptical that even authentic co-caring is going to overcome the difficulties of being with others. She thinks being-with an other is unachievable on the basis of care on its own. Rather, to be with an other in a genuine way requires working through our own subjectification as autonomously living human beings in a concrete time and space including our bodily being, belonging, and interrelations.

According to Irigaray, Heidegger's analysis of being-with remains predominantly mental and abstracted from fleshly physical being (CFN, 166–177; see also Scharff 2019, 49–84). His account of being-with does not allow for a full reckoning with the coming together of the comprehensive beings of two with one another. She explains Heidegger never completely gives up his commitment to the West's traditional hierarchy of consciousness over materiality. He does not appreciate that being-in-the-world's and being-with's equiprimordiality suggests incarnation and physicality are directly essential to being-with. Physicality is clearly and directly a component of being-in-the-world; yet Heidegger seems to think it only indirectly related to being-with through care. However, the very carnality that characterizes human life has to do with our capacity to be physically with one another (CFN, 114, 117). Irigaray's analysis in turn reveals a fundamental connection between being-in, being-with, and spatiality.

As Irigaray mentions in her interview with Andrea Wheeler in *Conversations*, "[a]s for the 'care' of Heidegger, I am afraid that it is too neutral and anonymous to take into consideration the other as such—the other here present with myself in an apparent same space and time but who, in fact, belongs to another world" (C, 53–72). Not only is it necessary to relate to the other in the "same" space and time as two being there together but the difference in our respective worlds also comes into play both as limit and as a threshold between us preserving our difference, albeit making possible a path between us. Space and spatialization link and mark the difference between our respective worlds that remain different even when with one another.

The caring relation as being-with, for Irigaray, is secondary to being-with in a more subjectified sense, that is, as subjects who shed their anonymity in favor of a subjective identity that makes them up as themselves and different from one another. This identity, for Irigaray, cannot be exclusively cultural, social, or biological but must consist comprehensively of "who" one is and amounts to "world" for the subject. Since these features of a subject's world, including bodily ones, are different depending on who one is, each subject is in or brings about a different world. Irigaray argues that this "who"-ness arises on the basis of what she calls "sexuation" that includes fleshly being but perhaps most particularly, self-self relation, "self-affection," and the relation of self to an other, "hetero-affection." "Sexuate subjectivity" for Irigaray is ontological or existential in that one is who one is on the basis of how one is (pre-)given but also how one gives themselves to themselves and is "given" (back) to themselves by others. The "who" of who we are *is* our world, including our carnal being. Our radical difference(s) compose a world that is both unique (singular) and in part shared with another/others when we encounter one another.

Being-with, according to Irigaray, is the bridging of these worlds and these "whos" on the basis of sharing in difference that can also be a relation in desire. Significantly, this sharing in desire, and sharing in a human space and time, sharing of breath and carnality, happens on the basis of sharing in touch, which depends in part on a physical context. Being-with is not a phenomenon merely of mutual caring, taking care together, but of a relational dynamic between two actually existing, living embodied subjects who are of different "worlds" and who encounter one another as different. Nevertheless, this encounter remains continually challenging since it means drawing on the comprehensive being of one's subjectivity and one's respective differences with an other in order for being with them to be "authentic." For Irigaray, to genuinely be with another is to be in communion with them, indicating that there is reciprocity to being-with demanding mutual sensitivity. Even more challenging than characterizing and understanding what is being-with is the project of enacting being-with in a living relation between two or more subjects. What follows is an exploration of the ways Irigaray, in contrast to and in conversation with Heidegger, addresses questions of being-with as they relate to space and spatialization, as well as indications of promising ways of addressing them.

Irigaray provides ways of understanding the differing modes of spatialization of objects and human beings, including analyses of Heidegger's later work concerning the end of metaphysics. I show links between Irigaray's discussions of technology and space and Heidegger's. This contrast makes clear some of the ways Heidegger intuited, on the one hand, the cruciality of with-being and human bodily being but misses the point of the significance of carnality and sensitivity to being-with. Irigaray, on the other hand, directly shows the fundamental necessity of carnal being to being with others. Contrasting the approach of Heidegger with Irigaray's and focusing on her critiques makes clear why it is so challenging to overcome the prejudices against bodily being in the Western milieu. The contrast also allows contemplation of not only Irigaray's theses but her approach, which can act as a model for being with one another.

Being with Others

In *Democracy Begins Between Two*, Irigaray articulates how a *heteros*, a difference across a divide, from one "side" to another, can be bridged if the subjective difference between the two is made explicit, given equivalent dignity, and if a context is established from which and to which each subject is empowered to be, especially as relating to radical difference (DB, 142, 155; see also Sares 2023, 21–22). Being-with necessitates a mediating grounded in difference to connect across a divide established in the specific respective identities of subjects. For Irigaray, these identities are fundamentally sexuate but that does not entail that they are based on or confined to a biological or even socially determined sex, which in our current milieu she contends can amount to byproducts of a patriarchal neutralization of difference. Sexuation rather arises as an interplay of fleshly difference, of global being.

Since being-with requires the mediation of difference, a mere spatial co-belonging is insufficient to establish a genuine "we" that is not merely an "I" projected from one onto the other, or a duplication of two of the same. Rather, being-with demands establishing a genuine mutual co-relation in difference. Co-belonging side-by-side to the same and in the same space is not sufficient, and in fact thinking in the manner of "being-alongside" presents an obstacle to thinking genuine being-with when that being-with, as Irigaray suggests, necessitates being together in difference. This in turn involves being in two different worlds/a shared world, which includes two differently arising spatiotemporal contexts, in part shared, but also in part not. Sharing with another in being with them in part amounts to sharing these orientations in space and time and is relative to our living organization and sharing with one another within and of space-time.

Spatiality itself is transformed, co- or re-constituted by a relation to and a relation with an ontologically different other. We (co-)inhabit different spaces—worlds, being(s)-in—that do not belong exclusively to the same space. There is an interval that is demarcated on both sides, from one to the other and from the other to one. In a relation of difference, without surrounding the other within a network of my own space and spatial relations, without recasting them as an object within a world of objects, and without retreating from them in reclusion or defense, I can maintain my difference from them and respect their difference from me when meeting them. Irigaray proposes that the relation can take place fruitfully if it is grounded in touch, specifically in recognition of sharing in breathing a shared atmosphere together.

Space, Ground, and Breath

In *The Forgetting of Air in Martin Heidegger*, Irigaray observes that if metaphysics is a history of the West's forgetting about air and about breath while constructing a ground on which to stand thinking, there cannot easily be a metaphysics that remembers breath and breathing with one another. Moreover, "[t]he metaphysician would be a trafficker in airs," she says (FA, 6), meaning they subject breath itself to the standard of solidity and objectivity set out by traditional Western metaphysics, even though breath moves fluidly and cannot be said to belong as a "property" solely to one subject or another or to the atmosphere. To do so is to cut off breathing from the sharing at play in being-with. On the contrary, understanding the relation between breathing and thinking does not have to contain breathing within a fixed volume.

In his later work, Heidegger proposes to find an end to or to put to an end the metaphysical quest of finding a metaphysical system that can contain all space and time and to look instead for a clearing, a place within which beings appear (see Heidegger 1993, 431–449). Irigaray notices that this still depends, even if he does not intend it to, on a solidified ground: "He wants this language he uses to ensure him a solid foundation. And if he is the one who lays this foundation, there is no risk of losing it too suddenly. Which can always occur if it proceeds from a female other:

should she absent herself, he is plunged back into the abyss" (FA, 38). This ground is, unbeknown to Heidegger, a false bottom, never truly a ground, because it depends on a false promise of a point of origin or of a figure-ground relation. Irigaray proposes that for this falsity to give way to a truer, sustainable frame that does not amount to a superficial construction, a suitable background for subjective co-relation would not amount to a foundation but an envelope where each subject provides not a total support or a perfect container but an opening, a horizon for the other, a subjective limit that responds to and challenges each one without closing in on them.

Irigaray writes, "[t]he life she gives is already prior to any possible demonstration. Without demonstration, she gives him that *Gestell* that is his living body. The mediation of this gift—or of this *from which*—is fluid: the blood" (FA, 33; emphasis in original). To give a frame, there must be some passage through or between voids. "Built on the void," Irigaray writes, "the bridge joined two banks that, prior to its construction, were not: the bridge made two banks. And, further: the bridge, a solidly established passageway, joins two voids that, prior to its construction, were not: the bridge made the void" (FA, 30). The void(s) do not become the annihilation of the world, though this is traditionally what a metaphysician fears. Rather the voids are the place(s) of thinking or the beginning of thinking and living. They are opened up in the passage from unthought to thought, or from birth to life, from the difference realized in carnal being. This is the birth of thinking, but also its limit—that is, how to bridge the void with language and with flesh, both necessary.

The flesh offers an envelope, the "first" of such envelopes, that which encircles the first bodily dwelling of the subject: their own flesh and the being that encircles them. But this fleshly envelope must not stay enclosed if it is to grow with a human consciousness that eventually matures as an autonomously living human. A subject opens an encounter with another, and this involves a double (at least) envelope, each one becoming an envelope of thinking, language, and living for the other. As Irigaray writes,

> In (the) place of the first receptacle—of him, or of her—in (the) place of their first "meeting," there is, now, void. To pass over it, from his side, in any case: a bridgeway. This bridge is for re-turning: the first empty envelope, the envelope of the void, into another one. This yields a double envelope or loop. The sign of infinity? The bridge is at the re-crossing-re-intersection

of these two envelopes. At this place, the inside passes into the outside, which comes back to the inside after having gone around. There is no longer any not-inside or not-outside here. Here the whole is: taken up again in a flawless double encirclement. There will be no breaching of this double boundary. Everything takes place "inside" this double enclosure: one comes and goes here from one side of the bank to the other, from one bank to the other nearly imperceptibly, and without noticing that one has changed sides. (FA, 30–31)

For Irigaray, it is essential that sexuate difference intervene as a mediation of the relations of subject to subject and subject to world. It ought not be, Irigaray insists, that the woman as maternal ground provide the perpetual or petrified envelope to the male subject. Rather, subjects should begin to provide a limit-frame to one another and to themselves as fully realized and free subjects. Failing that, the metaphysician posits an objective world to replace the ground and support of that first and subsequent envelopes provided by the other. To avoid the lonesomeness of autonomous breathing, as well as being a means of escaping a reciprocity with another that seems disorienting without a solid ground, the metaphysical subject forms an attachment to objects. As Irigaray writes, "[t]hey dwell in the outside. He senses them from the outside. He touches them: from the outside. They shrink from any approach other than that of contact. They come up-against [*contre*]—no further" (FA, 51).

As for the things, they may be "up-against" or "right-against" the subject (FA, 52) or may be consumed/consummated, but this does not solve the puzzles of existence for the metaphysical subject since the subjective other is still out of reach. The openness that Heidegger imagines as the dwelling place of things, the clearing where what we perceive comes to be, can also be a concealment of that which, for him, amounts to what needs to be forgotten (or concealed) in order for what is coming into presence to be revealed. Insisting on the sustained openness where objects come to be and pass away from experience amounts to demanding an availability without offering a retreat. It is to replace partnership with a subjective other with an externality that does not receive or give but that stays perpetually open: "Which means:" as Irigaray says, "for an entry into the absence of presence? There, it is night still. Where Being obtains-does not obtain" (FA, 52). This continual availability only reproduces the groundlessness it was designed to put to an end.

But what of the opening itself? Irigaray has discussed the openings of the body and their role in language as well as thinking in several texts, including in the well-known chapter "When Our Lips Speak Together" (TS, 205–218). In *The Forgetting of Air in Martin Heidegger*, Irigaray compares the understanding of space and time, Heidegger's notion of the opening, to a foreclosure of the porosity of "his" body and the perpetual openness of the female or feminized body to commerce, to penetration, to consumption. "Between these two mournings," she writes, "the expanse bearing the thinker's concerned comings-and-goings remains open. Mouth, or female loins, or eye, or body, or matter . . . always available, always open, left there, like that *present absence that makes entry into presence possible*" (FA, 55). The openness that is the complement to the subject's foundation and the encircled enclosed-ness of body and language is an incessant openness that is arrayed for him. Irigaray writes, "[n]ow all that is left is a ringed, encircled openness that is set-laid out before him, ready-to-hand. It takes up all the space: deposited, projected into the there" (FA, 55).

The imposed openness eliminates the possibility of withdrawal or of a threshold to allow the demarcation of a passage between one side of the opening and the other. Getting rid of permeability enforces perpetual openness: "Ever open, they are eclipsed by their openness. They are forgotten in the opening" (FA, 55). Rather, introducing a definite shape to the opening—one that provides a defined threshold that can be open but also closed—is necessary to allow a definition and integrity of the flesh as belonging to one or another. Irigaray asks,

> Without lips, how is the passage from one side of the openness to the other marked? How can the entrance to the opening be passed back through if lips have vanished? Where is the provenance, without lips—on this side or on the other? How can a passage from one mouth to the other, from here to there, take place without losing one or the other, or both, in an assimilation by a kind of distance in which the difference between the two is erased, and that once again amounts to sameness? (FA, 56)

Metaphysics as it has traditionally been done, including by Heidegger, remains insensitive to itself and its own economy of subjective relations in part because it lacks a basis in a carnality. Irigaray's critique is particularly important in reference to Heidegger because he has claimed to be returning to a supposedly more innocent, but also more conscious and ultimately more "existential," philosophy of the Pre-Socratics. Irigaray critiques an incompleteness of Heidegger's own metaphysical critique. He falls short of the task he set for himself of developing the existential phenomenological project past the stage of a metaphysics of presence(/absence) in having set up a phantom presence(/absence) beneath and surrounding the metaphysician-subject. His critique falters in his not perceiving the necessity for understanding and for living in a carnal relation both in oneself and with another.

Irigaray questioned Heidegger's clearing of the space of the subjective and surrounding the subject with a replacement consisting of objects, a metaphysical form of transitional object that Heidegger (and not only Heidegger) has used in place of the maternal (see, for instance, FA, 55). Irigaray also made related critiques of Merleau-Ponty, in particular, identifying his attribution "the flesh of the world" ([1964] 1968, 144, 146, 248, 250ff.) as a substitution of the objective surroundings with a projection of maternal flesh. Irigaray contends that Merleau-Ponty conflates an inanimate material objective world with a living flesh precisely because he does not differentiate himself as subject—and thus the world that he views as an extension of the subject—from the maternal (ESD, 157, 159). Merleau-Ponty and Heidegger do not make a sufficient differentiation from the maternal leading to an unacknowledged re-projection and rereading of the maternal back onto the world "of objects."

Yet, clues to a passage out of the traditional preference for solitary consciousness lie in the systematic avoidance of carnality by Heidegger and to some extent Merleau-Ponty when discussing relations between human existence and objects, and between subject and world. Heidegger propounds being-with's equiprimordiality with being-in-the-world ([1927] 2010, 114, 117). A co-priority of existing as being-in and being-with coincides with Irigaray's insistence that we ought to prioritize relations between subjects before relations with objects. Yet for Irigaray, to learn to be with others involves a recognition of human being as carnal (CFN, 10–12). If being-in-the-world and being-with are equiprimordial, then despite Heidegger's overall hesitancy to discuss body in relation to being-with, carnality is present in/as world, and this presence suggests carnality is a crucial element common to being-with and being-in. Irigaray elaborates the necessity of attending specifically to the role of carnality, especially fleshly being, as the privileged place of the possibility of communion with another subject.

How Returning to Flesh Returns Us
to a Living Space and Time

Irigaray takes up the question of the essentiality of a culture of carnality in her essay, "How Can I Touch You If You Are Not There?" (TBT, 94–102). In it she recounts experiencing others through mediation by technological devices and contrasts this with time spent together with another in the woods. Part of what is at stake in this anecdote is what it is for two human beings to encounter each other in their own flesh and, contrastingly, what happens to our ability to be with one another when we only interact through apparatuses of technological mediation that distance us from one another in space and time. In the piece, the telephone, the fax, the radio, the television, the answering machine, and the airplane serve to stretch out, to translocate, to displace, to sever, chop up and reconstitute, and thereby to flatten, distend, and transform, tangible physicality into a visual or auditory signal, restructuring the space between two. These technological devices replace bodily space and time with an informational space and time that has a fundamentally different and, most crucially, objectized quality to it. When we interact with these objects we are interacting with the artificial; we are no longer interacting in holistically human time and space, and this adds complication and confusion to our possibly being-with the other.

Irigaray comments, "what we receive through telecommunications often amounts to information which has already been selected, concentrated, focused in time, and is alien to the unfolding of everyday time" (TBT, 94). But just as importantly, these technologies also remove us from the familiar aspects of everyday space. Without the bodily presence of an other in a place near to me, the possibility for an intersubjective encounter that unfolds in a bodily human time and space is made largely inaccessible.

Through a dialogue with a concrete other, Irigaray brings into words the contrast between a living carnal encounter with another and an abstracted experience of being in the midst of technological mediation. The sometimes subtle, sometimes glaring, intervention of technology into the lives of humans is connected not only to the development of techniques of communicating but also to a history and tradition of valuing a rational and neutralized consciousness and intellect above living fleshly being. She writes, "placing the accent upon information, the language of telecommunications does not favor communication with whoever is watching or listening: there is not, or only in an exceptional manner, a dialogue between the person who sends the message, the one who speaks and the person who receives it, the one who listens to it. The exchange between the two is interrupted" (TBT, 94). With every new attempt to accelerate communication, we become acclimated to a spatial relation with technological interventions that can misplace or displace us. Irigaray writes, "[t]oday, contact means a telephone number, not touching each other through our senses, our skin" (TBT, 97). Attention that previously would have been given to one another in appreciation of each other's sensible qualities, and to our sensitive participation with them as another living being, is attracted to the various projections in media. Physical distance, displacement, and focusing on objects accustom us to giving up our sensuous relations. "It all began," she writes, "with a culture imposing on us an ideal which is unearthly and alien to our perceptions, to our corporeal senses. Such an ideal separates us, as does an abstract model, in theory valid for both of us but, in fact, impeding our coming into presence with each other" (TBT, 98). Looking beyond what is present here and now, in our immediate environment to our senses, causes us to lose our ability to sense. When we divert ourselves through technical mediation, we become disoriented to touching and feeling.

The displacement and de-spatialization remove us not just from one another's proximity but from each other's fleshly being. Digital technology increases this displacement through its attenuating and recomposing flesh as images and sounds. Yet Irigaray suggests that it is not technology alone that leads human beings away from each other but what technology affords: abstraction from living. "And have we not," she asks, "at last, returned love to the beyond? Loving what we could not touch with our hands, see with our eyes, hear with our ears. Desiring what was outside the reach of our senses without bothering to train our perceptions for desire: learning to look, to listen, to touch" (TBT, 99).

Irigaray here shows how it is that bodily presence is necessary to our being with another and how this presence has been overlooked in favor of a metaphysical replacement. The substitution of flesh with technique encourages forgetting the original with-breathing and with-being that we each benefited from in the initial moments of life and afterward. To encounter the other as mediated through technology is to encounter their reflection or projection, not to touch their flesh. In contrast, the flesh, she says, allows us to sense the other and the other to sense us, and to return to ourselves as whole beings. Irigaray comments of the incarnate other: "Being touched by you unveils that a meaning exists which must be perceived and become incarnate between us. [. . .] You remind me of being, notably by laying around me a space which allows me to collect myself, to gather myself together into a whole and so to remember to be" (CFN, 187). Proximity itself, while not solely responsible for our intimacy, facilitates it, in its allowing for a living dynamism in/as our flesh. The fleshly dynamic with an other brings about a returning to one's flesh as emplaced in a human time and space that is orienting and grounding and that allows a regathering of dispersed elements into a whole that is recognizably me.

Enframing as Displacement from Fleshly Being

Irigaray's discussion of flesh in "How Can I Touch You If You Are Not There" offers another contrast to Heidegger's analysis of technology in "The Question Concerning Technology" (Heidegger 1993, 307–341). His critique of technology hints at an implicit need for reevaluation of his lack of regard for the body, even though he does not perform it. According to Heidegger, the techniques associated with modern science, *technē*, gather momentum, appearing to arise from an external source; yet they are the result of a buildup of practices and attitudes accumulated in the modern era created by human beings. The techniques reproduce themselves and seem to take on a character of authority dictating how to view the world, even though they are constructed by and for mankind. They perform what Heidegger calls a "challenging forth" (326–341) asking of us to meet and recreate demands of a technological nature, imposing them on ourselves and our surroundings. This challenging forth creates a hierarchy of knowledge and changes the environment to fit technological aims through human labor and knowledge, reconstructing the world as a resource for technique. Heidegger writes, "[o]nly to the extent that man for his part is already challenged to exploit the energies of nature can this revealing that orders happen. If man is challenged, ordered, to do this, then does not man himself belong even more originally than nature within the standing-reserve?" (1993, 323). The hydrogen in water reveals itself as a potential source of energy, but this is even more so the case for human life that is revealed as producer and subject of technology and technique.

The total reconstruction of the means of perceiving the world as technological processes is called "enframing" (*Gestell*). Enframing's power is partly that it spatializes the world in terms of *technē*. It creates a spatialization of the natural world that reshifts from a natural place each and every being and transfers it (while also holding it still) into a frame that tells what each thing is: a scientific or technical object, including living plants, animals, and humans. Humankind is cut off from itself, both as a general phenomenon, and in the encounters human beings have with themselves, their own surroundings, and one another. The space surrounding each of us as human being becomes enmeshed with the technological so that the surrounds themselves become a space of technology even if there is no obvious artifice. The world itself becomes the space of knowledge and science, but this means it no longer holds natural significance and expels us from our belonging in it as people who dwell there.

If as Heidegger says, "[e]nframing means the gathering together of the setting-upon that sets upon man, i.e., challenges him forth, to reveal the actual, in the mode of ordering, as standing-reserve" (1993, 325), part of this revealing depends on a certain conception of space and time as technique. Heidegger articulates the need to uncouple from a fixed or overdetermined relation to *technē* and regain autonomy with respect to it (311, 313). Irigaray says, as in the case of a constructed culture, of which enframing is a part, "[o]nce more the question which must be asked is how we can both distinguish and articulate what comes from a natural origin with its properties on the one hand and what comes from a culture suitable for human beings on the other hand" (TBB, 28).

In having projected the frame of the world outside to this challenging forth "as if" we ourselves are the products and processes of scientific reason, we have reproduced a quasi-theological structure as an epistemic frame that delimits our relation to ourselves and to one another. As Irigaray writes, "[w]e have located the cause of enchantment beyond the other, outside of him, reducing him to an object of attraction, to a cause of sensations, to a seductive image, to a fascinating representation, without imagining him as a mystery to be examined, contemplated, embraced, and not sought in the beyond" (TBT, 99). In enframing, the other appears as a double or projection of us since they are automatically the same type of "technique," neutralized in their difference by an epistemic scene outlining us each as an instance of technology, as production or reproduction of a technological process, as biological and productive resource. By misidentifying the other as the same, we render each other, and ourselves, as the enframed production of a construction. Instead of being for ourselves and each other as living, the power of our life is transmuted into a power for the running of machinery, that is, a life process reduced to a mechanical piece in a scientific mechanical nature.

Our task, according to Irigaray, is to bring human life back into a living temporality and spatiality, and a living identity that supports a human becoming that allows us to return to our singularity as individual and relational human subjects. Irigaray writes, "[i]n reality, we have to open a clearing in a space filled with beings and their interrelations so that light can come into it again and enlighten us on the world to which we are handed over in order that we can interpret and transform it to make it more authentically ours" (TBB, 28). Heidegger's *Gestell* is for him the frame that structures our understanding of mathematical nature. It presents itself as a looming and oppressive edifice that imposes itself on thinking, causing man to be excluded from the "picture" or to be included as a mere object. In contrast, Irigaray identifies a frame in the form of sexuate difference that could contain in a positive sense, without *en*-framing the possibility of becoming (see TBB, 4, 25–30; CFN, 10, 170–205). Irigaray acknowledges the genuine need for constraints and limits in human being. She suggests that a subjective and carnal limit need not only exist but should be cultivated as a fleshly frame relying on difference and individuation, enveloping and steadying us, and making possible our opening to an other.

Limits could take the form of the limit between one's flesh and the flesh of someone who is radically different though in horizontal relation, such as the difference in fleshes between genders but including other dif-ferences as well. These relational limits serve not to fix a subject and object dualism but instead to produce a dynamic relation that offers boundaries without totalizing or sealing up a breathing relation between subjects.

Touch and Space-Time

Carnal touch establishes a relation with another in a living space and time. It not only enables our belonging to a space and time—or creates a space and time that belongs to us—but allows sharing a nearness, an intimacy, that reappropriates an internal space and time. Fleshly being subjectifies a space and time, creating an opening in the world for a genuine trans-formation to take place in it. Irigaray traces how this opening of space and time by human existence subjectifies time and space in a dynamic and living way contrasting with its being made into an extension of a metaphysician's consciousness.

The opening of space or clearing, made by human intervention and relation, manifests through an appreciation and valorization of touch, suggests Irigaray. A more carnal way of relating through space and time transforms them into a shared living dynamism suitable for human being. Space and time need to be rethought, according to Irigaray, as subject-relative, not in a generic sense but as differentiated according to their relations to and between individual subjects and as taking into account the dynamic between nature and culture. Irigaray writes, "[i]n this desire [for an other living being that is naturally different], two temporalities intervene, the one of nature and the one of culture, and fulfilling our desire compels us to take the two into account in order to elaborate a temporality suitable for the relationship between living beings" (CFN, 183). It is important to develop a similar relation between natural and cultural space that calls for our continual reenergization of living space through our own fleshly becoming: returning to dwelling with ourselves and responding to and adventuring to meet with another.

References

Heidegger, Martin. 1993. *Basic Writings: Martin Heidegger*. Edited by David Farrell Krell. Routledge.

Heidegger, Martin. (1927) 2010. *Being and Time*. Translated by Joan Stambaugh. State University of New York Press.

Merleau-Ponty, Maurice. (1964) 1968. *The Visible and the Invisible*. Translated by Alphonso Lingis. Northwestern University Press.

Sares, James. 2023. "The Ontological Negativity of Sexual Difference." In *What is Sexual Difference? Thinking with Irigaray*, edited by Mary C. Rawlinson and James Sares. Columbia University Press.

Scharff, Robert C. 2019. *Heidegger Becoming Phenomenological: Interpreting Husserl Through Dilthey, 1916–1925*. Rowman & Littlefield.

Part Two

Of Sensibility and the Elemental

Chapter Five

Affective *Poiesis*

Irigaray's Elemental Ontology

Ellen Mortensen

Between 1980 and 1983 Luce Irigaray wrote three books on the elemental: *Marine Lover: Of Friedrich Nietzsche*; *Elemental Passions*; and *The Forgetting of Air in Martin Heidegger*. In the first and the third book from this period, she undertakes a reading of Nietzsche and Heidegger respectively, where she investigates the two fluid elements—water and air—all the while raising the question of sexual difference. In the second book, *Elemental Passions*, Irigaray approaches the element of earth and its relation to all three fluid elements—water, air, and fire. In the following reading of *Elemental Passions*, I will explore what I call Irigaray's "affective *poiesis*" as it is articulated in her musings on the elemental, and above all on the element of earth, which she understands—together with the other three elements—as the condition of possibility for human existence and love between and among the sexes.

In my reading of *Elemental Passions*, after reflecting on some of the critical reception of the book and Irigaray's thinking on the elemental, I shall primarily focus on Irigaray's intervention into Heidegger's poetic meditations on the ontological conditions for human dwelling on earth. Irigaray's engagement with Heidegger's thinking has resounded throughout the better part of her work, from *Marine Lover* through *The Way of Love*, where she explores the possibility of a language and a practice of love.

Even though Irigaray repeatedly critiques Heidegger (see, among others, Mortensen 1994), her relationship to Heidegger's thinking is one of deep and prolonged engagement. In this respect, I agree with Maria C. Cimitile, who writes of Irigaray's critical relationship to Heidegger that, not only does this not mean "Irigaray does not engage in dialogue with others, a claim easily refuted," but it shows, quite to the contrary, "Heidegger to be Irigaray's most important and formidable interlocutor" (2007, 268). In *Elemental Passions*, it is above all Heidegger's understanding of poetic thinking as it relates to human dwelling on earth that Irigaray evokes, with a particular emphasis on his essay "Building, Dwelling, Thinking" from *Poetry, Language, Thought*.

The second part of my chapter will attempt to show how Irigaray's elemental meditation, which I read as a projection of "affective *poiesis*," might find nourishment in and shed light on the ethico-aesthetic project of Deleuze and Guattari. I am especially interested in how her notion of elemental passion relates to their concepts of affects and flow, particularly as these are laid out in *A Thousand Plateaus*.

An Other Love

A recurrent theme in Irigaray's work is love or, more specifically, the condition of possibility for love between and among the sexes under the present conditions on earth, a theme that is already present in *Speculum of the Other Woman* and that is also found in her later work *The Way of Love*. According to Irigaray, love has meager chances for creating individual and collective happiness given the state of affairs today. In *Elemental Passions*, she contends that in order for a veritable amorous encounter between the sexes to take place in our Western civilization, a new perception and a new language of love is needed. For this event to take place, metaphysical language has to be subverted to allow for sexual difference to emerge. This will require, first of all, that the speaking subject, an *I-woman*, establishes a relation, not only to the third person singular—a *she* of her own sex and a *he* (as well as a *you*) of the other sex—but also to a transcendent or a divine third-person instance, *She* or *He*, that is equally marked by sexual difference. Such a love between and among the sexes, while relating to a third, does not yet exist. Hence, Irigaray takes it upon herself to sketch out a path for such a figuration to emerge in the future. Such a language can only appear through a poetic meditation, which Irigaray hopes might open the possibilities of another "relation between natures and gods" (EP, 4), where the empirical and the transcendent could touch in a joyous encounter.

According to Irigaray, the kind of love that has existed between the sexes is a love that has been defined by man and his narcissistic project, which seeks to secure and prolong his paternal name, his earthly possessions, and the patriarchal institutions that he has erected on earth. In the process, *you-man* has appropriated woman, her feminine genealogy, and above all the earth, a necessary but forgotten element on which he has constructed his own identity while projecting beyond this earth a transcendent God, a *He*, that secures his terrestrial and spiritual being into eternity.

So far, all attempts to articulate another form of love have failed. Woman's feeble attempts to inscribe her sexed difference within a masculine discourse have for the most part fallen on deaf ears. If woman is to succeed in her quest for another form of passionate encounter, one in which her sexed difference might emerge, the *I-woman* has to pursue an alternative path. Such a passionate love cannot be sought through metaphysical language, where woman figures as the shunned and silenced other of the masculine subject. Only through sonorous song can an alternative language be sought and, accordingly, Irigaray makes an attempt to formulate a poetic language of love in which feminine difference may resound: "You have stopped my tongue. What remains is song. I can say nothing but sing. [. . .] Seeing, hearing, speaking, breathing, living, all these wait to be made fecund by an innocent potency" (EP, 7–8). For Irigaray, neither ordinary language nor the language of metaphysics is attuned to that for which the *I-woman* passionately yearns. But by poetically exploring what is opened up by the senses of the living body as it breathes, sees, hears, speaks, and sings, new possibilities may emerge.

The critical reception of *Elemental Passions* has focused on various aspects of Irigaray's proposed new economy of love beyond the patriarchal and masculine notion of market economy that is based for the most part on values such as masculine power, appropriation of the feminine, and accumulation of profit. Judith Still, among others, argues that Irigaray proposes an alternative economy—a gift economy—which at the same time informs her alternative notion of love in *Elemental Passions* (1997, 154). This economy of love, which Still deems "utopic," posits modes of exchange in potentially infinite supply instead of presuming infinite resources.[1] Linda Daley, for her part, takes issue with Still's understanding of Irigaray's logic of the gift and argues instead that "it is precisely by way of her interrogation of discourses of the market economy that she is able to locate the sexed conditions of possibility for the production of value" (2012, 61–62). For Daley, it is above all this interrogation that enables Irigaray to locate the resources for the reimagined symbolic order with which *Elemental Passions* experiments.

It is, however, Irigaray's entanglement with Merleau-Ponty's phenomenological thinking on the amorous encounter between the sexes that has above all caught the attention of many readers of *Elemental Passions*. Cecilia Sjöholm, for one, interprets *Elemental Passions* forcefully as a response to Merleau-Ponty's "The Intertwining—the Chiasm" in *The Visible and the Invisible*. Positing that the (masculine) narcissistic strain in Merleau-Ponty's chiasm is undercut by Irigaray's account of the sexes' amorous touching, Sjöholm characterizes the latter as a phenomenological understanding situating sexual difference as necessarily preceding the intertwining (2000).

In contrast, Dorothea Olkowski argues that Irigaray evades not only phenomenological commitments but any ontological commitments at all and that "[the] manner in which Irigaray constitutes the difference [between phenomenology and ontology] directly implicates a Bergsonian critique of the limits of phenomenology" (2000, 2). Focusing primarily on Irigaray's reading of Merleau-Ponty in *Ethics of Sexual Difference* but also on *Elemental Passions*, Olkowski ends up claiming that Irigaray's work "is *not* incompatible with a philosophical ontology other than that of phenomenology" (3). Her subtle analysis reveals that Irigaray is closely intertwined with, yet posits a clear demarcation from, Merleau-Ponty's phenomenology of the flesh. According to Olkowski, the direction toward which Irigaray instead moves is Bergson's thinking on the interval.[2]

Kelly Oliver, for her part, focuses on Irigaray's indebtedness to Merleau-Ponty's thinking on the interrelationship between the senses, above all vision and touch, which he elaborates in *The Visible and the Invisible*. Oliver acknowledges, however, that Irigaray diverts from Merleau-Ponty in her insistence on the primacy of the elemental, notably of air, in her understanding of vision. There is a development in Irigaray's thought, Oliver contends, whereby she moves from the denouncement of the privileging of the visual sense in Western metaphysics to a more nuanced and subtle understanding of the interconnectedness of all the senses, all the while acknowledging their indebtedness to the elements. Oliver highlights how air comes into play in vision, notably in *The Forgetting of Air in Martin*

Heidegger, where air becomes the element allowing vision to occur. This opens up, Oliver argues, a new theory of vision "that can ground Irigaray's more recent thoughts on intersubjectivity, particularly her carnal theory of vision and recognition" (2007, 124). I find Oliver's accounts of the development of Irigaray's thought convincing, and I believe that this new approach to vision plays a pivotal role in Irigaray's projections of love in *Elemental Passions*.

Although the readings of *Elemental Passions* cited above have illuminated Irigaray's work in important ways, especially as it relates to Merleau-Ponty's phenomenological thinking on the body and the interrelationship between the senses, my own reading of *Elemental Passions* will pursue two somewhat different paths of thinking I consider to be at work in the text. These paths lead us in two divergent directions, one Heideggerian and the other Deleuzian.

Irigaray published *Elemental Passions* in the time between *Marine Lover of Friedrich Nietzsche* and *The Forgetting of Air in Martin Heidegger*. It should therefore come as no surprise that Nietzsche's and Heidegger's thinking permeates *Elemental Passions* in different ways, in addition to other philosophers and texts. In their respective attempts at understanding man's earthly existence while unveiling that which metaphysics has forgotten or hidden from view, Nietzsche and Heidegger explore *poetic* thinking, which they oppose to metaphysical thinking. Irigaray follows the paths of their poetic musings in *Elemental Passions*, and the two male philosophers figure partly as dialogue partners, who are at times staged as the voice of *you-man* in the book. In addition, however, I believe that Irigaray's understanding of the affective exchanges required in a new understanding of love finds nourishment in Deleuze and Guattari's visceral ontology and, more specifically, in their understanding of affects and flows.[3]

Irigaray's Earth

By weaving in and out of philosophical texts, be these those of Merleau-Ponty, Nietzsche, or Heidegger, Irigaray attempts in *Elemental Passions* to challenge Western metaphysics' understanding not only of earthly and divine love but above all of the element of earth. Traditionally, the earth has been thought as a substance on which man founds his earthly existence, all the while projecting a transcendent world beyond this earthly ground.

Nietzsche constitutes for Irigaray *the* modern thinker of the earth who reevaluates the feminine by resurrecting the ancient, Pre-Socratic legacy of the feminine *chthonic* and its tragic insights into human finitude. But, at the same time, Irigaray contends that Nietzsche shies away from the element of water and the earth's dark, invisible, subterranean cavities. Instead, he paradoxically reaches for loftier insights while climbing mountains in search of his Dionysian "truths." Throughout *Elemental Passions*, Irigaray makes obvious allusions to Nietzsche's Zarathustra, the Overman, and his circle of eternal return. Yet, irrespective of the Overman's attempts to attain solitude and solipsistic self-possession, the shadow of the one that he has shunned, looms in the background:

> But, when you think you have rediscovered in yourself the hard kernel of your being, that circle where at last you would be restored to yourself, you still find me entwined. Still there holding you in my arms. And, when you want to repossess yourself in solitude, demarcate the territory which belongs to you, return to your own country, you are ever further in flight from yourself. You leave your home, seduced by what is distant. You fly off into an airy void. Charmed by the abyss where a secret echo of yourself could resonate. (EP, 12)

The echoes of the passage "At Noontide" in Nietzsche's *Thus Spoke Zarathustra* seem evident, where Nietzsche speaks of Zarathustra's desire to fly away from his earthly dwelling:

> And Zarathustra ran and ran and found no one else and was alone and found himself again and again and enjoyed and relished his solitude and thought of good things, for hours on end. About the hour of noon, however, when the sun stood exactly over Zarathustra's head, he passed an old gnarled and crooked tree which was embraced around by the abundant love of a vine and hidden from itself: from the vine an abundance of yellow grapes hung down to the wanderer. (Nietzsche [1883–1885] 1961, 286–287)

Irigaray claims that even in broad daylight, when Zarathustra believes that all his depths are visible to himself, a feminine shadow follows him, the shadow of her, *I-woman*, who dwells in a different illumination, that of the night, which haunts his mid-day, solar identity. And Irigaray asks: "Why should we not be illuminated by the night of our *jouissance*? Which casts a different light on things, on their contours, their spacing and their timing. [. . .] For sight is no longer our only guide. Seeing with an expanse which is dazzling and palpable, odorous and audible" (EP, 37–38). For Irigaray, earthy love between the sexes can no longer be guided exclusively by the visual sense, which has traditionally dominated masculine sensibility but must activate other senses as well: the olfactory sense, taste, the tactile sense, as well as the auditory sense. By being affectively oriented by the multiplicity of senses, changes will occur in our perception of both space and time. Western metaphysics has traditionally subjected the fluid elements to the perceived solidity and constancy of the earth, thought as matter and substance. Even though Zarathustra tries to escape the inner, watery cavities of the earth, Nietzsche's notion of the earth, invoking the ancient Greek Dionysian heritage, represents an exception from the traditional view of the earth as a solid ground. Despite his fear of the element of water, Nietzsche acknowledges the earth as infinitely volatile and destructive yet endlessly creative.

In my view, Irigaray's main project in *Elemental Passions* is to subvert the hierarchy of the senses, posited by metaphysics, whereby the visual sense is privileged. Instead, she attempts to uncover the multiple ways in which the workings of the fluid elements—water, air, and fire—continually open up and transform the earth's alleged self-identity. Partly harkening back to Nietzsche's Dionysian earth, but also to Empedocles' ontology[4] of the strife between the four elements, Irigaray invokes an earth that is attuned to all the other elements. Earth, air, fire, and water affect each other infinitely, thus causing the earth's constant metamorphosis.

Mark Paterson also invokes the passage from *Elemental Passions* cited above, where Irigaray refers to the "night of our *jouissance*," in his essay, "Caresses, Excesses, Intimacies and Estrangements" (2004). For Paterson, what Irigaray alludes to in this passage is an excess of *jouissance* where nocturnal caresses exceed the limits of that which is visible or can be established through the visual sense. There is, in Irigaray's amorous encounter, a wider understanding of sensation where all the senses are involved: notably, a kind of touching where the limits of the self and the other are lost, where an interpenetration between the two occurs, whereby "I become you" (EP, 79).

Contrary to Nietzsche's mountainous earth, Irigaray's earth is a living body, a dark, fluid, and porous element. In addressing the *you-man*, the

I-woman reminds him of this other earth, which is "[. . .] your blood, your air, your water. The place from which you draw life. In which you feel yourself to be alive. Through which you feel. Feel yourself. That place where you have forgotten that I already feel. Impalpably touching myself again and again. I am stirred everywhere and all the time. But the feeling is lost as soon as direction or dimension is imposed. Or rigid closing and opening" (EP, 19). It is *you-man*'s fear of the infinitely open and changing earth, Irigaray argues, that has made him privilege that which appears as solid and constant to the eye. Accordingly, metaphysics has privileged the solid and the massive—in short, what can be subjected to measurement and calculation. But Irigaray asks: "If we are living, how can we be pure crystal? And if your thinking aspires to the realm of crystal, how can we survive in it? How can I abandon my love of the vegetal? [. . .] And what does it signify, this attraction of yours for the mineral? A triumph over expansion through the cosmos? A means of avoiding change? Your need for mastery?" (EP, 33). Subsuming the fluid elements under that of the earth while privileging the latter's presumed permanence and solid ground is, Irigaray claims, in part the means by which *you-man*, the subject of metaphysics, has projected a self-image as a crystallized, self-identical entity. This presumed solidity allows *you-man* to demarcate a subjective circle around himself and to erect strict borders between the self and the other, all while projecting a supra-sensuous world beyond that is equally crystallized into an ideal realm, one that extends into eternity.

Heidegger's Earth

In addition to her engagement with Merleau-Ponty and Nietzsche, it is above all Irigaray's intimate dialogue with Martin Heidegger's ontological thinking that takes center stage in *Elemental Passions*. Here, Irigaray delves into Heidegger's meditation on the fourfold, dwelling, and the clearing, and repeatedly invokes his essay "Building, Dwelling, Thinking" where he writes: "The mortals are the human beings. They are called mortals because they can die. To die means to be capable of death *as* death. Only man dies, and indeed continually, as long as he remains on earth, under the sky, before the divinities. [. . .] This simple oneness of the four we call *the fourfold*. Mortals are in the fourfold by *dwelling*" (1971, 150). Irigaray listens to and inserts her difference into Heidegger's discourse. On the one hand, she mimes his thinking on the fourfold when she emphasizes the need for humans to meditate on the ontological conditions for our existence. But on the other, she accuses Heidegger, just as she accuses Nietzsche, of being consumed by the thought of death and nothingness. Heidegger's existential thinking on "being-towards-death" is, in Irigaray's view, both morbid and somewhat life-denying: "You have built an anaesthetic world. [. . .] Your world of anaesthetics kills insensibly. Irremediably. The more you go on producing fantasies, your preferred anaesthetics, the greater the danger: avoiding the passage through suffering which could still save" (EP, 55). By inserting death as a limit, *you-man* of the Heideggearian anaesthetic logos separates himself from the elemental movements of nature. And by erecting a wall around the clearing that gathers the four-fold—earth and sky, mortals and divinities—*you-man* builds a temporal and spatial horizon by imposing location, direction, and measurement on his dwelling on earth. For Irigaray's *I-woman*, these forms of temporality and spatiality do not exist: "For me, nothing is ever finite. What does not pass through skin, between our skins, mingles in our bodies' fluids. Ours. Or at least mine. And as mine are continuous with yours, there is no fixed boundary to impose a definite separation" (EP, 16). A porosity similar to that which exists in and between bodies likewise permeates the surfaces of all other beings, and above all the earth, which appears as a maternal, primordial body, endlessly open and giving: "My body is fluid and ever mobile. It brings you blood and milk, air and water and light" (EP, 25). Irigaray emphasizes the fundamental connection between the body of the speaking subject, the mother's body that has given her life, and the body of the earth, with her fluid elements: air, water, and fire. It is this multiple body, connected to the elements, that enables humans to flourish, sustain life, and dwell on this planet.

Aesthesis and *Poiesis*

In Heidegger's ontological thinking, language plays a pivotal role in the sense that it is in language that mortals find their place in the fourfold, with things *as* things. For Heidegger it is the poet—not as a living body, but as an impersonal, anesthetic voice—who is receptive to the call of in-human Being. Only the poet is capable of poiesis, the presencing or a letting-be of new beings, which he safeguards from the abyssal Nothingness of Being.

In contrast to Heidegger, who in his thinking on art and existence seeks to avoid *aesthesis*, the sensuous apprehension of the world, and who values the poet and his impersonal and inhuman language, Irigaray invokes in the dialogue between *I-woman* and *you-man* an *impassioned* language marked by sexual difference. This sensuous language gives voice to a living body that enters into a relation with the body of the other sex, the mother's body, and the body of the earth allowing humans of both sexes to dwell in her openness.

Irigaray stages a feminine voice, an *I-woman* that sings the sounds and the rhythms of the earth and the fluid elements. This song is attuned to elemental reverberations, the rhythms of a *sensuous transcendental*. Irigaray's affective poiesis, the saying that gives new possibilities for earthly existence, is fecund with drives and desires. Poietic saying allows the passionate difference between the sexes to resonate and come to presence in its free becoming. Her song is a poetic language where *jouissance* for both (or all) sexes is possible:

> And if the poison no longer comes into me, I may remember what came before. Resonant song kept back, exultation kept quiet, an appeal cried out, filling the universe with its clamour. What arises out of the furthest depth, emerging and unfolding, like an airy flower opening with the intensity of impatience. Petals already drenched in the gift of the expected consolation. Attentive vibration picking up the imperceptible tremor of your approach.
>
> For the first time, I saw you appear. And it was not midday. The sun was not any higher, nor the light more intense. But what made you visible came from you. Making you radiate from the inside outwards. (EP, 98)

The song that is remembered is one that connects the lovers to an anteriority that has been forgotten, a past that has been silenced, but that is now re-invoked in a poietic reverberation that requires a new sensibility attuned to another form of intensity. This sensibility is susceptible to minute and subtle tremors and airy flowering, poetic appearances that do not appear in broad daylight but rather emerge from the nocturnal and ancient depths of the earth.

Affects and Flow

Although Irigaray to my knowledge never explicitly invokes the works of Deleuze and Guattari, be it in *Elemental Passions* or in any other work,[5] there are numerous resonances between her elemental ontology and the ethico-aesthetic project of Deleuze and Guattari.[6] Without postulating who affects whom, one can note several textual instances in *Elemental Passions* where Irigaray's thinking reveals affinities to that of the two French philosophers, especially concerning the relation between the living body and the way in which art and language figures into the dynamic movements of the immanent world.

Deleuze and Guattari embrace—as does Irigaray—a thinking on art and poetic language that is grounded in *sense*, in *aesthesis*. All three are philosophers of difference, working with the legacy of, among others, Nietzsche and Heidegger. Above and beyond any other philosopher, Nietzsche figures prominently in Deleuze and Guattari's works, as he does in Irigaray's.

A key concept in Deleuze and Guattari's philosophy of immanence is *affect*, which they predominantly associate with art:

> What is preserved—the thing or the work of art—is *a block of sensations, that is to say, a compound of percepts and affects.*
>
> Percepts are no longer perceptions: they are independent of a state of those who experience them. Affects are no longer feelings or affection; they go beyond the strength of those who undergo them. Sensations, percepts, and affects are *beings* whose validity lies in themselves and exceeds any lived. They could be said to exist in the absence of man because man, as he is caught in stone, on the canvas, or by words, is himself a compound of percepts and affects. The work of art is a being of sensation and nothing else: it exists in itself (Deleuze and Guattari [1991] 1994, 164).

For Deleuze and Guattari, works of art—beings of affect and blocks of sensations—are capable of creating unfamiliar assemblages. Affects, which are compositions of speed and movement, may create symbioses of unnatural participations on the plane of consistency, which may in turn undermine and dissolve repressive molar identities on the plane of organization. Effective enhancement of affects has the power to create new becomings that may function as a form of liberation by connecting to the flow of immanence on the plane of consistency. Conversely, territorializations, colonizations, state institutions, and oppressive molar systems of thought and social organizations operate through regulation and policing of effects on the plane of organization.

The plane of consistency (or of immanence) is prephilosophical; yet it is what philosophy presupposes. Like "a section of chaos that acts like a sieve," the plane of immanence allows affects and flows to *be* (Deleuze and Guattari [1991] 1994, 42). The plane of organization is ontologically indebted to the plane of consistency but operates on a different plateau, in preformed fields where affects are "organized" or "composed." "Composition is the sole definition of art," Deleuze and Guattari affirm; composition in this sense is aesthetic and based on sensation and affect (191–192). However, there is also technical composition, the work of the material that draws on science, which is more susceptible to appropriation by instrumental thought.

In Chapter Ten of *A Thousand Plateaus*, entitled "1730: Becoming-Intense, Becoming-Animal, Becoming Imperceptible," Deleuze and Guattari write that all processes of deterritorialization have to pass through the "becoming-woman" ([1980] 1987, 232–309). It is possible to argue that Irigaray's poetic dialogue between *I-woman* and *you-man* in *Elemental Passions* partakes, as an instance of poetic thinking, in a process of minorization and deterritorialization, whereby the molar identities—that is, woman and man—are transformed and reconfigured to the extent that *I-woman* passes through "becoming-animal," "becoming-molecular" and eventually "becoming-imperceptible" (272–286). To describe this process, Irigaray repeatedly makes use of the terms *affect* and *flow*, as in the following passage: "When I am affected and reaffected by you in the profoundly distant totality, I rediscover the total expansiveness of my affections. The total space of my outstretching. The full extent of my flow. Of my fluidity" (EP, 45). According to Irigaray, "movements in the world of the senses are almost imperceptible" (EP, 91) and require an attentiveness that rigid, formal frameworks are incapable of detecting. For her, poetic language opens up for the flow of affects, where paradoxes and *polemos*, akin to Empedocles's vision, may thrive together, allowing new points of connection and new relations to occur:

> In golden light you flow. Firm density, so light. Before the separation of earth and sky, sea and continents, light and dark.

A mixture of rock, fire, water, ether. Where violence can still espouse gentleness. The heroic body overflowing with tenderness. Its weapons still those of a native innocence. Which blurs all sharp distinctions and brings all divisions back to their original nupitals. An alliance in which the opposing parties unite in an intense intermingling.

Waiting. Waiting for that wall which divides us to be made porous by your arrival. For its limit to be crossed. The line of the horizon temporarily effaced. (EP, 102)

In Irigaray's poetic universe, all things—human, animal, mineral, and vegetal—affect and are affected in such a way that everything touches everything else, "[s]timulating new flowering from the deepest buried depths or the infinitely distant. And nothing inert remained" (EP, 100). Elemental song, the song that embraces all that exists and will emerge, is the saying that might grant life to living human beings of different sexes as well as animal, mineral, and vegetal beings. Our dwelling is indebted to the elements, and the earth is the dwelling place that might open our connectedness to all the elements. The elemental—earth, air, water, and fire—is what grants our earthly existence and connects us with all other beings, past, present, and future. It is the flow and intensities of the elements, their internal strife, that grants us Being, but this indebtedness has been forgotten.

Conclusion

In my reading of *Elemental Passions* as a meditation on love between and among the sexes, I have discerned what I call Irigaray's affective poiesis, namely a sensuous mode of poetic thinking that is marked by sexual difference. Irigaray reworks and subverts key concepts and problematics in the history of philosophy: a Dionysian understanding of the earth and the eternal return in Nietzsche; the fourfold, dwelling, and the clearing in Heidegger; and the concepts of affect and flow in Deleuze and Guattari. Irigaray's affective poiesis—the sensuous presencing of becomings—reconfigures language in such a way that the sexed body, earthly yet transcendent, may touch thought in new and unexpected ways. For Irigaray, these affective *poietic* becomings may have the power to change the relation between living, desiring humans and the earthly abode in which we dwell. Poietic becoming, as a projection onto the future that allows for an affective touching between and of the sexes, will open up to new forms of love marked for the first time in human history by sexual difference. Irigaray's amorous language of affective poiesis announces the beginnings of an aesthetic practice that is attuned to the ebbs and flows of the elemental—calling on forces cosmic and earthly, human and in-human—a language that has the potential to create new worlds in which to dwell differently.

Notes

1. Irigaray has repeatedly meditated on the possibility of an alternative language and perceptions of love, based on a new logic of the gift, a thinking that can be found in texts such as "Women on the Market" in *This Sex Which is Not One, I Love to You,* and *To Be Two.*

2. Rebecca Hill makes a similar connection between Irigaray's thinking on the being and becoming of the relation "between-two" and Bergson's thinking on the interval in her book, *The Interval: Relation and Becoming in Irigaray, Aristotle, and Bergson.*

3. I am not the first to explore the connections between Irigaray and Deleuze and Guattari. Feminist theorists such as Rosi Braidotti in *Metamorphoses: Towards a Materialist Theory of Becoming*; Tamsin Lorraine in *Irigaray and Deleuze: Experiments in Visceral Philosophy*; and Elizabeth Grosz in *Time Travels: Feminism, Nature, Power* have successfully done so in their respective works.

4. Empedocles' ontology, where he elaborates on the strife between the four elements, were held to consist of two poems, in hexameter verse, entitled *On Nature* and *Purifications.*

5. It should be noted, however, that Irigaray in *Le Corps-à-corps avec la mère* denounces the fact that: "as soon as women are valorized in some way, men want to become women . . . i.e., not to lose the position of a subject who is in control of the situation and in control of discourse" [author's translation] (CAC, 64). Similar remarks that indirectly allude to Deleuze and Guattari are made in *This Sex Which Is Not One,* where she in a subtle way takes issue with Deleuze and Guattari's valorization of neurosis, which she claims is a masculine pathology. She differentiates neurosis from hysteria, which she claims is a more appropriate term for women. It is an ambiguous pathology in as much as it is a reserve of power and a paralyzed power (S, 138–140).

6. The French edition of *A Thousand Plateaus* appeared in 1980, the same year that *Amante marine* was published. And even though no direct connection can be established between the two publications, the books appeared in the

same philosophical environment in Paris at a time when the poststructuralist re-evaluation of the philosophical legacy of Nietzsche and Heidegger's thinking on difference was exceptionally active and dynamic.

References

Braidotti, Rosi. 2002. *Metamorphoses: Towards a Materialist Theory of Becoming.* Polity Press.

Cimitile, Maria. 2007. "Irigaray in Dialogue with Heidegger." In *Returning to Irigaray: Feminist Philosophy, Politics, and the Question of Unity*, edited by Maria C. Cimitile and Elaine P. Miller. State University of New York Press.

Daley, Linda. 2012. "Luce Irigaray's Sexuate Economy." *Feminist Theory* 13, no. 1: 59–79.

Deleuze, Gilles, and Félix Guattari. (1980) 1987. *A Thousand Plateaus: Capitalism and Schizophrenia.* Translated by Brian Massumi. University of Minnesota Press.

Deleuze, Gilles, and Félix Guattari. (1991) 1994. *What is Philosophy?* Translated by G. Burchill and H. Tomlinson. Verso.

Grosz, Elizabeth. 2005. *Time Travels: Feminism, Nature, Power.* Duke University Press.

Heidegger, Martin. 1971. "Building, Dwelling, Thinking," translated by A. Hofstadter. In *Poetry, Language, Thought.* Harper & Row.

Hill, Rebecca. 2012. *The Interval: Relation and Becoming in Irigaray, Aristotle, and Bergson.* Fordham University Press.

Lorraine, Tamsin. 1999. *Irigaray and Deleuze: Experiments in Visceral Philosophy.* Cornell University Press.

Mortensen, Ellen. 1994. *The Feminine and Nihilism: Reading Luce Irigaray with Nietzsche and Heidegger.* Scandinavian University Press.

Nietzsche, Friedrich. *Thus Spoke Zarathustra* (1883–1885) 1961. Translated by R. J. Hollingdale. Penguin Classics.

Oliver, Kelly. 2007. "Vision, Recognition, and Passion for the Elements." In *Returning to Irigaray: Feminist Philosophy, Politics, and the Question of Unity*, edited by Maria C. Cimitile and Elaine P. Miller. State University of New York Press.

Olkowski, Dorothea. 2000. "The End of Phenomenology: Bergson's Interval in Irigaray." *Hypatia* 15, no. 3: 73–91.

Paterson, Mark. 2004. "Caresses, Excesses, Intimacies and Estrangements." *Angelaki: Journal of Theoretical Humanities* 9, no. 1: 165–177.

Sjöholm, Cecilia. 2000. "Crossing Lovers: Luce Irigaray's *Elemental Passions*." *Hypatia* 15, no. 3: 92–112.

Still, Judith. 1997. *Feminine Economies: Thinking Against the Market in the Enlightenment and Late Twentieth Century.* Manchester University Press.

Chapter Six

To Speak of Immemorial Waters

Irigaray with Nietzsche

R‍EBECCA H‍ILL

For Luce Irigaray the giving of life precedes and exceeds the logic and language of western metaphysics. That this giving gives beyond reason and words has been largely forgotten in western thought since the time of the Pre-Socratics.[1] Diagnosing the oblivion of the giving of life and finding ways to express this giving is central to Irigaray's philosophical project. She deploys many concepts and formulations to express these ideas. They include woman, nature, the feminine, the becoming body of the mother, the lips, the envelope, and immemorial waters. These concepts are often interpreted by Irigaray's readers in ontic terms to designate present beings, especially cis women. While these concepts are related to cis women in her corpus, fundamentally, they designate the nontotalizable giving of life.

This chapter focuses on Irigaray's relationship with Nietzsche in her book *Marine Lover of Friedrich Nietzsche*. I argue that Nietzsche's thinking of life is a significant influence on Irigaray's philosophy of life and sexual difference. She is also critical of Nietzsche; Irigaray claims that at times his thought gets caught up in the web of his own discourse. Nietzsche's concepts of will to power and eternal return exclude the becoming of other wills and try to appropriate the becoming body of the mother into the figure of Zarathustra. This chapter concludes with a close reading of the speaking of immemorial waters from the first part of *Marine Lover*.

I relate the speaking of immemorial waters to Nietzsche's teaching of fidelity to the meaning of the earth and his affirmation of the eternal return. Before offering a reading of Irigaray with Nietzsche, I want to set up some orientation points on the status of life and sexual difference in Irigaray's oeuvre.

Several Senses of Sexual Difference

Irigaray's framing of sexual difference is commonly understood as anthropocentric. There is justification for this reading, especially if we focus on her works from the late eighties onward. For instance, in a well-known interview conducted in 1994, Irigaray speaks to the evolution of her thinking on sexual difference from *Speculum of the Other Woman* (first published in French in 1974) until the time of the interview. She characterizes her philosophy of sexual difference as consisting of three linked and overlapping chronological phases:

1. Sexual difference is a diagnosis of the way in which a single subject, historically the masculine, has constructed and interpreted the world exclusively according to his interests and perspectives.

2. Sexual difference is the elaboration of those mediations that would allow for the existence of a specifically feminine subject.

3. Sexual difference is the non-hierarchical relation between the masculine subject and the feminine subject who are understood as irreducible to one another. (Irigaray JLI 96–97)[2]

In this account, sexual difference is a practice of critical reading in the history of philosophy and a multifaceted task of invention. The diagnostic phase and the two generative phases are conceptualized in subjective terms. In the first instantiation, the philosopher of sexual difference finds that western metaphysics creates concepts and interprets the world according to the interests of the masculine western subject and disavows other relations to the world. In the second instantiation, there are elaborations of feminine subjects, feminine concepts, and feminine relations to the world. In the third case, sexual difference is a relationship between the feminine and the masculine as two irreducibly different subjects sharing a world.

There are dimensions of Irigaray's thought that exceed anthropocentric concerns, and these inhuman dimensions are crucial to the philosophy of sexual difference. A trace of these inhuman dimensions is legible in her didactic three-phase summary of sexual difference, if we pay close attention to her deployment of the concept of "relation." The relation between the sexes, which she also calls the interval, is *the* fundamental concept of her thought. In *An Ethics of Sexual Difference*, first published in French in 1984, the interval is figured as the nonlocalizable threshold generating the feminine pole of life and the masculine pole of life in a nonhierarchical dynamic (ESD, 54–55). As I read her, the interval is also sexual difference, beyond the sense of generating the sexuate intersubjectivity of human beings; the interval is a way of speaking of the giving of life. This is evident in her claim that for "this difference to be lived and thought, we must reconsider the whole problematic of space and time" (ESD, 7). Irigaray's corpus focuses on the sexuate giving of human life on Earth, though I read the giving of life as an affirmation that "everything" is alive. To be more precise, the interval is the pre-individual becoming of difference, beyond the giving of this universe, beyond totalization. The interval designates a reserve that is open to becoming other.

In works from the seventies and early eighties, published before *An Ethics of Sexual Difference*, Irigaray affirms a specifically feminine sense of difference. Feminine difference is more than a concept of woman as a sexuate human being irreducible to the subjectivity of western man. In this respect, her beautiful elaboration of feminine multiplicity in "When Our Lips Speak Together" can be read as a giving of life prior to the individuation of subjects (TS, 205–218). This cosmos birthing sense of the lips is not opposed to the intersubjective saying of the mother-daughter relation or to a discourse of lesbian lovers; these senses are implied and belong to the speaking together of the lips. In an elaboration of the giving of life as feminine difference from *Speculum of the Other Woman*, Irigaray reconceives Aristotle's *phusis* as "the becoming body in/as the mother" (*le devenir (du) corps de/dans la mère*) (S, 161). Becoming-body in/as the mother has several senses. In ontic terms, this phrase acknowledges the nonreciprocal maternal gift of mothers in contrast to Aristotle's overwhelming tendency to devalue and exclude mothers from his explicit theorization of the generation of human beings.[3] There is a far more fundamental sense of "becoming-body in/as the mother;" this giving, is a generative giving of universes as distinct from Aristotle's eternal first principle of the unmoved mover. Becoming body in/as the mother (is) the pre-individual becoming of life. Irigaray is not making a strategic argument. She is claiming that the giving of life as difference is feminine as such. This giving is not eternal; there are events of birthing that give worlds of difference.[4]

What is the relationship between the three subjective phases of sexual difference Irigaray summarizes in the 1994 interview and the postulation of life as feminine difference? The three phases are interdependent and build on each other: (1) critiques of the phallocentric conceptual world of western metaphysics and the exclusively masculine concept of the subject necessitate the (2) elaboration of feminine specificity distinct from the monologic of western man, and this generates a need to think (3) at least two sexuate subjects sharing a world. The strange open concept of life as feminine difference cannot be contained in a subjective or inter-subjective framework. Feminine difference is plainly juxtaposed to (1) the phallocentric edifice of western metaphysics, but feminine difference is not (2) a human idea of the feminine nor can feminine difference be read interchangeably with (3) the relation between the feminine and masculine given by the interval. I suggest that her aphoristic idea of life as feminine difference in the early works can be read in partial congruence with the articulations of Nature in Irigaray's later works such as *To Be Two* and *In the Beginning, She Was* (TBT, 1–17; IB, 1–50). Yet this congruence is only partial because the figuring of Nature in these more recent works is explicitly focused on the giving of life on Earth, whereas the earlier works speak much more abstractly of becoming mother as that which is indeterminable (S, 161).

There is another formulation of life as indeterminable in Irigaray in her aphoristic and brilliant book, *Elemental Passions*, first published in French in 1982. A feminine narrator describes her sense of the whole in juxtaposition to western man's sense of the whole:

> The whole is not the same for me as it is for you. For me, it can never be one. Can never be completed, always in-finite. When you talk about Infinity, it seems to me that you are speaking of a closed totality: a solid, empty membrane which would gather and contain all possibilities. The absolute of self-identity—in which you were, will be, could be.
>
> For me? A fluid expansion, never enclosed once and for all. Not even by projects or projections.
>
> There, the id-is-flowing cannot be halted. Without a limit, of whatever dimension or direction. A place where everything is

still possible. Prior to any difference of distinction. Giving only
a world of half-openings [*de l'entr'ouvert*]. Nothing determinable.
The foundation of all giving. A reserve of the dative. (EP, 89)[5]

The feminine narrator relates to the whole as a reserve of the dative. In
stark contrast, the addressee—the universal subject of western metaphysics—conceives of Infinity as if the whole is a closed totality. The narrator
of *Elemental Passions* calls on the addressee to acknowledge that he is
limited, that he does not master the whole, and to acknowledge the feminine narrator as a different kind of subject from him. On my reading,
the open whole—life as giving of difference—is not specifically feminine
difference. The foundation of all giving has no specific distinction or
character. "Nothing determinable." (Unless we read the fact that the giving of the open whole is revealed by a feminine subject as meaningful?)
    There are several senses of sexual difference in Irigaray. The fun-
damental sense of sexual difference is the nontotalizable giving of life as
difference. In many of Irigaray's texts, this difference is feminine, and in
some instances, feminine difference is specified as the becoming body in/
as the mother.[6] Arguably, there is also an inscription in Irigaray where the
open whole is not characterized as specifically feminine. What is consistent
in Irigaray's elaborations of sexual difference is the insistence that ways of
relating to the giving of life as difference need to be articulated in thought
and ethics. I agree wholeheartedly with her call to elaborate ways of relating to life as that excess which gives. This is crucial and urgent because
the dominant formations of western culture and the global framework of
modernity-coloniality are profoundly alienated from the vital and ordered
by values that are terribly destructive of life on Earth.[7] This is ontological
and political and significant, not only for feminist philosophy's efforts to
transvalue phallocratic thought and social relations but for the theoretical
(post)humanities, decolonial theory, queer theory, and trans theory. This
is also a central challenge for leftist activists, artists, and writers.

Irigaray as a Post-Heideggerian Philosopher

Marine Lover of Friedrich Nietzsche is one of Irigaray's most difficult
monographs. Like her other two "elemental" books from the early eighties,
The Forgetting of Air in Martin Heidegger and *Elemental Passions*, *Marine
Lover* is poetic and often allusive in its encounters with Nietzsche and

other thinkers. This means it is often far from obvious which sections of Nietzsche's corpus she is engaging. Moreover, her writing speaks at several levels simultaneously; she speaks to different ideas in his thought, to ideas in some of his precursors, such as Heraclitus and Aeschylus, and to the thought of other philosophers writing in the wake of Nietzsche. As Ellen Mortensen (1994) shows, Irigaray's *Marine Lover* is in implicit dialogue with Martin Heidegger and his thinking of the ontological difference between Being and beings.

Stephen Seely argues convincingly that while Irigaray must be read as Heideggerian, she is also critical of Heidegger (2017, 54). The German philosopher's diagnosis of the oblivion of the Being of beings in the metaphysical determination of being as presence and his sustained elaboration of the rise of planetary technicity are crucial to Irigaray. She agrees with Heidegger's reading of modern technicity, that is, of the reduction of all Being to the status of the objects for the human subject (Seely 2017, 45; Heidegger 1994, 307–343). Irigaray also follows Heidegger in comprehending technicity as a process of de-naturation that is fundamentally nihilistic (Seely 2017, 47–48). Where Heidegger emphasizes the forgetting of Being in Ancient Greek philosophy as decisive in the emergence of technicity, Irigaray argues that there is a forgetting prior to the oblivion of the Being of beings. This forgetting is the giving of life (Seely 2017, 54). Irigaray agrees that language is the house of Being—*es gibt*—but insists that language could not be articulated without the giving of life and that language is charged with forces of life (ESD, 127; Mortensen 1994, 15; 2020, 123). For Irigaray, Heidegger's postulation of the essence of *phusis* as the *logos* displaces the older sense of *phusis* or *phusein* as giving birth (FA, 86; Hill 2012, 84; Seely 2017, 54). In Irigaray, *phusein*—the becoming-body of the mother—gives time-matter. The task of sexual difference philosophers and artists is to find ways of speaking in relation to the giving of life, a giving which is not neutral, which is not one, and which can never be totalized.

Remain Faithful to the Earth

Nietzsche regards *Thus Spoke Zarathustra* as his greatest achievement (1989, 304–305). In this work, teachings are mostly elaborated through the figure of Zarathustra. Zarathustra repeatedly insists on the fundamental teaching: *"remain faithful to the earth."* This demands the making of knowledge and gift-giving that serves the meaning of the earth and does not get lost in a universe of timeless transcendent values (Nietzsche 1982b, 188, 125). For this writer, typing in Narrm on a breezy, overcast day in late summer, this teaching resonates with the Indigenous law common to the First Nations throughout Australia: to respect and to care for Country.

In Nietzsche, the command to remain faithful to the earth is dependent on a cluster of linked concepts: Zarathustra is the figure of superabundant life overcoming itself, the figure of endless metamorphosis, of eternal return that endlessly says "yes" to life, and the positing of new values (Mortensen [1962] 2006; Deleuze 2006, 16–17). Will to power is the force that impels the eternal return. More precisely, the will to power is a multiplicity of forces or wills becoming together. This becoming involves encounters between different forces in relations of strife, combat, and overcoming. The encounter of the wills is a differentiating, clashing, and combining in never-ending transformation. The forces do not resolve into a unity, nor do they issue from primal unity. In stark contrast to the postulation of the One as the source of all things that founds western metaphysics, Nietzsche conceives of identity as a mere fleeting after-effect of the movement of difference. Difference goes all the way down. For Nietzsche, this clashing, merging, and becoming of forces is life and "everything" is alive (Nietzsche [1880s] 1968, §618, §619; Lingis 1985, 40–41) The will to power is not to be confused with the metaphysical concepts of matter or psyche; the will to power consists of inner forces impelling the becoming of life as difference (Nietzsche 1968 [1880s], §618).

For Nietzsche, values must be interpreted in relation to the forces that will them. Values are elaborated by two modes of willing: (1) they are elaborated by a sovereign will creating what the sovereign thinks is worthy. For instance, the sovereign (master) valorizes "his" [sic] thought as good and "his" strength as noble. This is a yes-saying and active way of creating values. (2) Values can be posited by what Nietzsche calls "slaves" refusing the values of their oppressors and saying, "what the masters think is evil." Here, the slaves' first idea is a saying "no" to the values of the oppressive sovereign values. The slaves' idea of "good" is built on and shaped by the concept of evil the slaves attribute to the masters. "Good" in this instance is a secondary value that is posited after the slave has thought "what the master values is evil." The slave's idea of the "good" is what Nietzsche calls a reactive value. In Nietzsche's terms, for example, gentleness is an instance of slave morality thought up by oppressed people contemplating the cruelty of their rulers and reversing the norm of cruelty. In contrast, the master creates a new value in "his" deed or concept without reference to an exterior or opposed force. The master, like the slave, has a concept of "bad," but the master's concept of "bad" is posited as an after-thought and a side-production to "his" first and primary concept of "good." In the master's perspective, "bad" is "not-good." For instance, the master regards weakness as "bad," and this is the other and afterthought of "his" cherished idea of strength. While Nietzsche sometimes speaks of the master as if "he" is a subject in the metaphysical sense, the master is nothing other than the expression of "his" will/force. It is also necessary to read "slave morality" as an evaluation of force, of reactive force. For Nietzsche, "there is no doer behind the deed . . . the deed is everything" (Nietzsche [1887] 1989, 45).[8]

For many readers, Nietzsche's valorization of the master's active value creation and his critical evaluation of what he calls "slave morality" and "slave" postulations such as a universal ethics of gentleness is outrageous, especially if it is read subjectively. Yet Nietzsche's thinking on value creation is necessary reading for scholars and activists committed to critiquing and dismantling white supremacy, coloniality, patriarchy, heteronormativity, and other forms of oppression, and his influence is evident in significant decolonial, Black, feminist, and queer philosophy in the twentieth- and twenty-first-century readings of his work.[9] His account of active and reactive forces in life and thought remains an invaluable conceptual framework for decolonial feminist, queer, and leftist thinkers and activists.[10] For instance, a feminism that focuses excessively on the critique of patriarchal society and its dominant traditions of thought while offering no new values cannot get far. Feminist theory must posit new values, and these values must not be a mere inversion of patriarchal norms. Feminists need critique and feminists also need to affirm and invent feminine sexes in autonomous terms. This is precisely what Irigaray does with the lips that speak together. The Irigarayan affirming project of sexual difference is a project of value creation rooted in saying "yes" to the woman who loves her lips and to the lips of other femmes. Irigaray's lips are a saying yes to living milieus of the earth and yes to birthing rhythms of the cosmos.

The life-affirming Nietzsche/Zarathustra is the Nietzsche Irigaray loves and draws inspiration from in her effort to articulate the giving of life as sexual difference. Irigaray also goes into combat with him and refuses key aspects of his thought. It is impossible to summarize Irigaray's objections to Nietzsche in her complex three-part monograph. *Marine Lover* is highly poetic and unfolds her critique along with her affirmations of his extraordinary and varied writings. In this chapter, there are four points I wish to emphasize in Irigaray's disagreement with Nietzsche.

For Nietzsche, the figure of Zarathustra is less a man than a teacher who posits the affirmation of life as endless overcoming, and Zarathustra is unconstrained by any fixed values. Irigaray disagrees. She argues that Zarathustra is sexed masculine. This is evident, for instance, in Zarathustra's valorization of the "good war," his love of the phallic heights of the mountains, and his sun worship (the sun in the western tradition is consistently associated with phallic masculinity). And Irigaray reads Zarathustra's avoidance of the watery depths of the ocean and of darkness as symptoms of a masculine fear of femininity. Most of all, Zarathustra's audacious claim to speak "*the* meaning of the earth" [my emphasis] can be read as totalizing (ML, 15, 18, 21, 159). In this respect, the passage discussed earlier in which a feminine narrator says to an unspecified masculine addressee that he posits infinity as a closed whole can be read as an address to Nietzsche/Zarathustra (EP, 89).

Zarathustra does not make love with women or men—*though he might make love with animals and plants peopling the forest?*[11] In the famous song of the seven seals, life is a woman, and she is eternity:

> Oh, how should I not lust after eternity and after the nuptial
> ring of rings, the ring of recurrence?
> Never yet have I found the woman from whom I wanted
> children, unless it be this woman whom I love: for I love
> you, O eternity.
> For I love you, O eternity. (Nietzsche 1982b, 340, 341, 342, 343)

Irigaray argues that the postulation and double affirmation of the eternal return is predicated on a suppression/appropriation of the maternal. She writes: "And your whole will, your eternal recurrence, are these anything more than the dream of one who neither wants to have been born nor to continue being born, at every instance, of a female other? Does your joy in becoming not result from annihilating her from whom you are tearing yourself away?" (ML, 26–27).

Irigaray suggests that Nietzsche's greatest ressentiment is toward the maternal. I think his texts avow this in the very act of appropriating the maternal: one of his most famous images of the artist is of the artist as a "male mother" (Nietzsche 2001, §72). To return to the endless overcoming of Zarathustra affirming the eternal return eternally, conception, pregnancy, and birth are parts of him, so that Zarathustra has no need of a woman who is other to him. In contrast, in *Twilight of the Idols*, which was written after *Thus Spoke Zarathustra*, Nietzsche speaks directly and admiringly of orgiastic frenzy, the pains and pangs of maternal birth, and the sexual symbol of the phallus as the most valued symbol of all in the tragic Greek sense of eternal return. He writes:

> only in the Dionysian mysteries, in the psychology of the Dionysian state, that the *basic fact* of the Hellenic instinct finds expression—its "will to life." What was it that the Hellene guaranteed himself by means of these mysteries? *Eternal* life, the eternal return of life; the future promised and hallowed in the past, the triumphant Yes to life beyond all death and change; *true* life as the over-all continuation of life through procreation, through the mysteries of sexuality. For the Greeks the *sexual* symbol was therefore the venerable symbol par excellence, the real profundity in the whole of ancient piety. Every single element in the act of procreation, of pregnancy, and of birth aroused the highest and most solemn feelings. In the doctrine of the mysteries, *pain* is pronounced holy: the pangs of the woman giving birth hallow all pain; all becoming and growing—all that guarantees a future—involves pain. That there may be the eternal joy of creating, that the will to life may eternally affirm itself, the agony of the woman giving birth *must* also be there eternally. (1982a, 561–562)

Nietzsche's polemical figurations of woman are notorious. Irigaray devotes a close reading to his famous polemic on woman in Book II of *The Gay Science* in "Veiled Lips," the second part of *Marine Lover*. She argues that in Nietzsche *le feminin* becomes the stake in the game of his thinking, she becomes everything—*"woman has no essence"*—and this leaves no space for a woman other than the women that Nietzsche puts into play and ventriloquizes in his discourse (ML, 82–83). Nietzsche's women—mothers, little girls, old women, actresses, witches, feminists, castrated women, the Goddess Persephone, Dionysus' companion Ariadne, and so on—are figures caught in the web of his writing. For Irigaray, they are not faithful to the rhythms of the cosmic, the feminine as nontotalizable multiplicity, the feminine of the Earth.

Irigaray contends that Nietzsche's affirmation of endless becoming and eternal return is a flying over life, a desire to will everything, a desire to say everything. She suggests that there is no respect for alterity outside the metamorphoses of Zarathustra, there are no space-times of other worlds beyond the repetition (difference) of Zarathustra's circling. For Irigaray, this betrays the great teaching of Zarathustra to remain faithful to the meaning of the Earth. "In order to speak the meaning of the earth, is it necessary to exhaust all her stores? Is the reign of the superman at hand when the whole of the earth becomes sublime discourse, when all that remains of her is her praise in the memory of ghosts?" (ML, 18). In a Nietzschean essay on Zarathustra's becoming bird, Gary Shapiro suggests that while Irigaray's critique of Nietzsche is subtle and interesting, her approach is restrictively anthropocentric and misses Nietzsche's becomings-animal (2004, 85–86). An Irigarayan reply to Shapiro is that Nietzsche's Zarathustra carries the baggage of western man into his extraordinary effort to overcome the human and to affirm a philosophy of difference, a philosophy of endlessly becoming other. I also think, contra Shapiro, that there are passages in *Marine Lover* inspired by movements that are inhuman. Later, I develop the claim that there is an aquatic feminine animal speaking in her text and an oceanic speaking of immemorial waters.

The most persuasive and thoughtful criticism of Irigaray's reading of Nietzsche I know of is found in Mortensen's work. Her sustained engagement with *Marine Lover* in the essay "Will to Power in the Feminine" and her book *The Feminine and Nihilism: Luce Irigaray with Nietzsche and Martin Heidegger* read Irigaray in Heideggerian terms. Mortensen argues that Irigaray's reading of Nietzsche's will to power and the eternal return as an appropriation of maternal generation conflates ontology with the ontic (1995, 86). In a way, Mortensen is right—though Irigaray is not interested in being a "good" Heideggerian. Irigaray disagrees with Heidegger's framing of fundamental ontology. In a divergence from Heidegger, Irigaray audaciously elaborates a rethinking of the relationship between the ontic and ontological by placing the giving of life as sexual difference at the heart of her thought: the emergence of all beings comes into presence from the giving of life as sexual difference. Thinking must find ways of speaking respectfully in relation to this giving. In the concluding section I wish to show how this works in *Marine Lover*.[12]

La Mère / La Mer

How I should love you if to speak to you were possible.

—ML, 3

Irigaray is in open combat with Nietzsche/Zarathustra; she also imagines loving him, if it were possible to speak with him. To speak with him necessitates, not only that he would still be living but also that he would be willing to share the world with a different other, to listen to her speech with keen ears, and to respect that her sayings and her wills remain beyond the horizons of his sayings, his wills, and becoming-other. For the feminine narrator that opens *Marine Lover* to speak with him requires breath, air, water, earth, fire, and a sexuate interval between Zarathustra's becoming and the marine lover's becoming.

There are moments in Nietzsche's corpus where he avows difference between the sexes, and Zarathustra affirms the need for women and men to learn to love themselves and each other in the process of transvaluation (1982b, 183). I admire Nietzsche as an acute diagnostician of the motivations of misogyny in the western tradition and, arguably, in his own life and thought. In a remarkable aphorism in *The Gay Science*, he suggests that the will to create pure ideas and ideals and to devalue the body is impelled by male artists in reaction to their disgust at the "repulsive" maternal and bodily functions of women they love. At these moments, Nietzsche is close to a feminist thinker of sexual difference engaged in the critique of the pervasive phallocentrism of western philosophy.[13]

Mortensen suggests that there is a very close resonance between the conceptualization of will to power and eternal return as eternity (the only woman Nietzsche/Zarathustra loves) and Irigaray's sense of life as difference in the feminine (1995, 66; Nietzsche 1982b, 340, 341, 342, 343). The close resonance between Irigaray and Nietzsche is puzzling if we stick to what the text of *Marine Lover* says about Nietzsche/Zarathustra's appropriation of the mother. Irigaray, however, is a writer who works with the effects of silence, and this is important to making sense of her engagement with Nietzsche. There are movements in which her text thinks with Nietzsche's texts, though *Marine Lover* does this without explicitly avowing that Irigarayan difference in the feminine participates in the Nietzschean concept of difference. In other words, Irigaray's giving of life as feminine difference is indebted to Nietzsche's teaching of life as will to power. There is also divergence in their concepts of difference. For Nietzsche, will to power is eternally becoming other, while, as I have argued, in many of Irigaray's works, feminine difference is the becoming-body of the mother and has a beginning and perhaps an end. The giving of life is not infinite for Irigaray (S, 229).[14]

"Speaking of Immemorial Waters" (ML, 1–73) is a polyphony of feminine voices addressing the many masks of Nietzsche, as well as several of his readers and precursors.[15] Some of the feminine voices of Irigaray's text are inhuman. The marine lover who speaks to Zarathustra lives beyond the reach of the sunlight in dark waters in the depths of the sea. She is an aquatic animal. There is also a speaking of the sea (*la mer*). *La mer* is a pun on the French words for "the mother"—*la mère*. *La mer/la mère* is a saying of *phusis* as the mother. Addressing Zarathustra in the mountains, and Nietzsche in his walks near Rapello as he experienced the rapturous events of the coming of the figure of Zarathustra,[16] and the Nietzschean concept of eternal return, Irigaray writes:

> Yet is there any greater rapture than the sea? For he who climbs high to set his senses areel as if from good wine must still climb down again at last. And his rapture lasts only so long. And all kinds of depressions lie in wait, and the spell is often broken.
>
> But endless rapture awaits whoever trusts the sea. For as she rises and falls, so one's rapture swells and sinks. Whether the sea is rising or falling, nothing changes in the enchantment of living—moving about endlessly. And does it matter if the sea is pouring over the beaches or sinking back into its bed? Doesn't the one will the other, and the other the one? And isn't it the passage from one to the other that makes for eternal good fortune? (ML, 13)

In this passage the sea is written in the third person and figured as the great and endless rapture felt by a marine lover in contrast with the rapture of Zarathustra/Nietzsche on the earth, climbing, leaping, and dancing in the mountains. The marine lover participates in the rising and falling, the enchantment of the living becoming of the sea. This is the sea together with the marine lover as part of *phusis*, giving space and time and matter and form. In the following section, Irigaray's text shifts to speaking *as* the sea.

> Because both flowing over my banks and savoring my great depths are equal rapture for me. I do not wish to be measured out drop by drop. Drop by drop (I) do not care to live my time. For whole and entire (I) want myself at every instant.
>
> And what matter if it be ebb or flow? As long as, at each moment, (I) move as a whole. And, for me, ebb and flow have always set the rhythm of time. But (they) come at different hours. At midday or midnight, at dawn or dusk. One moment is worth absolutely no more than the other for the whole is

present in each. At each hour comes fortune, multiple in the winding of its becoming.

And (I) have no need to turn round and round to come back to the same or to enter into eternity.

For same have (I) been for all eternity, and, at the same time, ever different. And thus (I) come and go, change and stay, go on and come back, without any circle. Spread out and open in this endless becoming.

And without one direction ever being more important than another, without my ever wanting one rather than the other. For they are not distinct. Which is not to say that they are indistinguishable. (MA 14; AM, 20)

Parler mer is placed in counterpoint to Nietzsche's eternal return of the same. In Irigaray's text, the "same" is difference. The resonance and dissonance with Heraclitus, Nietzsche's favorite Pre-Socratic thinker, is striking: "The sun is new each day" (Heraclitus §XLVIIIA in Kahn, *The Art and Thought of Heraclitus: An Edition of the Fragments with Translation and Commentary*, 50–51).[17] Though perhaps Irigaray is not so different from Nietzsche, either, if we follow Deleuze, the eternal return of Nietzsche is difference (Deleuze [1962] 2006, 197–198)? Irigaray wonders if the circle of eternal return is a desire that there "will be no other but me" (ML, 15). While this is a criticism, it is an open criticism, because she addresses him in the form of a question, and this leaves open the necessary possibility that there are other space-times in the thought of Nietzsche. Irigaray's criticisms of Nietzsche should be read as open questions to tendencies in his thought rather than totalizing judgements.

I have written in this chapter about Irigaray's concept of life as feminine difference. In many of her works, this concept is posited as the becoming body of the mother giving birth. While open, feminine difference is not eternal. Yet there are also writings by Irigaray where feminine difference *is* eternal. The passages I have just quoted from *Marine Lover* are instances in which feminine difference is posited as eternal. I am not sure what to make of this oscillation in Irigaray's thinking of sexual difference. Perhaps we should read the eternal rapture of the marine lover as a reference to the aquatic animal praising the sea that gives her life and overflows her finitude? This would render "endlessly" and "eternity" in Irigaray as distinct from the sense of the eternity of eternal return that Irigaray faults in Nietzsche. Or perhaps we could read "endless rapture" and "eternity" as moments in which Irigaray affirms her own version of eternal becoming without return?

Irigaray's *parler mer* is not a refusal of Nietzsche's sun, or of the mountains. These figures are in conversation with the figuration of the sun and mountains in Nietzsche's discourse and the sun of Heraclitus' discourse. Irigaray is also gesturing beyond metaphor and seeking to connect with the sayings in Nietzsche that exceed metaphor. The sayings of the marine lover and the sayings of the sea are writings inspired and charged with the rhythms of the sea, with the movement of aquatic animals as singing becomings of an open world of difference. These songs belong in relationship with the singing earth, daylight, birdsong, rustlings of a small lizard, the forest, storms, thunder, and other becomings of life celebrated in Nietzsche's writing. In this sense, Irigaray's interventions are supplements to the language of Nietzsche that vibrates with the giving of life. Insofar as Irigaray's texts are inspired by the elemental, she is very close to Nietzsche's rapturous thinking of poetic and philosophic inspiration as encounters with life in which individuality melts away.

Notes

1. Édouard Glissant teaches us that the "west" is a project, not a place. Glissant, *Caribbean Discourse*, 2. In congruence with the theorists of decoloniality, I understand the western project as founded on the Coloniality of Being. See Wynter, "Unsettling Coloniality of Being/Power/Truth/Freedom." In Irigaray's terms, this project is constitutively phallocentric. For a discussion of close resonances between decolonial theory and Irigaray, see Seely, "Irigaray Between God and the Indians."

2. In recent work, Irigaray acknowledges that there are perhaps more than two sexuate subjects. I have argued elsewhere that this gives space for other kinds of subjects, including genderqueer or nonbinary subjects and trans women and trans men. See Hill, "At Least Two: The Tendencies of Sexual Difference" and Hill, "From the Exchange of Women to Sexual Difference."

3. An old meaning of *phusis* is slang for women's genitals, and an older term related to physis is *phusein*, meaning to give birth to. See Hill, *The Interval: Relation and Becoming in Irigaray, Aristotle and Bergson*, 23–24. The sense of maternal in the context of human reproduction is not limited to people with wombs who are thought to have the potential to birth children. For me, the maternal designates pregnancy, childbirth, care, and raising of children. For elaboration of this point, see Hill, "From the Exchange of Women to Sexual Difference."

4. In the essay "Immanent Maternal: Figures of Time in Aristotle, Bergson and Irigaray," I characterized the giving of life as feminine or what I called the

"immanent maternal." I qualified the characterization of the giving of life as the immanent maternal as a strategic gesture, the gesture of a feminist combatant refusing the phallomorphic projections that found and dominate western metaphysics. I am not satisfied with my argument for the cosmic mother as strategic in that text anymore, though I also hesitate to make the leap and affirm the living whole as feminine in Irigaray's sense. While I hesitate to make the leap, I admire Irigaray's audacity and regard this aspect of her thought as compelling. Irigaray's speculative argument for feminine difference and especially as becoming body in/as the mother has fascinating resonances with contemporary origins of life research in the sciences. See Annu Dahiya's excellent chapter, "The Conditions of Emergence: Irigaray, Primordial Wombs, and the Origins of Cellular Life."

5. Irigaray's formulation in this passage is reminiscent of Henri Bergson's philosophy. The open whole of the feminine narrator resonates with his intuitive conceptualization of the enduring whole, while the closed totality Irigaray attributes to western man aligns with Bergson's critical description of the intellectual reduction of the world in which everything is already given and the difference that duration makes is rendered invisible. See Bergson's "Introduction to Metaphysics" in *The Creative Mind*.

6. I will take up another instance of difference as the mother later in the chapter when we discuss Nietzsche.

7. The senses of alienation are at least two: (1) alienation by the enframing of global technicity that reduces Being to quantifiable beings described by Martin Heidegger in *The Question Concerning Technology* and other works, and (2) alienation in the Marxist sense by the reduction of everything to commodities on the market. See Marx, *Capital Volume 1*, 125–244.

8. This is a summary of some arguments from the first essay of *The Genealogy of Morals*. From reasons of brevity, I have left aside Nietzsche's brilliant analysis of the triumph of *ressentiment*, which issues from the reactive of will the "slaves." Deleuze's reading of "master morality" and "slave morality" in terms of active and reactive forces is an outstanding reading of Nietzsche's crucial text. Deleuze, *Nietzsche and Philosophy*, 39–72.

9. Decolonial philosopher Frantz Fanon's essay on the making of national literatures in *The Wretched of the Earth* calls on to decolonial writers to stop addressing the colonial masters and the traditions of coloniality and to think within and for the making of a new people and new earth. This is a yes-saying approach to creating literature that resonates with Nietzsche's idea of the sovereign creation of new values (see Fanon, *Wretched of the Earth*). Saidiya Hartman draws from Nietzsche's account of morality in her pathbreaking monograph *Scenes of Subjection*. Nietzsche's impact in continental feminist philosophy is widespread. In addition to Irigaray, see for instance, Grosz, *Volatile Bodies: Toward a Corporeal Feminism*; Grosz, *The Nick of Time: Politics, Evolution and the Untimely*; Grosz, *The Incorporeal: Ontology, Ethics and the Limits of Materialism*; Mortensen,

The Feminine and Nihilism: Luce Irigaray with Nietzsche and Martin Heidegger, Mortensen, "Nietzsche in the Feminine? Questioning Nietzsche's Will to Power;" and Oliver, *Womanizing Nietzsche: Philosophy's Relation to the "Feminine."* Also see the edited collection *Nietzsche, Feminism and Political Theory* (Paul Patton, ed.). Judith Butler draws on Nietzsche in their signature theory of performativity. *Bodies that Matter: On the Discursive Limits of "Sex,"* 121.

10. His work also attracts the admiration of fascists. Of course, Nietzsche's corpus was appropriated and distorted by the National Socialists under Nazism. This is all the more a reason for those of us on the left, in feminist, decolonial, queer, and crip, antiracist circles to read Nietzsche. On reading Nietzsche after National Socialism, see Derrida, "Otobiographies: The Teaching of Nietzsche and the Politics of the Proper Name," 1–38.

11. "I love the forest. It is bad to live in cities: there too many are in heat. Is it not better to fall into the hands of a murderer than the dreams of a woman in heat? And behold these men: their eyes say it—they know of nothing better on earth than to lie with a woman. Mud is at the bottom of their souls; and woe if their mud also has spirit!" Nietzsche, 1982b, 166.

12. Mortensen accepts Irigaray's divergences with Heidegger in a more recent essay. In "Between Heidegger's Poetic Thinking and Deleuzian Affect," Mortensen describes the main divergence between Irigaray and Heidegger in the following terms: "For Heidegger, Dasein enters into and receives language; language is the house of Being, the groundless ground that grants Being to all beings, which emerge in time through its *epoché*. By contrast, Irigaray does not understand language as devoid of life but instead as energized and mobilized by the forces of life, both negative and affirmative. Hence, language is alive and perpetually changing; it has a past (which may or may not be forgotten), a present, and a possible future." (2020, 123)

In this essay, Mortensen repeats the Irigarayan claim that Nietzsche (and other western philosophers) suppress and appropriate the maternal, and in this text Mortensen agrees with Irigaray (129–130).

13. We artists.—When we love a woman, we easily come to hate nature because of all the repulsive natural functions to which every woman is subject; we prefer not to think about it at all, but when our soul for once brushes against these matters, it shrugs impatiently and, as just said, casts a contemptuous look at nature: we feel insulted; nature seems to intrude on our property and with the most profane hands at that. In cases like this one refuses to hear anything about physiology and decrees secretly to oneself, "I will hear nothing of the idea that the human being is anything other than soul and form!" "The human being under the skin" is an abomination and unthinkable to all lovers, a blasphemy against God and love. Now, the way lovers still feel about nature and naturalness is how every worshipper of God and his "holy omnipotence" formerly felt; in every thing that was said about nature by astronomers, geologists, physiologists, and doctors, he

saw an intrusion on his choicest property and thus an attack—and a shameless one at that! Even the "law of nature" sounded to him like a slander against God; he would basically much rather have seen all of mechanics traced back to moral acts of will and choice—but since no one could do him that service, he *concealed* nature and mechanics from himself as best he could and lived in a dream. Oh, these people of former times knew how to *dream* and didn't even need to fall asleep first!—and we men of today also still know it all too well, despite all our good will towards waking and the day! We need only to love, to hate, to desire, simply to feel—*at once* the spirit and power of the dream comes over us, and we climb with open eyes, impervious to all danger, up the most dangerous paths, and onto the roofs and towers of fantasy, and without any vertigo, as though born to climb—we sleepwalkers of the day! We who conceal naturalness! We who are moon- and God-struck! We untiring wanderers, silent as death, on heights that we see not as heights but as our plains, as our safety." Nietzsche, 2001, §59.

In this aphorism love, hate, desire, feeling impel fabulation and world making that conceal nature from the artist. The misogynist reaction impelling the becoming idealist is one movement in Nietzsche's argument.

14. In Irigaray's recent and current work, her claim that life is nontotalizable is clearly distinguished from an idea that life is infinite or endless. See WDM, 1–3.

15. In the original French title "*Dire D'eau Immémoriales*" is a statement in the infinitive. And the verb *dire* is closer to the English "to say." I thank Antonia Pont for discussing the French sense of the title with me.

16. See the chapter in *Ecce Homo* on *Thus Spoke Zarathustra*.

17. "*O ilios ou monon kathaper o Hrakleitos phisi neos eph imeri estin all aei neos sunekhos.*"

References

Bergson, Henri. 1946. "Introduction to Metaphysics." In *The Creative Mind*. Trans. M. L. Andison. Philosophical Library.

Butler, Judith. 1993. *Bodies that Matter: On the Discursive Limits of "Sex."* Routledge.

Dahiya, Annu. 2022. "The Conditions of Emergence: Irigaray, Primordial Wombs, and the Origins of Cellular Life." In *Horizons of Difference: Rethinking Space, Place, and Identity with Irigaray*, edited by Ruthanne Crapo Kim, Yvette Russell, and Brenda Sharp. State University of New York Press.

Deleuze, Gilles. (1962) 2006. *Nietzsche and Philosophy*. Translated by Hugh Tomlinson. Columbia University Press.

Derrida, Jacques. (1984) 1985. "Otobiographies: The Teaching of Nietzsche and the Politics of the Proper Name," translated by Avital Ronell. In *The Ear of the Other: Otobiography, Transference, Translation*, edited by Peggy Kamuf. University of Nebraska Press.

Fanon, Frantz. (1963) 2004. *The Wretched of the Earth*. Translated by Richard Philcox. Grove Press.

Glissant, Édouard. (1981) 1989. *Caribbean Discourse*. Translated by J. Michael Dash. University Press of Virginia.

Grosz, Elizabeth. 1994. *Volatile Bodies: Toward a Corporeal Feminism*. Bloomington: Indiana University Press, 1994.

Grosz, Elizabeth. 2004. *The Nick of Time: Politics, Evolution and the Untimely*. Duke University Press.

Grosz, Elizabeth. 2017. *The Incorporeal: Ontology, Ethics and the Limits of Materialism*. Columbia University Press.

Hartman, Saidiya. 1997. *Scenes of Subjection: Terror, Slavery and Self-Making in Nineteenth Century America*. Oxford University Press.

Heidegger, Martin. 1994. *Basic Writings*. Translated by David Farell Krell. Routledge.

Hill, Rebecca. 2012. *The Interval: Relation and Becoming in Irigaray, Aristotle and Bergson*. Fordham University Press.

Hill, Rebecca. 2017. "At Least Two: The Tendencies of Sexual Difference." *Australian Feminist Law Journal* 43, no. 1: 25–40.

Hill, Rebecca. 2019. "Immanent Maternal: Figures of Time in Aristotle, Bergson and Irigaray." In *Antiquities Beyond Humanism*, edited by Emanuela Bianchi, Brooke Holmes, and Sara Brill. Oxford University Press.

Hill, Rebecca. 2022. "From the Exchange of Women to Sexual Difference." *Sydney Review of Books*. Writing and Society Research Centre, Western Sydney University.

Kahn, Charles H. 1979. *The Art and Thought of Heraclitus: An Edition of the Fragments with Translation and Commentary*. Cambridge University Press.

Lingis, Alphonso. 1985. "The Will to Power." In *The New Nietzsche*, edited by David B. Allison. MIT Press.

Marx, Karl. (1867) 1990. *Capital Volume I*. Translated by Ben Fowkes. Penguin.

Mortensen, Ellen. 1994. *The Feminine and Nihilism: Luce Irigaray with Nietzsche and Martin Heidegger*. Scandinavian University Press.

Mortensen, Ellen. 2020. "Between Heidegger's Poetic Thinking and Deleuzian Affect: Irigaray's *The Way of Love*." In *Thinking Life with Luce Irigaray: Language, Origin, Art, Love*, edited by Gail M. Schwab. State University of New York Press.

Mortensen, Ellen. 2006. "Nietzsche in the Feminine? Questioning Nietzsche's Will to Power." In *Sex, Breath, and Force: Sexual Difference in a Post-Feminist Era*, edited by Ellen Mortensen. Lexington Books.

Nietzsche, Friedrich. (c. 1880s) 1968. *The Will to Power*. Translated by Walter Kaufman and R. J. Hollingdale. Vintage Books.

Nietzsche, Friedrich. (1954) 1982a. *The Portable Nietzsche.* Edited and translated by Walter Kaufman. Viking Portable Library, Penguin.

Nietzsche, Friedrich. (1954) 1982b. "Thus Spoke Zarathustra." In *The Portable Nietzsche,* edited and translated by Walter Kaufman. Viking Portable Library, Penguin.

Nietzsche, Friedrich. (1887) 1989. *The Genealogy of Morals and Ecce Homo.* Translated by Walter Kaufman and R. J. Hollingdale. Vintage Books.

Nietzsche, Friedrich. (1882) 2001. *The Gay Science.* Translated by Josefine Nauckhoff. Cambridge University Press.

Oliver, Kelly. 1995. *Womanizing Nietzsche: Philosophy's Relation to the "Feminine."* Routledge.

Patton, Paul, ed. 1993. *Nietzsche, Feminism and Political Theory.* Routledge.

Seely, Stephen D. 2017. "Irigaray Between God and the Indians." *Australian Feminist Law Journal* 43, no. 1: 41–67.

Shapiro, Gary. 2004. "The Halycon Song as Birdsong." In *A Nietzschean Bestiary: Becoming Animal Beyond Docile and Brutal,* edited by Christa Davis Acampora and Ralph R. Acampora. Rowman and Littlefield.

Wynter, Sylvia. 2003. "Unsettling Coloniality of Being/Power/Truth/Freedom: Towards the Human, after Man, Its Overrepresentation, an Argument." *CR: The New Centennial Review* 3, no. 3: 257–337.

Chapter Seven

"A *Morphé* in Continual Gestation"

The Sensible Transcendental, Gesture, and Morphology in Irigaray

Athena V. Colman

According to Luce Irigaray, the problem of sexual difference reaches deeply into the thought and language of western philosophy and other reflective discourses like psychoanalysis.[1] It is, for her, the blind spot of tradition that can be confronted in this moment of history. Irigaray's methodology is affected by the impossibility of directly showing the problem of sexual difference without reproducing the very problem she is trying to over-come. As is widely known, the first aspect of her methodology is to show sexual difference *has not been*. For example, in texts like *Speculum of the Other Woman,* she demonstrates that *just* where the tradition of western thought deepens its investigation into the connections between the sexual, thought, and culture, it produces and reproduces a monosexual theory (for instance, Freud). In respect of the pervasiveness of the problem of the lack of sexual difference, or sexual *indifference*, Irigaray then also seeks to develop the *horizon* of sexual difference. This means she is seeking ways in which this difference is drawn out as a dynamic, developmental, and self-transformative process that requires the autonomy and connect-edness of one in relation to an other and in "the sharing of the world." Without this process, subjectivity and culture are blocked, and so there are no substantial ethical ties. For Irigaray, then, the problem of sexual difference is the problem of subjectivity, culture, and ethics. While many accuse Irigaray's thought of subordinating all other differences to sexual difference, perhaps one must remember that when she asked the question of sexual difference, she was not demanding an answer or offering an account—she was helping articulate the *question* as the horizon to make the very problem of sexual difference appear. Indeed, culturally speaking, western thought has yet to take the question of sexual difference seriously. And, if Irigaray's radical commitment to a culture of two in sexual difference may seem antiquated to some, and dangerous to others, her prescient insight that sexual difference is *the* question of our age has not been overcome or eclipsed by more recent theories of gender and sex (that is, queer theory and trans studies or transfeminism).[2] On the contrary, in many ways, such discourses reilluminate the problem of sexual difference, even, and maybe especially, where these discourses unfold at the site of its forgetting, thusly becoming the place where the logic of sexual *indifference* is reiterated.[3] For example, on Irigaray's view, the binary of masculine and feminine is the *appearance* of two that functions to secure an economy of one (that is, masculine sameness). Women have no separate symbolic. They are defined insofar as they are the denigrated other of the male subject from which he defines himself through her negation. Therefore, insofar as nonbinary subjects depend on the existing binary, the negation of which secures their subjectivity, they logically require and depend on the existence of the binary they repetitively reproduce. On this view, not only does a nonbinary subject reinscribe the monosexual culture, but in forming subjectivity and identity through a structural negation, they repeat the nonrelational violence that founds the masculine subject and, are thusly, a version of a masculine subject. For those who identify with either side of the binary, as a man or a woman, the same fate awaits. Again, on this reading, trans subjects who identify with either side of the binary also reassert that binary and, hence, inevitably reinvest the masculine subject at the level of the symbolic. Again, women, which includes trans women, do not have a separate symbolic through which to elaborate a different subjectivity. The societal anxiety that moves beyond transphobia to the specificity of transmisogyny enacted against trans women can be understood in terms of the absence of a culture of *a least two subjects* (that is, the absence of sexual difference).[4]

In what follows, I move beyond an Irigarayan critique of trans discourses to develop concepts in her thought that resource the importance of the question of sexual difference for all subjects, including trans subjects, in ways that open up a situated, relational context for subjectivity that does not leave trans women and men as incomprehensible, abject others. Toward this end, I develop Irigaray's thought in ways that index possibilities of difference in terms of the question of difference. I hope to extend moments in Irigaray's thought that show how resources for differences yet to be theorized at the level of embodiment and subjectivity are inextricably intertwined with the problem of sexual difference as such.[5] Such an account has the advantage of respecting Irigaray's own claim of sexuate identity as a relational identity, which is always a "way of entering into relation with oneself, with the world, with the other(s)" (KW, x) in which "[n]one of these [dimensions] can be sacrificed to the other without the connection with transcendence becoming ruined" (SW, 90–91).[6]

I begin with an account of morphology to reframe an approach to thinking sexuate subjectivity where relationality, meaning, and bodily life are inseverable from each other. The discussion of morphology anticipates and contextualizes a reading of Irigaray's notion of the *sensible transcendental*, which I develop to vivify the question of sexual difference and further specify by suggesting a moment of the sensible transcendental might be concretized in a morphological understanding of gesture. To clarify and develop this thought, I turn to Irigaray's thinking on gesture in subject formation. Irigaray's rereading of Freud's account of the little boy's entrance into language in *Beyond the Pleasure Principle*—an account that notably excludes an account of the little girl, positions the little boy's entrance into the symbolic as an acquisition of language that is marked in opposition to a dependency on the presence of the mother—and a concomitant mastery of the mother performed by a reduction of her to a body as a material, controllable object. Irigaray recovers the necessity of the meaningful bodily action of the gesture at the level of the materiality it putatively denies that supports and enables the little boy's linguistic achievement. The gesture is unknowingly preserved as the untheorized, unacknowledged, feminine-maternal-material support for the little boy's accomplishment and, indeed, the unacknowledged support of Freud's own account. In mapping the erasure of the feminine at the site of a dependency on her negation, Irigaray returns us to the psychoanalytic logic of the emergence of the symbolic. Irigaray's recovery of the necessity of the gesture, which is overlooked by Freud, destabilizes the solidity of the symbolic at the same time as situating its dependency in terms of the masculine mastery of the maternal-feminine.

Morphology Without Teleology

Morphology is an approach to studying forms and their variation in biology and linguistics. In biology, morphology "does not refer to deterministic analysis of forms in themselves, but to a method of discerning patterns of *relationships between* forms" (Robinson 2002, 93). As a subdiscipline in linguistics, morphology focuses on the *morpheme*—how differences in the material legacy of shapes or forms constituting words (written or spoken) accompany differences in meaning. For Irigaray, morphology uncovers meaning in its inextricability from the materiality of its expression.[7] Historically, the morphological features of language have been overshadowed by a focus on syntax.[8] Irigaray's own work diagnoses this disconnection in terms of the problem of sexual difference. The masculine symbolic order excludes the feminine while at the same time relying on the feminine to maintain itself. The masculine ideal of a universal subject reflects a psychic desire to distance itself from the maternal, the bodily, the irrational (an irrationality it constructs), and the feminine. It is the disavowal of this dependency that sustains the masculine symbolic, and thus, the feminine is the psychic support for her own erasure. In the absence of a feminine culture (in which such difference would be elaborated in and through the symbolic and imaginary registers), what can count as meaningful is theorized into an abstraction that is dependent on a severance from materiality, a severance that is shored up by syntax. The reduction of meaning to universalizing syntax relies on the assumption of a disembodied or "neutral" speaker that erases the specificity of the very bodies it depends on to speak. The universalizing version of syntax—that does not recognize itself as a particularity—subordinates the feminine speaking subject to a language that silences her.[9] Irigaray's response to this silence is to "[o]*verthrow syntax* by suspending its eternally teleological order" (S, 142), and her writing and philosophical methodology rigorously enact a frustration of syntax's teleology. She exposes the illusion of a universality unencumbered by material specificity and reveals that the masculine syntax-symbolic is subtended by an "empire of a morpho-logic"[10] (SN, 219) of the male imaginary "[w]hich, of course, knows no modification of its attributes, no change in morphology, no detumescence ever. Always identical to itself, no ups and downs" (S, 303). Irigaray discovers the neglect of the materiality of language deeply entrenched in the western tradition. She recalls the Platonic bifurcation of form and matter from the perspective of the missed moment of their reconnection in Aristotle, whose hyle-morphism rescued matter (*hyle*) from Plato's metaphysics—rejoining matter with form (*morphē*)—only to subjugate matter (associated with woman as passive materiality) to the primacy of form once again (where form is aligned with the active agency of man in developing and changing his world). In this way, the existing symbolic is propped up by denying any other morphology than its own. This *is* the problem of sexual difference. Hence, Irigaray tells us, "we must go back to the question not of the anatomy but of the morphology of female sex" (WE, 64).

How are we to understand this call to return to the morphology of female sex in Irigaray? Such a call may seem to resound the well-tread and much debated question of essentialism in Irigaray's project of sexual difference. However, it is important to notice how this charge of essentialism arises precisely at the limits where Irigaray's thought has discovered as problematic the absence of sexual difference itself. Indeed, her critique of the "ideal morphology of the Father's vision," which subtends the masculine syntax-symbolic, is that it enacts and enforces an exclusion of "all change, all alteration or modification" (S, 320). A return to the morphology of female sex cannot, therefore, be the positing of a new feminine "arkhē and telos" (S, 319 [*sic*]), since an arché as origin, or telos as goal or natural end, is only made possible by an exclusion of the feminine (S, 99). Moreover, a morphology of female sex must be discovered in its actuality and not in advance of its appearance: "Transmutations occur, always unexpectedly, since they do not conspire to any telos" (S, 233).

Elizabeth Grosz argues that Irigaray's distinction between anatomy and morphology shows her to be engaged in "a form of combat, a strategy for disarming phallocentric discourses in order to show what is at stake in them" (1993, 187). According to Alison Stone, Grosz' reading of morphology, which Stone claims is characteristic of most scholars, is only appropriate to Irigaray's earlier works where " 'morphology' denotes the form which a body assumes in culture. But the later Irigaray believes that bodies *naturally* assume form (*morphē*)" (2006, 109). There is no doubt that Irigaray's work is always engaged in the strategies suggested by Grosz and that there are threads in Irigaray that can be sewn together to suggest Stone's reading of the morphological. However, despite Stone's acknowledgment that Irigaray's notion of bodily form is never abstracted from "perceptually concrete terms" (109), her suggestion that 'bodies *naturally* assume form,' in effect, covers over what is specified by this concreteness and in so doing misses the transcendental moment in Irigaray's thinking.[11] Stone's intricate rereading of Irigaray through German philosophies of nature suggests that by "nature" Irigaray means a notion of *physis*: an "open-ended growth into presence" (14) realized as an "inner ordering principle (*logos*), namely, a rhythm" (109). According to Stone, the natural rhythm that regulated bodily formation becomes the identifiable morphological form.[12] Here, Stone's discernment of the importance of rhythm in sexuate difference is apposite (I reconsider rhythm in the discussion of gesture below), but her emphasis on its primacy in "nature," even when nature is understood to be an "open-process," risks absorbing the debt of maternal origins into a natural rhythm that precedes her. Such an account reduces rhythm to a teleology, to a plan that precedes sensible emergence, and thus reasserts the *transcendental as prior to the sensible*. The primacy of rhythm construed in this way also undermines Irigaray's claim for the ontological importance of birth, which her thought has salvaged from teleological accounts of reproduction in a return to the morphological.

Irigaray has specified that her account of sexual difference always includes, "[T]he morphology of the body and the relational context of birth" (CLB, 113). She implicates the morphological emergence from the body of the mother in terms of the subject position that one takes up in relation to her. For Irigaray, "[b]irth is distance before any form, or more exactly, it constitutes the entry into a morphology" (NL, 13). Since there is no form *before* birth, birth is nonteleological. Without a form that precedes, *informs*, or guarantees it, birth is the distance that grounds the possibility of relation; it enables the movement of self-relation in relation to another and to the world. In other words, birth is the separation that makes connection possible. A fine, if porous, line must be drawn between our maternal origins and Irigaray's ontology of birth. "Without telos or arché," birth makes the relation to our maternal origins possible (S, 229). Birth is our "entry into a morphology" because, for Irigaray, form is always *form of relation in relation*. Sexuate identity is thus relational identity (KW, 177). Here, the priority of sexual difference is realized in its ontological dimension: *sexual difference is the possibility of relation*. "[The subject] . . . has, and is, an incarnate form. It creates a morphology, and is one. The relation between the two is its story, with its projects, its generation, its loops, and its repetitions" (SN, 3).

The claim here is that our "birth has a debt beyond its social construction and that because the debt is to a time I cannot remember, or master in my memory, it is a latency—it is an absence in me that has allowed me to become" (Colman, 2022, 28). Birth is an actuality. As such, the movement of meaning is never divorced from the morphology birth initiates, "[a] *morphé* in continual gestation. Movements ceaselessly reshaping this incarnation" (ESD, 193). Respect for sexuate difference is not a parsing out of all identities into two possibilities. Rather, it is the acknowledgement that self-relation is already made possible by a relation to an other, which includes the otherness of our subjectivity that is never separate from intersubjectivity or the world. The embodied, historical, and sensible specificity of the way in which one takes up the relation to their birth reveals itself in, and as, a morphology constantly becoming. This is why Irigaray calls for a return to a morphology of the female sex while at the same time specifying that "no woman has the morphology of another" (SN, 243). Irigaray is not reducing sexual difference to women's anatomical features. Rather she is indexing the erasure of difference as an erasure of history, dependence, and multiplicity, which western thought has elaborated in terms of a denigration and negation of materiality, in turn, figured as woman or the feminine. The morphological never precedes sensible specificity and, as constituted and constituting in relation to an other, is never without transcendence: "A transcendence which now remains alive, sensible and even carnal . . . it remains irreducibly other" (KW, 148).

The sensible transcendental as a "future anterior"

Irigaray's notion of the sensible transcendental uncovers the deepest static, binarized, or dichotomous conceptions of thought. The problem is thus submerged *and* actualized in these conceptions. So, methodologically, to move those dichotomies is to contribute to developing the horizon of sexual difference. One of the broadest dichotomies in the philosophical tradition (if not *the* broadest) is that of the sensible and the transcendental. This dichotomy between the material and the ideal is present in all philosophical reflection in the western tradition; one might say this dichotomy organizes the history of western thought in which transcendence is meaningful only insofar as it directly or indirectly negates and denigrates the sensible and all things associated with sensibility.

Irigaray is not calling for the creation of an arbitrary philosophical concept. In writing in *relation* to various metaphysical concepts in the history of philosophy that have occluded sexual difference, Irigaray draws on the sensible transcendental to frustrate the binaries of western thought in an energetic deployment of meaning against itself.[13] Her notion of the sensible transcendental is corrective of a tradition that has misunderstood the nature of these terms in relation to each other, resulting in injustices. She subtly redresses these injustices by reordering the priority of the terms and locating the sensible as the entry point to the transcendental. Tina Chanter writes, "Irigaray's notion of the sensible transcendental conflates categories that traditionally philosophers have kept apart. The 'sensible transcendental' is nothing if not paradoxical" (1995, 180). However, beyond paradox, the sensible transcendental is "a remaking of immanence and transcendence" (ESD, 18) that "is the condition of an ethics of sexual difference" (Whitford 1991, 149), which anticipates and figures the time when the question of sexual difference is the horizon of self-relation, intersubjectivity, and world relatedness.

The sensible transcendental is then a claim about recognizing the present of sexual difference as well as a call to invoke its future in the most concrete sense. For this reason, Irigaray's reconfiguration of the relation between spatiality and temporality is central to her elaboration of the sensible transcendental. Traditionally, spatiality has been aligned with immanence and reduced to a passive materiality (associated with the feminine) if it is even acknowledged at all. Corresponding to this concept of spatiality, temporality has been the privileged modality of transcendence (associated with the masculine) that is made possible only by suppressing or forgetting the "spatial necessity" that provides the place from which transcendence arises (FA, 152). Irigaray's point is not simply to provide equal weight to spatiality; she is seeking a temporality that is not divested of its spatiality and a spatiality that is not forgotten in abstracted temporal constructs. Correspondingly, such a recasting transforms our concepts of the past, present, and future. As such, cultivating sexual difference means "the present will no longer remain only a bridge between past and future, future and past. . . . The temporal ecstasy of the present is thus articulated with a spatial ecstasy. But the two are just as well enstases" (SW, 85).

If the present is not to remain a mere bridge between the past and future that recedes beneath their connection, how are we to rethink this present? Such a rethinking is required if we are to understand the sensible transcendental as a "remaking of immanence and transcendence" (ESD, 18) that is both a future yet to come *and* a *recovering* of sexual difference in its actuality. To clarify this claim, Margaret Whitford's insight concerning the "future anterior" is helpful.[14] In addition to noting Irigaray's affinity for writing in the future perfect tense (*futur antérieur*)—a tense indicating that the past will be determined by an action in the future—Whitford notes the important connection between Lacan's concept of the future anterior and Irigaray's thought on sexual difference. For Lacan, the future anterior is "what I shall have been for what I am in the process of becoming" (Whitford 1991, 90). Accordingly, the future anterior is an indication of the inextricability of the imaginary and symbolic that captures the sense of the imaginary "as an *effect* of the symbolic; it is the symbolic that structures the imaginary, so there is a sense in which the imaginary does not exist until it is symbolized" (91). In other words, where the symbolic was ("what I shall have been"), there the imaginary shall come about ("what I am in the process of becoming"). Whitford is addressing the important question of how one can break with the masculine symbolic (and let us recall for Irigaray the "*imaginary* [is] transformed into the masculine symbolic" (90) in the absence of a "real *other*" (91). Hence, for Whitford, sexual difference is the future yet-to-come when a feminine symbolic can "effect" a feminine imaginary.

While Whitford is not mistaken on this point, her reading of sexual difference nonetheless emphasizes a notion of futurity that is still untethered from the present. The latter is left as a "bridge" and so Whitford overlooks the *actuality of the feminine* that Irigaray is seeking to retrieve, and actuality without which her claim to the nonrealization of difference, as sexual difference, would be incomprehensible. Whitford's view is also inconsistent with Irigaray's later works in which she has retrieved instances of the sensible transcendental. She proposes that the loss of some early Greek *morphological* forms in language, such as the verbal form of the middle voice, was the "loss of a sensible transcendental" (IB, 146).[15]

To articulate the sensible transcendental in such a way that futurity becomes, not just conceptual, but *sensible*, I turn to Irigaray's thought on gesture in her rereading of the psychoanalytic tradition in terms of subject formation. In particular, she examines the first elaboration of the little boy's entry into language. Not only does this moment provide an account of the little boy's development in terms of the symbolic in the formation of subjectivity but, significantly, Freud's text also constitutes the first symbolic inscription of the subject's entry into the symbolic in the history of psychoanalysis. Notably, the text bears another genealogical doubling as the little boy who becomes the site of the entrance into language is Freud's grandson.

Gesture in Subject Formation

Consider gestures. Gestures point to the indissolubility of the unconscious and conscious, and hence they seem to capture our own imaginary and that of our culture or sex. Frequently ambiguous, gestures often lack the precision of words but achieve a symbolic dimensionality. A body without gestures is a corpse, a body without relation. An attentiveness to gesture discloses the arising of meaning in its specific morphological form where it is never severed from the relational situation of the subject's birth or the unfolding of that meaning in the materiality of space and time. Concretizing the sensible transcendental in gesture reveals that the future of sexual difference realized in a sensible transcendental as a future anterior is not so much a future yet to come, when I shall have been, as it is a future to which we must return: "Become it as one recollects it? Make time of this source of time?" (ESD, 191).

As we have seen, the morphological "is not a structure of meaning but a sensible movement of meaning *in relation* that structures and restructures experience" (Colman 2022, 29). This means subject formation is always in process, always in formation and reformation. The processual formation of subjectivity is not a predetermined telos the infant passively undergoes as if subjectivity was *subject to* a telos in which subjectivity is the *end* result. Nor is the subject an *arché*, an imperfect material iteration of an unchanging, universal transcendental form. Such a subject would be predetermined, and subject formation would be reduced to an immediacy where the child's development is simply the expression of an already determined fate rendering sexuate difference to the anatomical result of an arché or telos.[16] Irigaray emphasizes the morphological is not teleological, it is not a "blind immediacy" (JTN, 35) but an ongoing process of relationality that is dependent on the mother's (the other's) bodily and material support—the denial and negation of which founds the ideal subject (that is, the male subject) who, as I will detail below, turns the mother into a "thing" to be mastered.[17]

Irigaray's critique of nonrelational, teleological, or universal types as a determinism of sex are helpful insights for thinking trans subjectivities and embodiment. Again, Irigaray has been unrelenting and adamant in her claim that sexual difference must be raised as a question for our time. Her critique of telos and arché are vital to her rethinking of subject formation as an ongoing relational process. The little boy and the little girl take up different relational attitudes to their birth as "[t]he first world of the subject is an other" (SW, 105). Irigaray writes, "[s]exed identity implies a way of constituting subjectivity in relation to the world, to the self, and to the other, that is specific to each sex. This specificity is determined in part by corporeal characteristics as implying a *different relational attitude*" (KW,

177; emphasis in original). Crucially, in her rereading of psychoanalysis, Irigaray undertakes an analysis of specific ways in which the relational attitudes of the little boy and the little girl are elaborated and supported by gestures, which are, in the same space-time, both the *material possibility and realization of meaning in expression.*

Irigaray contends the little boy has a harder time developing a relation to an other as a subject, whereas the little girl, born of one who is like her, has a more difficult time finding herself as an other apart from the mother. In the discussion of the little boy and the little girl that follows it is important to keep in mind that Irigaray is not attempting to present a universal theory of subject formation. Rather, these accounts point to how morphological aspects of the subject's formation as supported by gesture become phenomenologically and analytically available in her engagement with and critique of the psychoanalytic tradition.

Irigaray finds the neglect of gesture in the subject's entrance into the symbolic in psychoanalysis has caused it to overlook aspects of the maternal and corporeal that support the little boy's entrance into language and subsequently sustain him there. Moreover, it is only by disregarding an account of the importance of gesture that psychoanalysis has been able to avoid providing a full account of the way the little girl forges her own subjectivity.

In particular, Irigaray rereads Freud's observation of *his* grandson's game of *fort-da* (gone-there), which notably focuses on a little boy and which considers the male child's entrance into language as compensation for, or mastery over, the absence (or loss) of the mother. In the context of his overall consideration of repetition compulsion in *Beyond the Pleasure Principle*, Freud narrates and interprets the game of little Ernst who *performs* the absence and return of his mother through the manipulation of a wooden reel tied to a string. The child "plays gone" with the reel by throwing it under his curtained cot while exclaiming "o-o-o-o" (interpreted by Freud to be the German word *fort*—or "gone") and then subsequently expresses a pleasurable "a-a-a-a" (interpreted to be *da*—or 'there') when he pulls it back from under the cot into view again. Freud notes that the boy finds greater pleasure in making the reel return ([1920] 2006, 141). There is little doubt that the ability to make the reel return at will and the realization of that ability in the act of drawing the object forth from the recesses of the cot toward himself is the source of this greater pleasure. Hence, little Ernst gains pleasure from mastering the object, which is a substitute for his mother, in controlling the presence and absence of the mother-as-object. Freud interprets this game as a "great cultural achievement in successfully abnegating his drives . . . [that allows] his mother to go away without a great fuss" (141). In this way, Freud concludes the game of "gone-there," or *fort-da*, can be interpreted in two ways: to manage the absence of the mother by controlling her through a substitute object or to take revenge on the mother by exercising control in sending her away. Psychoanalytically, this text is read as the boy's entrance into the symbolic order, which is the prerequisite and compensation for the loss of the mother. The little boy repeats the same linear motion over and over, setting up and reinforcing the control he holds over the object. Substituting the object for the mother, he annihilates her; she becomes disposable and retrievable at his will. The little boy thus assuages his anxiety about his inability to control his mother's absence (and so also her presence) by making her into an object that he can control. Ernst's "great cultural achievement" of disposing of his need for the mother is the entry into culture. "She must be thrown over there, put at a distance, beyond the horizon, so that she can come back to him, back inside him, so that he can take her back, over and over again, re-assimilate her, and feel no sorrow" (SG, 31). Freud's explanation of this mastery focuses on the child's use of the words *fort* and *da* but not on the gesture of throwing the reel, which allowed the child to accomplish this task in the first place and enabled the syllabic expressions to be appropriate, or accurate. That is to say, the uttering of *fort* and *da* would be meaningless without the gestural motion of the arm, which, in accomplishing the movement of the object from one place to the next, allows the connection *between* the moment of the "gone" and the "there." The mastery of this game could not be fulfilled without the gestures of throwing and retrieving, but notably, they are not included in what is registered as criteria for entrance into the symbolic order. Irigaray states, "it is with a gesture of the hand and arm, accompanied by certain spoken syllables, that the little boy masters the absence of his mother and is thus able to enter the symbolic universe. What happens later to those meshed articulations of arm and sound-making apparatus?" (SG, 96–97). Irigaray asks why the little boy's gestures, so vital to hooking words onto the world, have been excluded in Freud's psychoanalytic theorization.

Ernst's gesture of the arm repelling the object and then drawing it back signifies his mastery over the mother in addition to, or perhaps even more fundamentally than, the speaking of the words *fort-da*. Irigaray's expression "sound-making apparatus" intimates the way in which the little boy's mouth, tongue, teeth, and vocal cords will slice up space around him—including any others in it—to produce an instrumentalized world. A world where he controls the appearance and reappearance, not of the mother, but of the objects he has filled his world up with in place of her.

Irigaray notices Freud also overlooks the materiality of the cot's curtain or veil underneath which Ernst would throw his reel, allowing him to play "gone" in the first place. The veil made it possible for the reel to return to him again and again insofar as it was the medium, or material, which enabled Ernst to hide and recover the object. Irigaray states "[t]he veil is necessary as a setting, a mediation for the performance of presence in absence" (SG, 30). Moreover, it is the string that psychically enables his means of control in throwing her away or in retrieving her at will. The string, which is always present and makes the game possible, is covered over by the Ernst's words *fort-da*, and by Freud's own interpretation, "disappearance-appearance." The string is also the way the little boy remains attached to the maternal object, sustaining the success of the game of her renunciation. The "string is a tie which therefore never really allowed a definitive departure, so that any return is not so much a product of reattachment as it is the result of refusal to let go properly in the first place" (Chanter 1995, 261).

But exactly what is made possible by this gesture of the fort-da? A "division—of time, of space of the other, of the self" (SG, 102). Ernst is not really playing a game; like his grandfather Freud, "he is framing a theory" (SG, 31), which "authorizes the confusion or substitution of reality and unreality" (SG, 32). Significantly, Irigaray calls attention to the fact that Ernst is not walking when he performs his fort-da. "He is not using his legs to find his mother. [. . .] He looks for his mother with arm and mouth" (SG, 97). The little boy reorders space by his temporalizing gestures of repetition from *one* static, seated position—his own—the center of the world around which other things revolve.

With his fort-da, the little boy cuts out his autonomy from the mother in severing the two moments—fort/da—apart. Refinding these words as "originally" severed from each other, from their maternal legacy in dependence on another, and from his own body's gestures. The little boy's entry into language, into the masculine symbolic-syntax, is made possible by the condition of forgetting what made such an entry possible. The little boy's game allows him to forget the connection that allowed meaning to part them in the first place. Irigaray does not find it surprising that it is the "father" of psychoanalysis who overlooks the gesture even as he memorializes it.

Freud's account of the little girl's entrance into language is summarized in the single insight that the little girl enters into language earlier than the little boy. The brevity here is surprising as Freud already implies the little girl's journey to language is more complicated than the little boy's since the little girl, as identified with the mother, will have to switch love-objects (heterosexuality is implied here). In this way, Irigaray tells us that "a whole economy of gestural and verbal relations between the mother and daughter are forgotten in so-called normal language" (SN, 258). Freud's account of the entrance into the symbolic *is part of the symbolic*—his focus on the little boy and the maternal absence and material exclusion, which supports and sustains his entrance into the symbolic, is related to the absence of an account of the little girl, and thus, it is also an account of the exclusion of the feminine from the symbolic.[18]

Irigaray retrieves the little girl in a recreation of her entrance into the symbolic. The description Irigaray offers of the little girl's entrance into language stresses movement, flexibility, and intersubjectivity.

> [Girls] enter language by producing a space, a path, a river, a dance, a rhythm, a song. . . . Girls describe space around themselves rather than displacing a substitute object . . . *they whirl about in different directions*. . . . They whirl . . . around themselves and within themselves. . . . Girls can find no substitutes for the mother except the whole of nature. . . . This *with* has to try to become a *with self*. . . . The girl-subject does not have objects as the boy does. It splits into two . . . by a gesture, to touch both perhaps so that birth is repeated. . . . Women do not try to master the other but to give birth to themselves (SG, 99).

The little girl "speaks *with* the mother, not in her absence" (SG, 99). Even in the case where the little girl becomes despondent at the absence of the mother, she does not seek to psychically interiorize or incorporate the mother through an object. Rather she moves, she "throws herself on the floor" (SG, 97). If the little girl takes up an object such as a doll, she relates to that object as a "quasi-subject." She does not attempt to master the mother in a fort-da. Rather, when the little girl is not restricted, she forms in her own movements a "vital subjective space" (SG, 97). She creates her subjectivity out of movements and gestures, contouring herself away from the mother without absenting her from space. The little girl's twirling is the morphological instituting and delineating of form that helps her articulate her relational identity to the mother. It is here that we can reclaim the sense of rhythm from Stone's account of morphology without, however, claiming its primacy over the relation that engendered its emergence. The little girl dances in circles—returning back to herself before she can walk in a straight line and away from others. Finding her autonomy by walking, she does not want to be still (SG, 100). Irigaray states that the "paralysis of female hysterics described by Freud and Breuer affects the *legs*" (SG, 100). Recall that Freud documented but did not theorize the immobility of Ernst's legs in his fort-da game of mastery and control.

The little girl's subjectivity is in formation and reformation and because of her morphology, "*form is never complete in her*" (S, 229). The morphé in "continual gestation" is also birth as an expression of the limit, which ensures her sexuate difference. Here, birth references the temporality of a becoming that is not already determined by a principle more primary than the movement of her own becoming. A morphological teleology would reinstate a transcendental that is primary and transcendent to feminine subjectivity. In Irigaray's feminine morphology, the limit is also the possibility for self-affection, intersubjectivity, and world relation. Each gesture is a self-composition and can be understood in terms of the girl's self-affection. Irigaray's inscription of the little girl's entrance into the symbolic enacts a *sensible* retrieval of her morphology as a contouring of meaning and experience through her gestures. "A transcendence that cannot be reduced to a mental idea or belief, but is incarnate, also in another" (KW, 148). In this way, the gesture is already realized in the simultaneity of the world and self and heralds a future articulated in respect for sexuate difference always to be-come—again. This is a future anterior glimpsed in the little girl's gestures where there is an inextricability of materiality and meaning which is indicated *as a possibility in bodily meaning*: this "birth of women is still to come (or to come again?) in its own forms" (NL, 13). Gesture concretizes the sensible transcendental that bears the relational identity of its otherness in the singularity of its expression. Without telos or arché, but in relational identity and its morphological forms, the transcendental we find here is one that is immanent: "a space of breath and gestation which is not the void," a sensible transcendental as such (NL, 13).

Conclusion: Different Sexuate Subjectivities in a Time of Sexual Indifference

Irigaray's rereading of Freud tracks the genealogical moment of the history of the entry of the symbolic as a theory in the symbolic, which, in turn, reveals the symbolic as dependent on the negation of the material feminine, and all associated with her, at the same time as he inadvertently records the absolute reliance on her. The lack of feminine counterpart for the little girl in this entry into symbolization already demonstrates her barred entry to the symbolic. Arguably, Irigaray follows Freud across the individual and cultural moments of the symbolic. She reads the developmental account of the little boy's entrance into the symbolic at the same time as marking the moment of its theorization in the canon. The very logic of the problem of sexual difference is shown up in the symbolic as the accomplishment of the negation and mastery of the feminine that ultimately depends on her. While Irigaray points to the differences in developmental accounts of the little boy and girl, her recovering of Freud from Freud's own account simultaneously shows the difference between the little girl and boy even where Freud has no interest in preserving such a difference.

Irigaray's rereading retrieves the imaginary morphology of the ways in which the little boy's relation to materiality is figured in its nonrelationality by Freud. Irigaray is not only seeking to "add" feminine subjectivity to the current monosexual culture. The logic of the culture is of that oneness, which means there is only, culturally speaking, *one subject*. Hence, she writes that her "research attempts to suggest to women a morpho-logic that is appropriate to their bodies. It's aimed at the male subject, too, inviting him to redefine himself as a body with a view to exchanges between sexed subjects" (JTN, 59). While Irigaray does not address trans subjects directly, I argue the implications and importance of her thought are available and vital for thinking about trans in ways that do not offer a singular theory of the trans subject, which would assume that such a theory would outstrip the problem of sexual difference, on the one hand, that is, assume that trans subjects are not "real" men and women, or, on the other hand, assume that there is an account of trans subjectivity that homogenizes all experiences of trans subjectivity and embodiment. The very desire for such an account is the place where the logic of sameness returns with a vengeance.

To reiterate, to claim a unitary account of trans subjectivity in abstraction or to suggest there is a universal recovery of an account of trans subjectivity would already assume that all trans subject formation occurs in childhood *and* that such a formation has been preserved by a tradition that has excluded an account for the little girl and only indirectly preserved the feminine through the sheer necessity of its negation and exclusion in the erection of the current symbolic. Such an historical revisionism would assume trans subjects are not little boys and little girls or that all trans subjects must have always already been trans. If trans subjectivity and embodiment could be read and recovered through a symbolic that has denied difference, it is unclear what that would mean for trans subjectivity. Again, such an account would assume an ahistorical account that trans is an essence available in childhood for *all* trans subjects. To suggest all exclusions of difference in the canon are equally the same and can be equally recovered is once again to assert and perpetuate a logic of sameness. On this reading, Irigaray can be read as an entry into the problem of how difference can be and often is occluded.

The problem of a monosexual culture is replicated in trans precisely because there are not yet two *cultural* subjects for there to be either two or at least two. There is no language for more than one. In western thought, embodiment is not possible to think outside of the binarization of matter/form. Hence, different embodiments are left locked out of imaginary and symbolic elaboration. This moves the question of sexual difference into the forefront of thinking trans. The question of sexual difference is a call to develop this ethical horizon, which moves beyond capturing bodies in a symbolic that erases them and toward forms of life in which there is respect for more than one form of life.

Notes

1. Two terminological points are necessary. First, in her later texts Irigaray uses the term "sexuate" or "sexed" difference (*la différence sexué*) with increasing frequency. Irigaray's recent clarification of "sexuate," which is not a departure from sexual difference but a way of "talking about subjectivity or identity, and not only of sexual choice . . . to clear up misunderstandings which result from reducing our sexuate identity or subjectivity to a sexual particularity or choice" (Irigaray and Müller, 2022, 179). Thus, I use these terms interchangeably.

2. For an insightful and concise elucidation of the many ways Irigaray's concept of sexual difference has been interpreted, critiqued, and mobilized in terms of her prioritization of difference as sexual difference, see Hill, "The Multiple Readings of Irigaray's Concept of Sexual Difference."

3. The engagement with Irigaray's thought in either recasting her critique (for instance, of the form-matter distinction or in critiquing the ontological primacy of sexual difference) is vital to the development of some of the discourses, which have forgotten her contribution to that thought. For example, Lynne Huffer traces the erasure of Irigaray's legacy to Judith Butler's seminal texts on performativity, which resourced key moments in queer theory. Huffer writes, "Irigaray's subsequent absence from queer theory is evidence of a forgetting of her radical feminist practice as an always already queer method." Huffer, *Are the Lips a Grave? A Queer Feminist on the Ethics of Sex*, 42.

4. Elsewhere I have argued these points to demonstrate Irigaray's importance to thinking trans subjectivities without reproducing an exclusionary logic that masquerades as difference. See Athena Colman, "Tarrying with Sexual Difference: Toward a Morphological Ontology of Trans Subjectivity," which also provides a more sustained articulation of a morphological ontology of trans feminine subjectivity. To be clear, the reading of Irigaray I am offering is not one she would necessarily endorse. She has made some questionable and, quite frankly, unclear claims about trans subjectivity in the past (JTN, 61–62) and, again, more recently (Irigaray and Müller, 2022, 179). However, in this paper, I am following Danielle Poe ("Can Luce Irigaray's Notion of Sexual Difference Be Applied to Transsexual and Transgender Narratives") and reading Irigaray against herself in ways that I take to be faithful to the philosophical implications of her thought, which includes her rich pursuit of difference.

5. I am using "trans" in a broad, but nonuniversalizing sense, which may or may not index subjects who are transgender, transsexual, nonbinary, genderqueer, and genderfluid subjects (noting that not all of those who identify with these subject positions identify as trans). I cannot, and do not wish to, homogenize or claim to speak to all gender/sex identifications. In light of Irigaray's thought, it is unclear any identities but the one, the masculine one, are symbolically available in the first place. Indeed, the problem of sexual difference is reflected in the struggle for different sexuate subjectivities to appear *in their difference* and not as aberrations of the universal ideal, masculine, monosexual culture, which responds to sexuate difference with violence, oppression, and, too often, death.

6. I suggest that gesture unfolds elements of Irigaray's thought in all three dimensions: the gesture in subject formation; the intersubjectivity of the caress; and style as world-relation. Although it is beyond the purview of this paper to explicate all three moments, the paper develops the groundwork for this overall claim and offers an account of gesture in subject formation.

7. I take this insight to be central to Irigaray's influence on and contribution to *new materialism*.

8. This was particularly the case when generative grammar rose to its position of dominance over structural linguistics. This did not, however, entail suppressing consideration of the morphological within linguistic analysis but rather,

as Katamba and Stonham note, an ever more expansive generation of "readjust-ment rules . . . which were morphological rules in disguise" (*Morphology*, 10–11).

9. Marjorie Hass develops this thought in terms of the distinction between *l'énoncé* and *l'énonciation* in Irigaray's empirical language studies. Hass, "The Style of the Speaking Subject: Irigaray's Empirical Studies of Language Production."

10. There is good reason to want to characterize the masculine rigidifica-tion of the morphological in terms of a "morpho-*logic*" in contradistinction to a feminine "morpho*logy*." Chris Peers assumes this distinction in "Freud, Plato and Irigaray: A Morpho-logic of Teaching and Learning." However, Irigaray's texts are not entirely consistent in her usage of the distinction in this way. For example, Irigaray suggests women develop a "morpho-logic that is appropriate to their bodies" in JTN (59). This translation is consistent with the original French, "morpho-logique" (*Je, tu, nous. Pour une culture de la différence*, Paris, Grasset, 1990, 73).

11. To be fair to Stone, Irigaray's work suggests this reading. I am extending Irigaray's thought to offer a critique based on a curated selection of her corpus and extending an interpretation of Irigaray, which is dependent on developing her most radical thought on the ontology of sexual difference to its logical conclusion.

12. For a perspicacious critique of Stone's construal of rhythm in Irigaray, see Mader, "Somatic Ontology: Comments on Alison Stone's Luce Irigaray and the Philosophy of Sexual Difference."

13. Rachel Jones reads Irigaray's notion of the sensible transcendental as a response to Kant in *Irigaray: Towards a Sexuate Philosophy* (126).

14. In addition to Whitford, other thinkers have used the resonances of the future anterior to characterize the nature of Irigaray's thought on sexual difference (Harvey and Krier, *Luce Irigaray and Premodern Culture: Thresholds of History*, 18; Cheah and Grosz, "The Future of Sexual Difference: An Interview with Judith Butler and Drucilla Cornell," 19–42). However, it is important to note Irigaray does not consistently use this tense when writing about the sensible transcendental.

15. Outside a binarized economy of activity and passivity, Irigaray retrieves the moment of the movement of self-affection in the Greek middle voice as the appearance of a form capable of expressing self-relation and reciprocity (that is, I act from, and upon myself. I receive my actions from the other that is me) (IB, 147).

16. While I am drawing on many of Irigaray's texts for developing this emphasis on *telos* and *arché*, Irigaray's use of these terms together in the history of philosophy can be found in S (319, 320, 329.)

17. From Irigaray's view, the legacy of the binary of form/matter that persists in defining matter as a passive *thing* to be mastered and used as a resource has resulted in today's global climate crisis. Arguably, the lack of a *genuine*, collective global response can partially be explained by the persistence of the operative hier-archical binaries, which also indicate the lack of a culture of sexuate difference, which for Irigaray, is a culture that respects life.

18. The exclusion of the feminine is particularly pressing when one remembers the little boy's mother in this case was Freud's own daughter.

References

Chanter, Tina. 1995. *Ethics of Eros: Irigaray's Rewriting of the Philosophers*. Routledge.

Cheah, Pheng, and Elizabeth Grosz. 1998. "The Future of Sexual Difference: An Interview with Judith Butler and Drucilla Cornell." *Diacritics* 28, no. 1: 19–42.

Colman, Athena. 2022. "Tarrying with Sexual Difference: Toward a Morphological Ontology of Trans Subjectivity." In *Horizons of Difference: Rethinking Space, Place, and Identity with Irigaray*, edited by Ruthanne Crapo Kim, Yvette Russell, and Brenda Sharp. State University of New York Press.

Freud, Sigmund. (1920) 2006. "Beyond the Pleasure Principle." In *The Penguin Freud Reader*, edited by Adam Philips. Penguin Books.

Grosz, Elizabeth. 1993. "Irigaray's Notion of Sexual Morphology." In *ReImagining Women: Representations of Women in Culture*, edited by Shirley Neuman and Glennis Stephenson. University of Toronto Press.

Harvey, Elizabeth D., and Theresa Krier, eds. 2014. *Luce Irigaray and Premodern Culture: Thresholds of History*. Routledge.

Hass, Marjorie. 2000. "The Style of the Speaking Subject: Irigaray's Empirical Studies of Language Production." *Hypatia* 15, no. 1: 64–89.

Hill, Rebecca. 2016. "The Multiple Readings of Irigaray's Concept of Sexual Difference." *Philosophy Compass* 11, no. 7: 390–401.

Huffer, Lynne. 2013. *Are the Lips a Grave? A Queer Feminist on the Ethics of Sex*. Columbia University Press.

Irigaray, Luce, and Tobias Müller. 2022. "The Emergence of a New Human Being." *Angelaki: Journal of the Theoretical Humanities* 27, no. 5: 174–181.

Jones, Rachel. 2011. *Irigaray: Towards a Sexuate Philosophy*. Polity Press.

Katamba, Francis, and John Stonham. 2006. *Morphology*. Palgrave Macmillan.

Mader, Mary Beth. 2008. "Somatic Ontology: Comments on Alison Stone's Luce Irigaray and the Philosophy of Sexual Difference." *Differences: A Journal of Feminist Cultural Studies* 19, no. 3: 126–138.

Peers, Chris. 2012. "Freud, Plato and Irigaray: A Morpho-logic of Teaching and Learning." *Educational Philosophy and Theory* 44, no. 7: 761–774.

Poe, Danielle. 2011. "Can Luce Irigaray's Notion of Sexual Difference Be Applied to Transsexual and Transgender Narratives." In *Thinking with Irigaray*, edited by Mary C. Rawlinson, Sabrina L. Hom, and Serene J. Khader. State University of New York Press.

Robinson, Hilary. 2002. "Approaching Painting Through Feminine Morphology." *Paragraph*, 25, no. 3: 93–104.

Stone, Alison. 2006. *Luce Irigaray and the Philosophy of Sexual Difference*. Cambridge University Press.
Whitford, Margaret. 1991. *Luce Irigaray: Philosophy in the Feminine*. Routledge.

Part Three

Feminine Genealogies

Chapter Eight

Simone de Beauvoir and Luce Irigaray

A Genealogy Reconsidered

GAIL SCHWAB

Genealogical Difficulties

Spatially and temporally, genealogy establishes a complex relation—a topology of closeness and distance, intimacy and alienation, acceptance and rejection. The intellectual relationship between Simone de Beauvoir and Luce Irigaray exhibits this inherent genealogical complexity. In 2003, Debra Bergoffen wrote that "Irigaray, however much she may respect Beauvoir, does not recognize her genealogical debt" (2003a, 18); I would add here that Beauvoir reciprocated the negligence.[1] Neither woman ever fully recognized the importance of their intellectual kinship. This essay will examine the Beauvoir-Irigaray genealogy, looking closely at those texts where Irigaray specifically discusses Beauvoir, as well as texts where their respective thinking exhibits similarities or affinities. Irigaray has never done a close reading of any particular text by Beauvoir but has only commented briefly on her oeuvre as a whole in: "A Personal Note: Equal or Different?" (JTN, 9–14); "The Other: Woman" and "You Who Will Never Be Mine" (ILTY, 59–68, 103–108); and "The Question of the Other" (DB, 121–141). Thus, the intense engagement throughout Irigaray's early work with thinkers such as Plato, Freud, Lacan, Descartes, Marx,

155

Sartre, Merleau-Ponty, Levinas, Nietzsche, Heidegger, and Hegel was never extended to Beauvoir.

It is true that Beauvoir consistently eschewed the official title of "Philosopher" for herself. By choice and by intent, she had never engaged in the construction of a totalizing philosophic system, finding, as she writes in *La Force de l'âge*, system-building to be " 'a concerted delirium' requiring that philosophers give their 'insights the value of universal keys' " (Simons 2004, 2). Sara Heinämaa explains that Beauvoir, "introduc[ing] us into an alternative understanding of philosophizing" (2003, 4), preferred pursuing her ideas in narrative, in the concrete problems, passions, and actions of fictional and historical human characters. Thus, her method is not univocal or monologic; as Heinämaa describes it, "her text invites the reader to enter into a dialogue with the characters and to reflect" on the problems presented in the relationships among them and in the plot (2003, 7). Irigaray, another experimental writer who never constructed a philosophic system, does not create fictional characters or construct novelistic plots, but her texts are neither academic nor (traditionally) logically argumentative, but rather epigrammatic, poetic, allusive, and dialogic. Irigaray's text, like Beauvoir's, invites the intersubjective participation of her reader and creates an intratextual encounter between her and another thinker or writer. Effectively, Irigaray and Beauvoir share a refusal to occupy the position of the philosophical One. It could be that this nonsystematic approach to making philosophy comprises one of the most striking features of the topology of their genealogy.

In "A Personal Note: Equal or Different?" Irigaray writes, "I was never close to Simone de Beauvoir. [. . .] When I sent her *Speculum* [. . .] I was hoping for a careful and intelligent reading from her, a sister, who would help me with the academic and institutional problems I was having because of the book. Nothing came of this, unfortunately!" (JTN, 10). It seems Irigaray expected, or wished for, some help or support from Beauvoir that was not forthcoming. We cannot know in any objective sense what transpired between them after the publication of *Speculum*. What we do know is that Irigaray clearly thought a great deal about Simone de Beauvoir's lack of response to *Speculum*, wrote about it in *Je Tu Nous*, and then again in *I Love To You*, and then rewrote the story yet again in *Democracy Begins Between Two*, where she seems to take some responsibility for the distance maintained between them: "I can now see just how much the subtitle of *Speculum* may have irritated Simone de Beauvoir. [. . .] I didn't remember what the problematic of the other in her work was" (DB, 125).[2]

Sexual Difference and Equality

In "A Personal Note," Irigaray briefly highlights what she considers one of the major differences in intellectual background between her and Beauvoir: Beauvoir and Sartre were "wary" of psychoanalysis, whereas her own expertise in and practice of psychoanalysis had prepared her for "theorizing identity as sexual" and allowed her to push her "thought on women's liberation beyond simply a quest for equality between the sexes" (JTN, 11). Irigaray seems to be implying that Beauvoir was unable to understand the importance of sexual identity. However, Sartre's low opinion of psychoanalysis[3] does not automatically translate into a Beauvoirian neglect of sexual identity, for however egalitarian the liberal—or the Marxist—legal and political foundations of *The Second Sex* may be, it is still unavoidably about "theorizing identity as sexual" and about sexual difference. Bergoffen writes that *The Second Sex* "calls for a transvaluation (not an eradication) of sexual difference [and . . .] a future in which sex and gender are lived differently" (2003, 17), and Heinämaa further explains that "for Beauvoir, women and men are two different variations of the human way of relating to the world. [. . .] So, the principal difference is the experiential difference between two types of living bodies, women's bodies and men's bodies" (2003, 84). Many oft-cited passages of *The Second Sex* are devoted to descriptions of the experiential specificity of the female body and to differences from male bodily experience. Indeed, Beauvoir actually closes *The Second Sex* with the concept of sexual difference. In her conclusion, she writes: "Certain differences between man and woman will always exist; her eroticism, and thus her sexual world, possessing a singular form, cannot fail to engender in her a sensuality, a singular sensitivity; her relation to her body, to the male body, and to the child will never be the same as those man has with his body, with the female body, and with the child" ([1949] 2010, 765). Beauvoir's reference to the "sexual world" and especially the "singular form" of female eroticism unavoidably brings to mind Irigaray's emphasis on the "morphology" of the two lips, just as her reference to the mother-child relation also calls to mind the Irigarayan development of sexual difference from relational identity (discussed in some detail below in the section entitled "Becoming"[4]).

In "A Personal Note," Irigaray criticizes the principle of equality itself and implicitly places her philosophical and feminist relationship to Beauvoir under the broad heading of "equality versus difference." She writes: "To whom or to what do women want to be equalized? To men? To a salary? [. . .] Women's exploitation is based upon sexual difference;

its solution will come only through sexual difference" (JTN, 12). Irigaray appears to be subordinating a concept of "equality" to the principle of "difference" and thus to be implementing the type of hierarchical binary logical and linguistic operation that she has criticized across her oeuvre.[5] However, she goes on to write, at the end of "A Personal Note," that "equality between men and women cannot be achieved without a *theory of gender as sexed* and a rewriting of the rights and obligations of each sex, *qua different*, in social rights and obligations" (JTN, 13; Irigaray's emphasis), deliberately undermining the binary she appeared to be establishing. Ultimately, sexual difference is *about* equality. Although Irigaray has often insisted that equality means "sameness," she is perfectly aware that, when applied to life in society, rather than to mathematical abstractions, "equal to" comprises many legal and political nuances regarding civil rights and protections and civic duties. Indeed, what are the equivalent rights proposed by Irigaray, including in two of the other essays in *Je Tu Nous*,[6] if not the way to make sure that women participate in public and private life on an equal footing with men?

It is fascinating to read in this context Simone de Beauvoir's description of a society where civil rights and protections for women would be guaranteed.

> A world where men and women would be equal is easy to imagine because it is exactly the one the Soviet revolution *promised*: women raised and educated exactly like men would work under the same conditions and for the same salaries; erotic freedom would be accepted by custom [. . .]; marriage would be based on a free engagement that the spouses could break when they wanted to: motherhood would be freely chosen—that is, birth control and abortion would be allowed—and in return all mothers and their children would be given the same rights; maternity leave would be paid for by the society that would have the responsibility for the children. ([1949] 2010, 760)

Many of these rights in Beauvoir's description of the promised socialist utopia of gender equality resemble the rights specifically discussed by Irigaray in her calls for equivalent rights, and they very clearly take sexual difference into account in the areas of rights to sexuality, birth control, marriage, divorce, motherhood, and of society's recognition of its responsibilities toward the care and well-being of children. Irigaray, reflecting more contemporary data and attitudes about rape, incest, and pornography, is more radical in her demands for women's rights to life and bodily integrity and to appropriate and nonexploitative representations in the media, as well as in her calls for mothers' rights to protect the civil identity and bodily integrity of their children.[7] Beauvoir also emphasizes an identity of education and of labor conditions for women and men that would be rejected by Irigaray, who insists that it is only through fostering institutions and customs respectful of sexual difference in the workplace and in the education system that girls and women can begin once again to make significant progress toward feminist goals. The divergences between Beauvoir and Irigaray in this area seem, however, to be differences of degree and temporal perspective, rather than deep-seated ideological differences stemming from a pseudoconflict inherent in the false binary of sexual difference and equality.

For Beauvoir, the first goal women should aspire to is financial independence, and she places far more emphasis on the economic aspect of the feminist project than Irigaray does. She is nevertheless careful to acknowledge that "the question of women's work is complex" ([1949] 2010, 721) and that "one must not think that the simple juxtaposition of the right to vote and a job amounts to total liberation" (721). Beauvoir is highly cognizant of the exploitative, "second shift" structure of women's labor: "most working women do not escape the traditional feminine world; neither society nor their husbands give them the help needed to become, in concrete terms, the equals of men" (722). Thus, sexual difference issues play an important role in both Beauvoir's and Irigaray's respective understanding of the problems for women in the workplace. However, I would note Irigaray's shift of emphasis away from the primacy of economic equality toward equal opportunity to undertake creative projects. Irigaray writes in "How Could We Achieve Women's Liberation?": "We are mistaken when we consider that the liberation of woman can stop at an economic and social level. This can only provide us with a framework thanks to which reaching freedom can happen, and no more. Going no further makes us productive machines or social products without the creative ability that characterizes humanity as such" (HCA, 26–27). Beauvoir also speaks of the importance of allowing women access to creativity and to taking initiative, to "proudly and happily participate in building" a new world ([1949] 2010, 722), as she writes in *The Second Sex*. While both philosophers insist that economic independence is important for women, both are also careful to point out that women's liberation will entail much more than enhanced social status and adequate financial success.

Which Other Woman?

In "The Other: Woman," Irigaray clarifies one of the goals she had established for *Speculum*: "I wanted to question [. . .] female alterity defined from a male subject's point of view. I questioned myself as identified in this way: the other of/for man and man alone" (ILTY, 63). Despite the (unintended?) reference to the introduction to *The Second Sex* that many readers have sensed in the title of *Speculum of the Other Woman*, Irigaray asserts that the "other woman" of *Speculum* bears no relation to Beauvoir's description of woman as Man's other. Her goal is the creation of something totally new; she will seek to create an "Other Woman" who would be not a second sex but a different subject—an Other irreducible to the "universal" (male) subject. For Irigaray, Beauvoir's other woman of/for man "implies the cancellation of the possibility of any subjectivity other than man's" (DB, 122–123); she concludes: "My work on female subjectivity develops in the opposite direction to that of Simone de Beauvoir's work as regards the question of the other" (DB, 123).

Tina Chanter has argued that "Beauvoir's preliminary attempt to theorize woman as other has been underestimated" (1995, 74), demonstrating that, although Beauvoir accepts, following Lévi-Strauss and the structuralists, the Self/Other binary as a fundamental structure of human thought, she also maintains that in the usual course of human history the Other eventually throws off its label and status as Other and comes to define itself as the One/the Self, casting the original One into the role of the Other. Women, Beauvoir claims, have never done this.[8] She asks: "Where does this submission in woman come from?" ([1949] 2010, 7). As Michèle LeDœuff notes, the Self/Other binary as the foundation of reasoning was never called into question in the existential philosophies of Sartre, Merleau-Ponty, and Levinas, or in the psychoanalysis of Lacan. On the contrary, this binary was also embraced as the basis of sexuate differences. LeDœuff writes with typical irony: "If the fundamental and primary dimension of consciousness is the duality of the Same and the Other, it is only a short step from this to deduce the metaphysical duality of the sexes: man is the Same [Self], women the Other. [. . .] That is how it is" (1991, 107). According to LeDœuff, however, Beauvoir's analysis of the problem was nuanced in an important way that differentiates her from her fellow existentialists-phenomenologists, as well as from Lévi-Strauss and Lacan, because she "reintroduces [. . .] the notion of reciprocity" (108). Beauvoir clearly understood that in the case of men and women the binary had taken hold not in relative terms, but as an Absolute—that the Self(Man)/Other(Woman) structure had somehow "malfunctioned," making itself permanent—and she sets out to try and understand the problem.

Beauvoir concludes that this failure of reciprocity, this one-sided, permanent submission by women to their status as Other, is rooted in the areas of human creativity, initiative, and risktaking—types of activity that, in prehistory, as well as through much of recorded history, human females had been less freely able than human males to undertake, because doing so could have potentially endangered their offspring and communities, given the bodily realities of pregnancy, childbirth, and lactation. Chanter finds that Beauvoir's attempt to understand the lack of reciprocity between men and women "takes shape around the idea that while men risk their lives, create values, and introduce novelty into the world, women do not. [. . .] Having set up the problem in this way, the only solution she can find is for women to become more creative, more like the subjects that they fundamentally are—less feminine, more masculine. [. . .] To become to all intents and purposes like men" (1995, 75). Establishing what is meant in this context by either "feminine" or "like men" is complex.

In a discussion in *The Second Sex* of a survey taken among women working in a Renault factory, Beauvoir reports that the women expressed a preference for forty hours of weekly work at home over forty hours of weekly work in the factory. What these results show, according to Beauvoir, is that these women "[did] not escape the *traditional feminine world*" ([1949] 2010, 722; my emphasis), by which she means women's forced second shift of childcare, housework, and in-home labor, which the women of Renault could not escape, even as they put in forty hours a week at the factory. Beauvoir reasons, however, that had they been "part of a world that would be their world, that they would [have] proudly and happily participate[d] in building" (722), their preferences might have been quite different. The Renault factory world that they had not participated in building was not theirs, not exclusively because they were "feminine," and not because they were insufficiently "like men," but rather because the creativity, initiative, and risktaking had all been accomplished by the wielders of power and capital—undoubtedly men. However, the building of the Renault factory world had little or nothing to do with their "masculinity" and everything to do with their power and capital. The male workers on the assembly line at Renault were in, if not the exact same position as the women, at least a very similar position (except, of course, that they most probably did not have to assume the second shift at home after work); the factory was not their world, and they had not built it with their own creativity, initiative, and risktaking. Were those men not "like men?" Were they "feminine?" Trying to understand this situation in terms of "masculine" and "feminine" is not illuminating. "Creating values," "introducing novelty into the world," and "taking up initiatives" signify neither "femininity" nor "masculinity," but only moving beyond, exploring possibilities—that is, transcendence, which Beauvoir advocates for all, both men and women.[9]

For Beauvoir, reciprocity between two means Self and Other, Other and Self, each staking their own competitive claim to be the One/the Self, because for her, subjectivity—Sartrean and Hegelian—is One. Her "other woman" partakes of the Platonic conceptualization of the Other as a more or less imperfect copy of the perfection of the singular, supposedly universal, Ideal. For Irigaray, reciprocity can only be established in the relationship—created across an interval of recognition, love, and respect—between Two, two irreducible Others, each with their own subjectivity. In thinking "the question of the other," Beauvoir is not prepared, or unable, to go so far as to assert reciprocity between two separate and irreducible subjectivities. It will take Irigaray to come along and complete the journey to Woman the Subject, irreducible to Man the Subject. Thus, I conclude, along with Chanter, that Beauvoir "does not carry out her own project of thinking woman as other, from a woman's point of view" (Chanter 1995, 75). Beauvoir never quite gets there. Nevertheless, it is an exaggeration to conclude, as Irigaray does, that Beauvoir's problematic of the other developed in the "opposite direction" of Irigaray's. Rather it was a start—urging women in the right direction toward transcendence, risk-taking, initiative, and creativity.

Becoming

"One is not born, but rather becomes, woman" (Beauvoir [1949] 2010, 283). Irigaray paraphrases Beauvoir's famous dictum: "It's not as Simone de Beauvoir said: one is not born, but rather becomes a woman (through culture), but rather: I am born a woman, but I must still become this woman that I am by nature" (ILTY, 107). We need to look in some detail at both Beauvoir's statement and Irigaray's paraphrasis if we want to understand what the differences and the similarities (if any) are between them in the areas of becoming woman and becoming more generally. In her well known 1986 article, Judith Butler oriented feminist thinking toward conceiving Beauvoir's becoming (not born as) woman as a radical rethinking of the relation between the body and gender, and many subsequent readers subscribed to this social constructivist interpretation of becoming (not born as) woman.[10] However, feminist thought on this issue is not monolithic, and many writers have also brought philosophical clarifications and/or objections to the strict social constructivist interpretation. For example, Moira Gatens writes that "to maintain, as Beauvoir does, that the capacities of the body—understood in naturalistic or biological terms—always require interpretation, is not equivalent to maintaining that the body is itself an interpretation or pure social construction" (2003, 273). It is important to emphasize, however, that theorists who try to nuance the social constructivist argument do not claim that there is an established "truth" about what a woman *is*. There is no preordained female (or male) nature; there are only lived bodies that experience life, the world, and each other. How should we then understand Irigaray's unexpected paraphrasis of Beauvoir, where the emphasis seems to be exclusively on "nature?" What can it mean to be "born a woman" and to "become the woman one already is by nature?"

Irigaray has given extensive thought to the phenomena of birth, of intrauterine and early postnatal life, and of the foundations of the relationship between child and mother and their crucial importance to the development and grounding of sexual difference in what she calls *relational identity*. I have discussed the issue of relational identity in some detail in a previous article, arguing that, beginning within the womb,

> there is an aspect of the embodied connection between mother and child that communicates a "relational style" [. . .] that begins the structuring of a relational identity for the child. I would extend this reasoning to children's embodied relations with their fathers or any other primary caregiver[s], relations that are less intimate prenatally, but nevertheless not nonexistent, and that develop postnatally according to rhythms that can be sensed by children just as the mother's rhythms can be sensed. (Schwab 2016, 142; see 140–143 for full argument)

This sensitivity to, or—as Alison Stone puts it (2006, 135)—this "non-conceptual" awareness of, these pre- and postnatal rhythms, forms the rudiments of a sexually differentiated relationality for the child; this, I believe, is the sense in which, for Irigaray, a woman is "born a woman." It would be absurd to suppose that Irigaray intends to say that nature develops these relational identities in conformity with strictly delineated, preexisting definitions of "woman" or of "man." Nature only prescribes bodily relationality, and differences in bodily relationality then generate sexual difference. It is important to emphasize that this prediscursive relationality is fluid; there are no linguistic boundaries to limit its development to a binary gender system or to any other type of preordained structure.[11]

As regards Beauvoir's "becoming woman," Heinämaa claims that it has often been misinterpreted: "Beauvoir is thought to offer an account of how women—as individuals and as a group—have become 'what they are.' [. . .] We—as women and men—are not anything, but constantly in a process of becoming" (2003, 84). Heinämaa, Butler, and Gatens all insist on the importance for Beauvoir of moving beyond a static concept of what women "are," as well as on the importance of "the possibilities open to them to create a new future beyond what she takes to be the 'historical facts' of their past conditions of existence," as Gatens writes (2003, 274). Becoming is all about change and transformation over time, about the open future and multiples of possibilities.

Certainly, for Irigaray as well, becoming is about change and transformation; however, Irigaray's open future is not quite the same as the existentialist's open future envisioned by Beauvoir. For Irigaray, who has consistently refused to accept any individual woman's success within the current structure of society as a definitive indicator of feminist progress, the becoming of an individual woman is always contextualized within the becoming of women as a group. Thus, there are certain limits in the becoming of the individual, limits not always taken into account in Beauvoir's existentialist perspective.[12] It is important to emphasize, however, that group belonging does not mean belonging to a defined entity, fixed and immutable. Just as any individual's identity comes to exist only in relationality, genders exist only in relation to each other. As Elizabeth Grosz points out, gender differences, or "sexual difference is not a comparative relation between two entities, two sexes, that are independently given, like apples and oranges. It is not a comparison or contrast of two autonomous entities, but it is a relation that is constitutive of the two sexes, which do not preexist their differentiation" (2016, 159).[13]

In a pointed critique of Hegel, Irigaray claims that a generic (group) identity "rules out all forms of totality" (ILTY, 106). "The relation between man and woman, men and women, [. . .] is without definitive resolution or assumption, always *becoming* in the outward and return journeying between one and the other, the ones and the others, with no end or final reckoning" (107; my emphasis). Thus, after having been born a woman "by nature"—that is, by virtue of having lived a particular intrauterine and postnatal bodily relationality—I must strive to become within the context of the continuous and unending development (or becoming) of the world of women, in dialectic with other worlds. These worlds all develop and change endlessly, together and separately; they can never be totalized or finalized as One or Ones, but are still and always becoming, and the dialectic is never-ending; there is never any closure—only evolution, becoming, and "becoming undone."[14] I would propose that Simone de Beauvoir's existentialist conception of becoming, even with its grounding in individual agency and intention, is not so very different from this. As Bergoffen describes it in her introduction to *Pyrrhus and Cineas*: "I am a way of being that makes myself be by reaching beyond myself toward something other than myself. I am [. . .] a going beyond without end" (2004a, 83).

The "One + One + One" and the "One of One"

Irigaray has been intensely committed to the centrality and primacy of sexual difference, despite fairly unanimous sustained criticisms from other feminists for whom sexual difference is one difference out of many.[15] Irigaray's conceptualization of the problem of difference has often been found inadequate,[16] insensitive to, and inappropriately dismissive of differences among women.[17] In "Toward a 'New and Possible Meeting': Ambiguity as Difference," Emily Anne Parker envisions a "far wider world of difference" beyond sexual difference and expands difference to its maximum amplitude in her concept of "elemental difference" (2018, 85, 87)—that is, difference that establishes singularity and uniqueness, the "one of one." We might briefly contrast Parker's "one of one" with Irigaray's "one + one + one." For Irigaray, the one + one + one represents the anonymous generality of the endlessly proliferating copies of the generic subject of Western civilization. The becoming and the open future that sexual difference represents for Irigaray are a way out of the stifling uniformity of the one + one + one (see Schwab 2020; and TBT, 31–32). For Parker, however, it is Irigaray who is seeking "the comfort of generalization" (2018, 104); a "world of women"—gender identification and identity—would comprise just another series of avatars of that universal subject. In "elemental difference," devoid of those "comforts of generalization," there are only bodies and persons, the one of one; there is no generalized group identification.

Like Irigaray, Beauvoir has frequently been criticized for her insensitivity to various types of difference(s) and for her "false universalism."[18] One of the goals of Parker's chapter is presumably to create an alternative reading to these criticisms by mobilizing Beauvoir's concept of ambiguity in an argument against "generalization." She cites *The Ethics of Ambiguity*: "each one has the incomparable taste in his mouth of his own life" and "[l]et us try to assume our fundamental ambiguity. It is in the knowledge of the authentic conditions of our life that we must draw our strength to live and our reason for acting" (Parker 2018, 101, 102; and Beauvoir [1947] 1948, 9), and Parker then concludes that ambiguity signifies "singularity: a mutual lived visceral alterity." For Parker, "freedom [. . .] has never given rise to homogeneity [. . .], and uniformity is always something forced" (101, 96).[19]

Even as we recognize that Parker's one of one is not synonymous with individualism, we should note that Beauvoirian "ambiguity" does place emphasis on the individual and that there can be some risk involved in focusing too heavily on singularity. In Beauvoir's view of her own life and work, in her self-image as created in her autobiographical writings, she very often presents herself as an existentialist subject, acting freely as an individual to carry out her project, unencumbered by the sexual differences she described in detail in *The Second Sex* or by the social, political, and economic differences she discussed in *Pyrrhus and Cineas* and the *Ethics of Ambiguity*.[20] Beauvoir's personal individualism at times even seems to contradict her avowed political Marxism, and her criticisms of Marxism, as it was implemented in the mid- to late-twentieth century, are often expressed as a defense of individualism and individual experience and achievement (Simons 1995, 251, and passim.).

Leaving aside Beauvoir's habits of self-representation, which reflect literary as well as philosophical concerns, it is important to note that ambiguity, by its very definition, is complex, and that, in addition to singularity and uniqueness, Beauvoir's conceptualization of ambiguity comports commonality. According to Sonia Kruks, as Beauvoir develops it in *The Second Sex*: "the 'lived experience' of woman's situation [. . .] is, of course, *individually* lived. Extensive citations from women's memoirs, novels, etc. give her account an intensely personal and subjective foundation. Yet, at the same time, Beauvoir wants also to be able to evaluate that experience as a whole. [. . .] Human experience is individual experience, but it also has *generality*" (1990, 107). In existentialist terms, it has the generality of "situation." Irigaray will make a similar claim for generality, arguing for a cultural—or an historical—group generality: "Each individual of an historical era belongs, to a great extent, to the same world. What they consider to be their own—subjectivity, thoughts, feelings—is, in a way, common to a group, to a culture. Their most intimate beliefs or emotions are shared by many" (SW, 65). The Beauvoirian generality of social and historical situation is obviously not precisely the same as Irigaray's "subjectivity, thoughts, feelings" that are "shared by many," but it does constitute the possibility of groups of individuals whose history can be clarified in a study, for example, *The Second Sex*, and about whose life experiences and whose situation(s) generalized statements carrying truth value can be made. Thus, there are women, and a woman is one out of many, in addition to being one of one.

Relationality and Freedom

Parker also offers a highly fruitful, nuanced interpretation of Beauvoirian ambiguity—that is, ambiguity as "the mutually creative relations among singularities" (2018, 95)—and I would like to explore this idea of mutually creative relations in the conclusion that follows. Kruks argues that Beauvoir had moved beyond, possibly as early as *Pyrrhus and Cineas* (1944) and certainly by the time of the *Ethics of Ambiguity* (1947) and of *The Second Sex* (1949), the solipsistic isolation of Sartrean freedom and subjectivity, as well as his Hegelian analysis of human relations. She attributes the evolution of Beauvoir's thought in this area at least partly to the influence of Merleau-Ponty; Beauvoir characterized his conceptualization of perception as "communication and communion" between the subject and the world (Beauvoir 2004b, 162), and his understanding of subjectivity as intersubjective. "Intersubjectivity [. . .] exists insofar as I and another are both situated in, perceive, and can communicate about the same natural and social world. We cannot ever have the identical perception, since we are separate existences, each a body-subject with its own unique situation. Yet there can be such overlap between our perceptions as to create between us an 'interworld,' a primordial communication" (Merleau-Ponty [1945] 1962, 357, cited in Kruks 1990, 124).[21]

There is an undeniable sense in Beauvoir that humans share a great deal and that what they share is just as important as what separates them. She writes in the *Ethics of Ambiguity* that "the privilege [. . .] of being a sovereign and unique subject amidst a universe of objects is what [we] share with all [our] fellow-men" (1948, 7). Thus, our very uniqueness, our singularity, is a source of commonality. Our aloneness in the universe of objects is—paradoxically, or ambiguously—tempered by that "interworld of primordial communication." Irigaray will assess the human situation in similar terms, envisioning our place in the world ambiguously, noting our vulnerability to "the terror experienced in the face of a vast freedom and solitude" and our common experience of nature—a domain that for us founds "inter-worlds, [. . .] a universal that is shareable by all" (SW, 66–67).

It is true that Beauvoir and Irigaray appear to differ significantly on the idea of freedom. For Beauvoir, despite her philosophical independence from Sartre, humans—within the always unavoidable limits of their individual and collective situation(s)—are free beings, for whom and by whom all values and meanings arise from our freedom to transcend, to choose projects, and to bring them to fruition. Irigaray rejects even the Beauvoirian modified concept of existentialist human freedom; she describes what she calls the "networks" of relations among all beings and all objects in the world in which each of us is caught up: "One who is born enters a world that predetermines their point of view, their choices, their present intentions or their future plans—inside a horizon they believe they give in complete freedom to their world" (SW, 64–65). Irigaray's description of networks might be read as an extreme rendering of "situation," or even compared to Beauvoir's immanence, where women have traditionally been trapped and where transcendence seems impossible.

Thus, it would appear that Irigaray conceives our freedom as completely circumscribed by those networks; however, she opens the possibility of transcendence through the ethical relation to the other. Irigaray's very conceptualization of transcendence as horizontal, as dependent not on a vertical relation to a god or gods, but on other subjectivities and my ethical relation to them, precludes thinking transcendence as the strictly individual effort to accomplish a project: "It is no longer only by myself that I transcend [. . .] through projecting myself into the beyond; rather

it is through accepting to stop before the irreducibility of the other. [. . .]
The sense of the other [. . .] makes me enter into another world of meaning, in which the relational weaving is still to be elaborated" (SW, 77). It
is only the other who will help me break out of the situation constituted
by my network and find my freedom, through revealing their own world:
"availability towards the transcendental dimension opened by the other
undoes the weaving of the relations that structured the world for me
[. . .]. To this world, I will never return unchanged: I will have gained a
new freedom" (SW, 89). Of course, transcendence does not mean that I
remain within the other's world, beyond my own. That would be nothing
more than a different situation, a different network, where the freedom
gained in relating to the other is lost in what would eventually be only
a different immanence. Having been a visitor to that other world, I must
return to my own, bringing originality, creativity, possibilities that were
not there before. I bring new values and new meanings to my world—the
very definition of Beauvoirian transcendence.

Beauvoir writes in *Pyrrhus and Cineas* that "a man would be nothing
if nothing happened to him, and it is always through others that something
happens to him, starting with his birth" ([1944] 2004a, 125). Thus, for
Beauvoir as for Irigaray, any particular individual's efforts are insufficient
to create values and meaning totally on their own, and the cooperation
and dedication of others are required for the advancement into the future
of that meaning and those values. "Mutually creative relations among singularities" are crucial to any endeavor, to the success of any project, and
the success or failure of my project depends not only on the freedom of
others but also on their well-being. This, indeed, is the principle founding
Beauvoir's political and social activism, her support of the Resistance, her
feminism, her opposition to the Algerian war, her horror at the appalling
behavior of the French in the conduct of that war, her public opposition
to the American war in Vietnam. . . . Despite the inevitable conflicts that
will arise when the differing projects of disparate freedoms come into
contact with one another, without the other, both our values and our
projects are empty, meaningless, going nowhere. As Beauvoir writes in the
Ethics of Ambiguity: "Only the freedom of other men can extend beyond
our life" ([1947] 1948, 71–72). Bergoffen elucidates in her introduction to
Pyrrhus and Cineas: "I bring value and meaning to a world without value
and meaning of its own. I cannot, however, support these values alone.
They will find a home in the world only if others embrace them; only if
I persuade others to make my values theirs. As radically free, I need the

other" (2004, 83–85). Irigaray would claim that without the other, I would remain inside the weaving and interlacing of the network holding me in place. For both thinkers, relationality is the basis of freedom.

What both Beauvoir and Irigaray have brought to Western philosophy and to feminism is incalculable. Their relationship to each other was not close, not as open and direct as Irigaray, at least, would have liked; despite the distance maintained in acquaintance and in feminist points of view, their thinking on relationality emphasized its crucial importance to the development of the potential of human freedom and subjectivity and reveals an affinity and—dare I say it?—a genealogy of philosophy in the feminine. So let us particularly acknowledge this genealogy of freedom through relationality and extend it. Indefinitely . . .

Notes

1. Beauvoir does mention Irigaray in an interview and declares that she has "found some very interesting things in Irigaray," although she also finds Irigaray "too ready to adopt the Freudian notion of the inferiority of women." Beauvoir and Wenzel, "Interview with Helene Wenzel," 12. I have found no other references to Irigaray in her work.

2. It seems clear that Irigaray, for whom female genealogies were becoming increasingly important, perceived a problem in her genealogical relationship to Beauvoir and tried in several different places to deal with it. Regrettably, she never did this in any extended philosophically analytical way.

3. Beauvoir actually cites Freud with some frequency in *The Second Sex* (Index 779). This does not turn her into a proponent of psychoanalysis, but she was obviously familiar with Freudian texts. In the interview mentioned above in n1, Beauvoir writes that she "admire[s] Freud on a great many points." Beauvoir and Wenzel, "Interview with Helene Wenzel," 12. She also quotes Lacan once in *The Second Sex*, 783.

4. I have also discussed relational identity in some detail elsewhere. See Schwab, "Creating Inter-Sexuate Inter-Subjectivity in the Classroom?" 140–143. See also Louise Burchill, "Life-Giving Sex versus Mere Animal Existence," 161–162, and Phyllis Kaminski, "Daughters, Difference, and Irigaray's Economy of Desire," 200–201, for useful takes on relational identity.

5. Erla Karlsdottir and Sigridur Thorgeirsdottir emphasize this point in their incisive critique of Irigaray's relationship to binary thinking in "Nature, Culture, and Sexuate Difference," 107 and passim.

6. See "The Right to Life" and "Why Define Sexed Rights?" in JTN (75–80, 81–92). See also, "How Do We Become Civil Women" and "Civil Rights and Responsibilities for the Two Sexes" in TD (39–64, 67–87).

7. See the texts referred to in the preceding note. Despite Judith Butler's criticisms of Irigarayan sexuate rights discourse as being "all about mom and motherhood and not at all about postfamily arrangements or alternative family arrangements" (Pheng and Grosz, "The Future of Sexual Difference" 28), Irigaray's claims regarding a mother's right to protect her own life and bodily integrity, as well as that of her children, actually appear to be highly appropriate to alternative family and postfamily arrangements, especially for single women. See Schwab, "Women and the Law in Irigarayan Theory," 146–177.

8. Beauvoir writes that "the subject posits itself only in opposition; it asserts itself as the essential and sets up the other as inessential, as the object, but the other consciousness has an opposing reciprocal claim. [. . .] In order for the other not to turn into the One, the Other has to submit to this foreign point of view." *The Second Sex*, 7.

9. For a brief discussion of Irigarayan transcendence, see below, "Relationality and Freedom."

10. For example, see Gatens "Beauvoir and Biology," 273–274, 276–277; Bergoffen "Simone de Beauvoir," 248–249, 252; Julie K. Ward, "Beauvoir's Two Senses of 'Body' in *The Second Sex*," 238–240, for nuanced interpretations of "Beauvoirean social constructivism."

11. See PP, 43–49, for a detailed elaboration of relational identity.

12. Beauvoir will also nuance her position on group belonging and individual limitations. See "Relationality and Freedom" below.

13. Grosz developed this idea as far back as 1994 in "The Hetero and the Homo" (344).

14. Grosz's book on Darwin, Bergson, Deleuze, and Irigaray is entitled: *Becoming Undone: Darwinian Reflections on Life, Politics, and Art*.

15. Contrary to recent criticisms, Elizabeth Grosz, while arguing for the primacy of sexual difference, acknowledges the importance of many other differences besides sexual difference (see Grosz "Irigaray and Darwin on Sexual Difference: Some Reflections," 158).

16. *Between East and West* represented a concerted effort on Irigaray's part to deal with other differences beyond sexual difference. Undertheorized, it lacks references to texts that treat other differences effectively.

17. Does this mean that Irigaray, as has often been claimed, is heterosexist, gay-phobic, "intersex-phobic," or transphobic? As for heterosexism, I have argued elsewhere that sexual difference is not heterosexuality and will not rehearse that argument again (see "Sexual Difference as Model" and "Reading Irigaray [and Her Readers]"). Ofelia Schutte argued persuasively back in 1997 that Irigaray's "phenomenology of the caress rejects compulsory heterosexuality" ("A Critique of Normative Heterosexuality," 55–56).

18. See Pilardi "Feminists Read *The Second Sex*," 38–39, for a "catalog" of such criticisms, and Al-Saji, "Material Life" for a detailed analysis of the problem specifically with reference to Muslim women.

19. This passage is the one emphasized particularly by Audre Lorde in her famous lecture at the conference on the *The Second Sex* in 1979. See Parker, "Toward a 'New and Possible Meeting,'" 87, 108n7, and 109n14, n21; and Card, "Introduction: Beauvoir and the Ambiguity of 'Ambiguity' in Ethics," 9, for a discussion of the circumstances of the conference where this lecture was delivered and its ramifications over the years.

20. See Pilardi "Feminists Read *The Second Sex*," 32–34, 35–36, for references to feminist critiques of this aspect of her writings. See also Al-Saji, "Material Life," 21–53; and Kruks "Simone de Beauvoir: Teaching Sartre about Freedom," 80.

21. See also Kruks, "Simone de Beauvoir."

References

Al-Saji, Alia. 2018. "Material Life: Bergsonian Tendencies in Simone de Beauvoir's Philosophy." In *Differences: Rereading Beauvoir and Irigaray*, edited by Anne van Leeuwen and Emily Anne Parker. Oxford University Press.

Beauvoir, Simone de. (1947) 1948. *The Ethics of Ambiguity*. Translated by Bernard Frechtman. Citadel Press.

Beauvoir, Simone de. "Pyrrhus and Cineas." (1944) 2004a. Translated by Marybeth Timmermann. In *Philosophical Writings*, edited by Margaret A. Simons. University of Illinois Press.

Beauvoir, Simone de. (1945) 2004b. "Review of the Phenomenology of Perception." Translated by Marybeth Timmermann. In *Philosophical Writings*, edited by Margaret A. Simons. University of Illinois Press.

Beauvoir, Simone de. (1949) 2010. *The Second Sex*. Translated by Constance Borde and Sheila Malovany-Chevallier. Knopf.

Beauvoir, Simone de, and Helene Wenzel. 1986. "Interview with Helene Wenzel." *Yale French Studies* No. 72: 5–32.

Bergoffen, Deborah. 2003a. "Failed Friendship, Forgotten Genealogies: Simone de Beauvoir and Luce Irigaray." *Bulletin de la Société américaine de philosophie de langue française* 3, no. 1.

Bergoffen, Deborah. 2003b. "Simone de Beauvoir: (Re)counting the Sexual Difference." In *The Cambridge Companion to Simone de Beauvoir*, edited by Claudia Card. Cambridge University Press.

Bergoffen, Deborah. 2004. "Introduction to Pyrrhus and Cineas." In *Philosophical Writings*, edited by Margaret A. Simons. University of Illinois Press.

Burchill, Louise. 2020. "Life-Giving Sex versus Mere Animal Existence: Irigaray's and Badiou's Chiasmatic Conceptions of 'Woman' and Sexual Pleasure." In *Thinking Life with Luce Irigaray: Language, Origin, Art, Love*, edited by Gail Schwab. State University of New York Press.

Butler, Judith. 1986. "Sex and Gender in Simone de Beauvoir's *Second Sex*." *Yale French Studies* 72: 35–49.

Card, Claudia. 2003. "Introduction: Beauvoir and the Ambiguity of 'Ambiguity' in Ethics." In *The Cambridge Companion to Simone de Beauvoir*, edited by Claudia Card. Cambridge University Press.

Chanter, Tina. 1995. *Ethics of Eros*. Routledge.

Cheah, Pheng, and Elizabeth Grosz. 1998. "The Future of Sexual Difference: An Interview with Judith Butler and Drucilla Cornell." *Diacritics* 28, no. 1: 19–42.

Coates, Ta-Nehisi. 2015. *Between the World and Me*. Spiegel & Grau.

Gatens, Moira. 2003. "Beauvoir and Biology: A Second Look." In *The Cambridge Companion to Simone de Beauvoir*, edited by Claudia Card. Cambridge University Press.

Grosz, Elizabeth. 1994. "The Hetero and the Homo." In *Engaging with Irigaray*, edited by Carolyn Burke, Naomi Schor, and Margaret Whitford. Columbia University Press.

Grosz, Elizabeth. 2011. *Becoming Undone: Darwinian Reflections on Life, Politics, and Art*. Duke University Press.

Grosz, Elizabeth. 2016. "Irigaray and Darwin on Sexual Difference: Some Reflections." In *Engaging the World: Thinking After Irigaray*, edited by Mary C. Rawlinson. State University of New York Press.

Heinämaa, Sara. 2003. *Toward a Phenomenology of Sexual Difference: Husserl, Merleau-Ponty, Beauvoir*. Rowman & Littlefield.

Kaminski, Phyllis H. 2020. "Daughters, Difference, and Irigaray's Economy of Desire." In *Thinking Life with Luce Irigaray: Language, Origin, Art, Love*, edited by Gail Schwab. State University of New York Press.

Karlsdottir, Erla, and Sigridur Thorgeirsdottir. 2020. "Nature, Culture, and Sexuate Difference in Luce Irigaray's Pluralist Model of Embodied Life." In *Thinking Life with Luce Irigaray: Language, Origin, Art, Love*, edited by Gail Schwab. State University of New York Press.

Kruks, Sonia. 1990. *Situation and Human Existence: Freedom, Subjectivity, and Society*. Unwin Hyman.

Kruks, Sonia. 1995. "Simone de Beauvoir: Teaching Sartre about Freedom." In *Feminist Interpretations of Simone de Beauvoir*, edited by Margaret A. Simons. Pennsylvania State University Press.

Le Dœuff, Michèle. (1989) 1991. *Hipparchia's Choice: An Essay Concerning Women, Philosophy, etc.* Translated by Trista Selous. Blackwell.

Merleau-Ponty, Maurice. (1945) 1962. *Phenomenology of Perception*. Translated by Colin Smith. Routledge & Kegan Paul.

Parker, Emily Anne. 2018. "Toward a 'New and Possible Meeting:' Ambiguity as Difference." In *Differences: Rereading Beauvoir and Irigaray*, edited by Anne van Leeuwen and Emily Anne Parker. Oxford University Press.

Pilardi, Jo-Ann. 1995. "Feminists Read *the Second Sex*." In *Feminist Interpretations of Simone de Beauvoir*, edited by Margaret A. Simons. Pennsylvania State University Press.

Schutte, Ofelia. 1997. "A Critique of Normative Heterosexuality: Identity, Embodiment, and Sexual Difference in Beauvoir and Irigaray." *Hypatia* 12, no. 1: 40–62.

Schwab, Gail. 1996. "Women and the Law in Irigarayan Theory." *Metaphilosophy* 27, nos. 1 and 2: 146–177.

Schwab, Gail. 1998. "Sexual Difference as Model: An Ethics for the Global Future." *Diacritics* 28, no. 1: 76–92.

Schwab, Gail. 2007. "Reading Irigaray (and Her Readers) in the Twenty-First Century." In *Returning to Irigaray: Feminist Philosophy, Politics, and the Question of Unity*, edited by Maria C. Cimitile and Elaine P. Miller. State University of New York Press.

Schwab, Gail. 2016. "Creating Inter-Sexuate Inter-Subjectivity in the Classroom? Luce Irigaray's Linguistic Research in Its Latest Iteration." In *Engaging the World: Thinking After Irigaray*, edited by Mary C. Rawlinson. State University of New York Press.

Schwab, Gail. 2020. "Freedom, Desire, and the Other: Reading Sartre with Irigaray." In *Thinking Life with Luce Irigaray: Language, Origin, Art, Love*, edited by Gail Schwab. State University of New York Press.

Simons, Margaret A. 1995. "The Second Sex: From Marxism to Radical Feminism." In *Feminist Interpretations of Simone de Beauvoir*, edited by Margaret A. Simons. Pennsylvania State University Press.

Simons, Margaret A. 2004. "Introduction." In *Philosophical Writings*, edited by Margaret A. Simons. University of Illinois Press.

Stone, Alison. 2006. *Luce Irigaray and the Philosophy of Sexual Difference*. Cambridge University Press.

Ward, Julie K. 1995. "Beauvoir's Two Senses of 'Body' in *The Second Sex*." In *Feminist Interpretations of Simone de Beauvoir*, edited by Margaret A. Simons. Pennsylvania State University Press.

Chapter Nine

Luce Irigaray and the Fate of Antigone

Respect for Sexuate Identity

Marguerite La Caze

Sophocles's *Antigone* (c. 441 BCE) presents a rich source for interpretations in the history of philosophy concerning law, ethics, and sexual difference. Luce Irigaray's multiple readings of the character of Antigone across her writings create a rich topology of interlocking meanings. In the play, Antigone, daughter of Oedipus and Jocasta, feels she must bury her brother Polynices although he is regarded as a traitor and she is forbidden to do so by King Creon of Thebes, Jocasta's brother. Her two brothers, Polynices and Eteocles, have killed each other in a battle for Thebes, Eteocles as defender of Thebes, Polynices as attacker. Eteocles is given a proper burial by Creon due to his role, and Polynices is refused burial for attacking the city. Antigone's sister, Ismene, says she must follow Creon's command. When Creon discovers Antigone has buried Polynices, he orders that she be locked in a tomb, left there to die. After persuasion by Haemon, his son and Antigone's fiancé (and cousin), and the wise man Teiresias (as well as the chorus) to change his mind, Creon buries Polynices and rushes to the tomb only to discover Antigone has committed suicide, and she is followed by Haemon and Eurydice, his mother. Creon is left alone to bemoan the events.[1]

This chapter examines the differences between Irigaray's reading of *Antigone* in "Between Myth and History: The Tragedy of Antigone," a chapter of her book *In the Beginning, She Was*; the readings of the play in her earlier work; and comments on sexuate difference elsewhere within *In the Beginning* itself.[2] In "Between Myth and History," (BMH) Irigaray identifies with Antigone's exclusion and asserts the brother-sister relationship as the basis for conceptualizing sexuate identity and difference. This is oddly dissonant with her earlier readings, which affirm neither an identification with Antigone nor the brother-sister relationship as representative of a sexuate identity. In earlier work, Irigaray argues that the man and woman of the couple provide the basis for an ethics of sexuate difference. In *An Ethics of Sexual Difference* Irigaray writes of the "space of freedom and attraction" between man and woman, which "might take place at the time of their first meeting, even prior to the betrothal, and remain as a permanent proof of difference" (ESD, 13–14). The tension in Irigaray's thought is also shown by her comment at the beginning of the book that the brother-sister relationship is not different enough to represent sexuate identity (IB, 18). I explore the distinctive possibilities for sexuate identity presented by this reading of *Antigone* and ask what it means to valorize Antigone today, considering the connections that Irigaray draws between Antigone's actions and valuing our earthly environment.

Hegel's Readings of *Antigone*

Irigaray's interpretation of *Antigone* develops against the background of G. W. F. Hegel's readings. In the *Phenomenology of Spirit*, Hegel describes Antigone as the one who "knowingly commits the crime" as she knows the law and the power that she is acting against ([1807] 1977, ¶470). Moreover, in relation to Antigone, he exalts the brother-sister relationship over that of husband and wife, or parents and children, arguing that brother and sister "are the same blood which has, however, in them, reached a state of rest and equilibrium. Therefore, they do not desire one another, nor have they given to, or received from, one another this independent being-for-itself; on the contrary, they are free individualities in regard to each other" (¶457). Hegel further contends that because of the purity of this relationship, "the loss of the brother is therefore irreparable to the sister and her duty towards him is the highest" (¶457), the principle he sees exemplified in *Antigone*.

In his lectures on aesthetics, Hegel discusses *Antigone* in more detail and reads Antigone as representative of divine law and the family, in contrast to the man, who has to leave the family and adhere to the laws of the state. His view is that Sophocles's play develops

> the opposition [. . .] between ethical life in its social universality and the family as the natural ground of moral relations. These are the purest forces of tragic representation. It is, in short, the harmony of these spheres and the concordant action within the bounds of their realized content, which constitute the perfected reality of the moral life. [. . .] Antigone reverences the ties of blood-relationship, the gods of the nether world. Creon alone recognizes Zeus, the paramount Power of public life and the commonwealth (1962, 68).

The gods of the netherworld are "the instinctive Powers of feeling, Love, and Kinship" (1962, 178). In her reading, Irigaray questions whether Antigone is tied only to the gods of the underworld or to those of the world of light as well. Hegel explains how Antigone and Creon are bound by the other's obligations to the state and to the divine law and the family: Antigone as daughter of a king (Oedipus) and fiancée of Haemon, and Creon as husband and father himself (73–74). He also stresses that Creon, like Antigone, is punished for his failure to fulfill one aspect of his obligations, namely, his son Haemon and wife Eurydice die as a consequence of Antigone's death (74, 186), while he still lives, but without happiness. These elements of Hegel's interpretation of *Antigone* help highlight how Irigaray's view works in counterpoint to his and goes through a number of evolutions.

Irigaray's Earlier Readings of *Antigone*

Irigaray's best-known earlier reading of *Antigone* is in *Speculum of the Other Woman* in the section "The Eternal Irony of the Community," following Hegel's claim that woman is that irony (S, 214–226; Hegel [1807] 1977, ¶475). Irigaray mimics Hegel's idea that women have a duty to bury the body of the man, transforming the physical into the spiritual and universal (S, 214–215). She states that Antigone's brother is returned to "*the womb of the earth*" in an action that is "the divine law, or *positive* ethical action, as it relates to the individual" (S, 215; emphasis in original). However, Irigaray reminds us that, for Hegel, individual and family ties threaten the totality of the community. She links the threat of death from the state in his work with a cult of death and suggests that human law and divine law come together in this cult such that "the relationship between man and woman is possible" in Hegel's ethical realm (S, 216).

Here, Irigaray traces Hegel's focus on the brother-sister relationship, untainted in that they have the same blood but do not feel desire for each other and are not enmeshed in parent-child relations. She concludes that brother and sister come together and are balanced through the sublation of red blood into a process of semblance or white blood (*sang blanc*). Red blood for Irigaray connects mother and child and symbolizes the matrilineal link.[3] She sees Hegel's interpretation as connecting matriarchy and patriarchy in this relation between brother and sister. However, Irigaray cautions: "But this moment is mythical, of course, and the *Hegelian dream* outlined above is already the effect of a dialectic produced by the discourse of patriarchy" (S, 217). Hegel himself, she argues, reveals there is an asymmetry between brother and sister. He concedes that the brother represents the recognition the sister does not have as mother and wife, while the sister does not represent recognition the brother is lacking as father and husband. For Hegel, the brother already has recognition as a man and therefore does not need it for his social role.

Irigaray describes Ismene as "indisputably a 'woman'" in weakness and obedience, whereas Antigone threatens the masculinity of Creon by defying him (S, 218). On this interpretation, Antigone chooses to die unmarried to honor her mother's son and the link with the gods of the underworld. She accepts an unjust punishment for protecting her brother and anticipates it by killing herself. Irigaray sees Antigone as choosing the younger, weaker brother through identification with her mother, motivated by "tenderness and pity" (S, 219). However, Sophocles's plays indicate that Polynices is the older brother: it was his "younger brother" who exiled him from Thebes.[4] Irigaray must, therefore, be using other sources here.

What Irigaray takes from Hegel's interpretation is the description of Antigone as the "*living mirror*" of Polynices and the development of masculine identity (S, 221; emphasis in original). She concludes that the unity between brother and sister is perverted by the different recognition they are given by Thebes. Although Polynices is not allowed a burial, Irigaray sees Antigone as representing Polynices's autonomy rather than her own. There is a parallel here to how the woman in Hegel's dialectic loses her "living, autonomous subjectivity" according to Irigaray (S, 22). She argues that following the triumph of patriarchy represented by Creon's kingship, women and men become more separated from each other. This idea of separation leads Irigaray to search for the ethical moment when the peaceful relationship between brother and sister was broken down. She traces it to the idea of a femininity that is at fault in disobeying the law—such as Antigone's insistence on burying her brother. Shifting to a psychoanalytic register, she considers how the female is connected to the unconscious and is unable to differentiate herself from the maternal or masculine to affirm her own link to self as a singular universal. Woman preserves memory and prevents "at least the soul of man and of community from being lost and forgotten" (S, 225). Irigaray asserts that Antigone is in revolt because "she would set up the strength of youth possessed by the son, the brother, the young man, for in them, much more than in the power of government, she recognises a master, an equal, a lover" (S, 226). These are an interesting choice of words since she is reintroducing desire to the account of the sister and brother. Irigaray admits that Antigone's actions are only seeds of revolt and have no power, since they are not connected to the goal of the community. Yet in *In the Beginning*, as we shall see, Irigaray views Antigone as making a full and successful revolt that could inspire contemporary political action and thought.

In distinction to *Speculum*, Irigaray's discussion of *Antigone* in *Sexes and Genealogies* finds Hegel's reading supported by Sophocles's plays (SG, 2). Antigone tries to transcend her brothers' crime in killing each other, Irigaray states, by respecting the divine laws and "cultural obligations owed to the mother's blood, the blood shared by the brothers and sisters in the family" (SG, 2). That Antigone is forbidden to pay respects to her blood ties reveals Sophocles's play as marking the transition to a patriarchal order. Irigaray's contention is that this patriarchal legacy continues, where the husband's genealogy replaces the female genealogy and where men transfer their love for their mothers to their wives as a substitute. Antigone does not represent the female gender on this account; she "is already the desexualized representative of *the other of the same*" (SG, 111; emphasis in original).[5] Women are expected to focus on the children of the male and to view the man like a child. Irigaray also links Antigone to the loss of identity through her "incarceration [. . .] in the stone cave outside the city" (SG, 134)—an interpretation in contrast to her more recent claim that Antigone asserts a feminine identity. Such interpretative shifts undoubtedly reflect the fact that *In the Beginning* is a different phase of Irigaray's work, a phase beyond the critique of *Speculum*, past the feminine imagery of her second phase and focused on an ethics of sexuate difference (JLI, 96–97). Her understanding of Antigone has changed because she is looking for something different.

Irigaray's Interpretation of *Antigone* in *In the Beginning, She Was*

In the Beginning outlines an ethic of flourishing reciprocity and respect where we become "more perfectly ourselves through being and letting each other be. Freedom is re-expressed as a space of availability for something different in the future" (IB, 62). In that context, Irigaray's interpretation focuses on Antigone's freedom and independence, her respect for her brother Polynices, and her suggestion of a pathway for us to follow. However, in the book's introduction, Irigaray explicitly states that sexuate difference, *qua* an "irreducible human difference," finds its "most universal paradigm" in the relationship "between man and woman, a man and a woman who are naturally different, without any similarity through blood—the sexuate transcendence between a brother and a sister keeping a share in sameness—and who affirm their cultural difference" (IB, 18). This relation between man and woman has yet to be created and established, she argues. So why does Irigaray say that the brother and sister relationship represents sexuate identity later in the book (IB, 118)? I center on the quote from Irigaray's introduction to show how surprising it is that she returns to the brother-sister relation in her interpretation of *Antigone* in the same text and how this reveals a sense of ambivalence in her elucidation of the play.

An important point Irigaray makes is that art is more critical than morality for the task of creating relations between us (IB, 22). She believes we return to Greek culture in search of something lost, an incompleteness we feel (IB, 145). Thus her reading fulfills the broader purpose of acknowledging and developing the crucial role of art in creating new relations between us in accordance with what she has outlined elsewhere. In *Speculum*, Irigaray sees Antigone as adhering to a female line and identifying with her mother, a point preserved in the later reading as she consistently refers to Polynices as "son of Antigone's mother." In both readings, Irigaray is responding to Hegel's interpretation; yet there is a shift since she first rejects nostalgia for the brother-sister relationship and then asserts it. The chapter's change of perspective is prefigured in *Thinking the Difference*, where she suggests that girls and women can identify with Antigone, that her views are similar to Antigone's, and that human organization must be based on the cosmic (TD, 70–72). The questions that arise here are: Can the myth of Antigone enter into History, as the Western tradition conceives it? Should we identify with Antigone and her tragic fate? Does Antigone represent a respect for life, generation, and genealogy? How does the brother-sister relation represent sexuate differentiation and identity?

To some extent, Irigaray's reading is an elaboration of her earlier ones, where she discerns Antigone as honoring a female genealogy and a female spirituality, but significant differences exist. Noting how difficult it is to ascertain the meaning of Antigone's "will and act" (IB, 113), Irigaray distances herself from recent approaches positioning Antigone as representative of an eternal feminine that is psychologized. While she has said that women *can* identify with Antigone, here Irigaray personalizes the identification. She identifies with Antigone's exclusions, which she believes are due to her attempts to reveal truth, stating, "I have shared Antigone's tragic fate: the exclusion from socio-cultural places because of my public assertion of a truth that has been repressed, or at least not recognized as such, that thus disturbs our usual order" (IB, 115). However, this exclusion—and consequent return to nature—has enabled her, she claims, to see the meaning of Antigone's tragic destiny. This represents a significant change from *An Ethics of Sexual Difference*, where she states, "I will not identify with" the character of Antigone (ESD, 118). One might wonder—as Judith Butler notes, for example—what is at stake here in identifying with a woman born into an incestuous family who commits suicide (2000, 2, 72). Irigaray meets these concerns by reversing the logic, arguing that it is Creon who is incestuous and that, despite appearances, Antigone is choosing life rather than death.[6] So we need to see how this argument develops. Furthermore, Irigaray says she is distancing herself from Hegel to a greater extent than she did in *Speculum*: "Because I have been expelled from social places, from the belonging on which Hegel founded his reading of Sophocles's tragedy, because in a way I have been buried alive in the natural world, and also because the truth that I tried to unveil, after arousing enthusiasm and bedazzlement, has again been covered and hidden by the arbitrary and subsequent blindness of our civilization, the mystery that envelops Antigone has become more familiar to me, indeed more intimate" (IB, 117). Irigaray values "Antigone's rationality and wisdom in contrast to Creon's irrationality and madness" (IB, 117–118), unlike Hegel. It should be noted that Creon comes to see the wisdom and rightness in Antigone's action, burying Polynices and going to release Antigone, albeit too late. Moreover, Antigone recognizes the force of Creon's command by burying Polynices symbolically rather than "properly." The sentry reports: "The corpse was covered from sight-/ Not with a proper grave-just a layer of earth-/As it might be, the act of some pious passer-by" (Sophocles 1947, 253–254).[7] Irigaray argues that "Sophocles's tragedy takes place in the passage from a manner of thinking faithful to life, love, and desire towards a reasoning which leads only to destruction, hatred, and death" (IB, 118). Her contention is that, rather than intentionally creating a disruption, Antigone had to obey a higher order and unwritten laws—with these latter being of a different order than state, or human, law. Irigaray sees Antigone as respecting three sets of unwritten laws: that of the living universe and living beings, that of generation and not just genealogy, and that of sexuate difference.

Irigaray distinguishes between "sexuate," understood as pertaining to sexed specificity, and "sexual," understood as pertaining to sexuality or to its restraint. If Antigone had been concerned with sexuality, she would have privileged her fiancé Haemon. Hegel's mistake, Irigaray contends, was to consider that Antigone's duty was related to the constraint of sexuality. Instead, Antigone reveres the singular and concrete sexuate identity of her brother *qua* "the son of the mother." According to Irigaray, the duality of man and woman must be respected first "as a sort of frame" before sexual desire or attraction (IB, 119). This is interesting, as it moves the idea of the irreducible two away from the heterosexual couple to man and woman. However, it appears to conflict with her claim in the book's first chapter and elsewhere that the brother and sister are too similar to represent sexuate duality. In contrast to her reading in *Speculum*, where she is caustic about Hegel's stress on the "unsullied" brother-sister relationship (S, 216), Irigaray is closer here—despite what she maintains—to Hegel's interpretation and valuing of that relationship. Another feature of Irigaray's reading is her attempt to consider the myth of Antigone in relation to patriarchal History, "a tragic gesture" as sexuate desire is for the infinite (IB, 135–136). As she says in *Thinking the Difference*, myth expresses history, and "[h]istory as expressed in myth is more closely related to female, matrilineal traditions" (TD, 101).

Irigaray argues that Antigone must bury her brother Polynices to respect his unique identity—an identity more unique than that of a fiancé, who is substitutable—and not let him become just physical matter (IB, 119). She stresses, in conformity with her remarks in *Speculum*, Sophocles's claim that Polynices is born of the same mother as Antigone. Sophocles himself provides a kind of retrospective justification for Antigone's actions in *Oedipus at Colonus*, written after *Antigone*, where Polynices asks both sisters to bury him after he is killed by and kills his brother Eteocles, in fulfillment of Oedipus's curse (1947, 1371, 1441). For Irigaray, we should therefore see Antigone as respecting the cosmic order, the generational order, and sexuate differentiation; hence, I will examine each of these in turn.

The Cosmic Order, Life, Death, and Self-Sacrifice

Irigaray accepts that Antigone is aligned with the divine laws but goes further in contending that she acts to maintain the harmony between light and darkness, the world of the living and the underworld. This view is contrasted with a focus on the made world that neglects any harmony between nature, gods, and humans. While this feature of her argument is compelling, the end of the play shows Creon now brought to see his error on that score and to acknowledge the importance of divine law. Irigaray argues that Antigone is trying to maintain respect for cosmic order by reverencing Zeus and Hades and thereby "maintain[s] a fragile harmony between the two gods and their mutual realms" (IB, 120). She differs from Hegel in valorizing Antigone's decision and asserting that the unwritten laws are the more important ones. Significantly, she argues that what appears to be Antigone's choice to die is really a choice of life.

"She cannot accept survival instead of living," Irigaray writes of Antigone. First, on this view, existing is not living; true living is to live well. Antigone cannot cultivate her life and make it flourish, which could only happen after "giving thanks to those who brought her into the world, after securing a valid memory for her brother" (IB, 124). She must carry out this act of respect before she can marry her fiancé Haemon. Conversely, to wish to merely survive rather than to flourish is to choose death. Irigaray argues: "But is it not surviving at any cost that testifies to a wish to die rather than to really live?" (IB, 125–126). She observes that even the chorus is alarmed by Creon's determination to punish whoever has symbolically buried Polynices: "But he that, too rashly daring, walks in sin/In solitary pride to his life's end/At door of mine shall never enter in/To call me friend" (Sophocles 1947, 368–371). For Irigaray, the chorus's alarm comes from the unbalancing of the world's cosmic harmony, an imbalance she connects with the destruction of nature. Likewise,

Teiresias warns Creon that his failure to "pay to the dead his due" (1026) is disruptive of nature. Irigaray's first step in reclaiming Antigone is this argument that the choice of death is in reality a choice of life—that is, a flourishing life lived in a harmonious world, with this a choice thus "accomplishing life and making it blossom" (IB, 123). "She wants to live and not to die," Irigaray concludes (IB, 126), on the basis that Antigone shows her valuing of life and respect for the world through her desire to bury her brother. Furthermore, in *Through Vegetal Being*, she adds that Antigone wishes to restore her brother's body to its most appropriate element, the earth (TVB, 126).

However, Antigone not only accepts her punishment but takes it further by killing herself, thus not allowing the possibility of survival and life. In *An Ethics of Sexual Difference*, Irigaray explains Antigone's suicide simply by saying, "[s]uicide, the only act left to her" (ESD, 119). Yet now she sees Antigone as choosing death *as* life since true life is impossible, and mere existence, when harmony cannot be maintained, is not worthwhile. But does not this recommend and condone self-sac-rifice?[8] What meaning has life without survival? Even if we understand Antigone's choice and agree that in these times life is flawed through the destruction of the environment, how can that be a model for us? Irigaray claims that Creon's action in entombing Antigone is paralleled today: "In a way, all of our patriarchal system amounts to this killing without openly committing a murder; that is to say, little by little depriving us of the surroundings that allow us to live, by polluting, annihilating the equilibrium of the environment, destroying the plant and animal worlds, and finally humanity itself" (IB, 125). Furthermore, she adds that some people commit suicide rather than wait for the planet to die. However, even if *that* is true, it cannot be something we recommend rather than fighting to save the planet. Sometimes to survive is to triumph, as when the destruction of a group of people is attempted. Sometimes we might need to follow Ismene as our model, to consider that there has been enough suffering and to put an end to it, and to live.[9]

In *Speculum* Irigaray asks of Antigone: "*is mourning itself her jou-issance?* . . . Does she thus anticipate the decree of death formulated by those in power? Does she duplicate it? Has she given in? Or is she still in revolt?" (S, 219; emphasis in original). Irigaray answers in *In the Begin-ning* that Antigone has chosen to affirm genuine life over survival. But in choosing suicide, not just accepting Creon's decree, Antigone seems to have chosen death. A messenger reports to Eurydice that "There in the furthest corner of the cave/ We saw her hanging by the neck" (Sophocles 1947, 1218–1219). Even though the idea of true life as against mere survival can make sense in certain situations, seeing how the choice of death can be commended to us is difficult, especially when we consider the hasty nature of Antigone's choice. But perhaps we will progress if we consider Antigone's choice to bury her brother.

Respect for Generational Order and Genealogy

In relation to respect for generational order, Irigaray states the need for the sustaining conditions of human life, and for limits, provided through genealogy and sexuate difference (IB, 127). The lesson of Antigone is that the paternal genealogy has attempted to suppress the maternal one when what is needed is an alliance. According to Irigaray, the maternal genealogy values life, growth, and generation and favors daughters and the youngest son as heirs of generation itself. This approach, she argues, is exemplified in Antigone's concern for her younger brother, Polynices, who does not inherit power, "the son of her mother." Irigaray contends that the chorus, the soothsayer, and the conversation between Ismene and Antigone when they debate the question of Polynices's burial, all support the values of a maternal genealogy (IB, 128).[10] However, as Hegel's interpretation anticipates, Creon's changing his mind shows that he also respects this genealogy and the need for obedience to it as well as obedience to state law. Creon says, "Now I believe./ It is by the laws of heaven that man must live" (Sophocles 1947, 1113) and arranges for Polynices's burial and for Antigone to be released. The contrast between the two, Creon and Antigone, need not be stressed so much by Irigaray.

The maternal order is distinguished by the way it values love not confined to the institution of the family, according to Irigaray. Thus, the chorus claims that Aphrodite is the winner in the struggle of love and desire over patriarchy, after Haemon threatens suicide and leaves his father: "At the side of the great gods/ Aphrodite immortal/ Works her will upon all." (Sophocles 1947, 794–796). Like the chorus, Irigaray sees Haemon as rebelling because of his love for Antigone, although he says to Creon that the cause he is pleading for is "*yours*, and mine, and that of the gods of the dead" (752; emphasis in original). She also wishes to show that incest does not come from the maternal order, rather, it "comes from a regression provoked by a truly problematic establishment of patriarchy"

(IB, 129). The patriarchy, Irigaray argues, does not allow the mother her identity and leads to a "nostalgic regression to an initial state" (IB, 129). In patriarchy, maternal and feminine differentiation are not respected, so the mother cannot be seen as who she is. Oedipus, for example, after realizing he has made love with his mother, takes out his eyes, making it more likely that he will make a mistake, contends Irigaray (IB, 130).[11] As she observes, Antigone became Oedipus's guide (in *Oedipus at Colonus*) because she recognizes the ethical need to respect life and generation. Irigaray details here the autonomy and differentiation of the maternal order, which, if valued, would involve respect for sexuate difference, not the "neuter individual of the polis, the state" (IB, 131).

Respect for Sexuate Differentiation Between Brother and Sister

Irigaray argues that nature is filled with differentiation that is not based on hierarchical or quantitative differences. She maintains that human beings have a special role in using difference to access transcendence, writing that "[t]he place where human difference appears is between sister and brother" (IB, 131). Yet Irigaray states in her introduction that the brother and sister relation cannot be the universal paradigm of irreducible difference between two because "the sexuate difference between brother and sister keep[s] a share in sameness" (IB, 18), as I mentioned. Thus, we need to examine what, if anything, has changed here.

Irigaray observes that the traditional family serves to reproduce the species and does not respect sexuate identity since men and women are seen only in terms of their reproductive and parental roles. Hegel, she says, links man with Creon or Oedipus and woman with Antigone or Ismene, thinking only of roles or functions (IB, 132). For Irigaray, Oedipus and Creon do not reach their sexuate identity but either stay too close to the mother (Oedipus) or rebel against her through misogyny (Creon). However, Creon realizes his mistake when he is persuaded by Haemon and then Teiresias that we should live by the laws of heaven and accepts his guilt: "My hands have done amiss, my head is bowed/With fate too heavy for me" (Sophocles 1947, 162).

In contrast, Antigone shows that sexuate identity exists and comes through brother and sister, Irigaray claims, such that "there is an appearance of transcendence of sexuate identity with respect to the body" (IB, 133).

For her, Antigone testifies to the existence of this sexuate identity and the need to respect it. Sexuate identity is bodily and cultural in that the distinct bodily identity "creates a world different for man and woman" (IB, 133). Burying Polynices represents a recognition of the transcendent world of his different sexuate identity, according to Irigaray. The transcendent aspect is its going beyond our comprehension, remaining a mystery for us. We cannot see, understand, or substitute what meaning the body has for the other sexuate being or for how their subjectivity is constructed. This is a robust account of the significance of sexuate differentiation, consolidating Irigaray's assertion that this transcendental dimension "exists, or ought to exist" (IB, 134). We need to respect this difference through Antigone, Irigaray contends, to allow the myth of Antigone to enter into History. Her claim is that male and female genders belong to different worlds and "have to elaborate a third world through their relations in difference, a third world that does not belong to one or the other, but is generated by the two with respect for their difference(s)" (IB, 135). This world involves developing what Irigaray calls a relational culture that recognizes specificities. Yet, why does the brother-sister relationship represent this difference rather than the couple or friends, as Irigaray contends elsewhere (ESD, 12–14; ILTY, 9–11)?

Irigaray focuses on the strange lines—considered by some interpreters as a later interpolation into the text—that assert Antigone's relation with her brother to be less replaceable than other relations.[12] This is an assertion Irigaray takes extremely seriously, subscribing to Antigone's argument that she could have another husband, or sons, but not another brother, since her parents are dead: "O but I would not have done the forbidden thing/ For any husband or for any son./ For why? I could have had another husband/ And by him other sons, if one were lost;/ But, father and mother lost, where would I get another brother?" (Sophocles 1947, 904–909). Here Irigaray restates that the sexuate other concerns "the most basic, universal, and irreducible otherness" (IB, 134). She also says that this otherness first appears between brother and sister, possibly referring to the ordering of the life cycle, if we see sexuate otherness as beginning with birth. The problem with this claim is that first, it applies specifically to Antigone, in that both her parents are dead, and second, that an argument for a hierarchy of relationships that takes some as replaceable and others as not fails to respect the individuality and preciousness of each person. While Antigone literally cannot get another brother, experientially she cannot get another Haemon either, although she could have another fiancé.

Antigone and Irigaray appear inconsistent in saying that some individuals are more important than others rather than each person should be respected since Antigone initially argued that both brothers should be buried properly. Irigaray differs from most commentators in following Antigone's logic rather than questioning it.[13] She seems to be coming closer to Hegel, who argued that the brother-sister relationship was unique because it was not confused by eroticism or by the dependence of children on parents (Hegel [1807] 1977, ¶457). Irigaray suggests here that the brother-sister relationship has more potential than the heterosexual couple, being nonsexual.

Irigaray argues that the world of the other sexuate being is transcendent to us in the sense of being organized in a different way, so not fully understood by us, and a proper object of wonder. Yet the brother-sister relationship, the couple relationship, friendship, and other relations are worthy of wonder.[14] The brother represents for Antigone in Irigaray's eyes "an identity different from her own" (IB, 133). Both these representations have positive elements that mean they could be *one* representative of differentiation along with others, such as race, class, ethnicity, sexuality, or families and friendship, although of course Irigaray interprets sexual difference as ontological, as "given (*Es gibt*) by life itself or by nature" (Seely 2016, 110).[15] Finally, what does it mean to affirm Antigone's tragic fate? Should we accept this tragic turn?

A Tragic Vision?

Irigaray calls the fate of Antigone an insurmountable tragedy and claims that cultivating our sexuate identity must involve tragedy. Not only do we have to embody our own gender alone but "our sexuate desire longs for the infinite and the absolute while History is limited and human. Furthermore, sexuate truth is and must remain dual, each one having to accomplish alone, with respect for the other, one's sexuate identity" (IB, 136). She also suggests there is a tragic necessity in distinguishing sexuate belonging from sexual attraction, as Antigone has to bury her brother before marrying her fiancé. Moreover, Antigone's burial of Polynices protects his sexuate identity from being just a body and limited to a role in Creon's dictatorial rule. Irigaray says that difference, in both the play and our contemporary society, is replaced by "public functionalism," here meaning that men and women have to take up appointed roles (IB, 136).

Irigaray notes that Hegel implies Antigone's mission could be greater than that of Jesus Christ in texts other than *Phenomenology of Spirit*. In his lectures on the history of philosophy, Hegel compares Antigone to Socrates, mentioning "the heavenly Antigone, that noblest of figures that ever appeared on earth" (1962, 360). This idea has some foundation, Irigaray argues, as what is distinctive about the laws Antigone follows is that they are unwritten and do not distinguish between civil and religious duties. Irigaray concludes we must follow the unwritten rule of respect for life, respect for all children of the human species (IB, 137). This conclusion implies less a tragic fate than an optimism that we will respect the laws as Antigone does.

We return to *Antigone* because of its fascination and because we admire Antigone's renunciation and faithfulness. Could the brother-sister relationship have more potential than the heterosexual couple because it is nonsexual, as Irigaray suggests in her interpretation of *Antigone*? While this idea is intriguing and we can see why she is tempted by it in places, just as Hegel was, it is difficult to show that the brother-sister relationship is more important than other relationships—in either this particular case or, even more so, in general. Irigaray's ambivalence on this point is demonstrated by her comment at the beginning of her book that the brother-sister relationship is not different enough to represent sexuate identity. The brother-sister relation is no more representative than the heterosexual relationship is of all relationships, powerful though it may be in contrasting with the unequal and nonreciprocal traditional couple. The possibility of an ethical future can be represented by couples, friends, family, and other configurations.

The other problematic aspect of Irigaray's argument is the idea that the concept of "life" as a value rather than a reality is more precious than actual survival, as she expands the meaning of life in her interpretation of Antigone. In more recent work she stresses the significance of the vegetal world in ensuring our life and natural survival (WDM, 5). As Irigaray writes in *Through Vegetal Being*, it is necessary "to recover breathing first to survive and, then, to discover how to cultivate life" (TVB, 26). It is problematic for Antigone, and in general, especially considering Antigone's suicide, even though the concern her character expresses is with indefinite life beyond mortal existence and beyond human existence. Survival itself can be a value in a range of circumstances. Furthermore, why should life remain tragic, even if it is tragic while we struggle to cultivate sexuate identity? Insofar as we believe in the possibility of positive change, we may turn toward the more optimistic aspects of Irigaray's work on loving and respecting others.

Acknowledgments

I would like to thank the organizers of the Topologies of Sexual Difference Conference at Royal Melbourne Institute of Technology University, especially Rebecca Hill, for inviting me to present a keynote, and Louise Burchill and Rebecca for their helpful editorial suggestions.

Notes

1. Ismene also survives, although we do not hear from her.

2. Irigaray published this essay earlier in S. E. Wilmer and A. Audroné Žukauskaité, *Interrogating Antigone in Postmodern Philosophy and Criticism*, 197–212.

3. See Sabrina Hom in Irigaray (T, 120–25) for a discussion of the significance of blood for Irigaray. Rachel Jones, *Irigaray*, 206, contrasts red blood with white blood, "the father's sperm."

4. In *Oedipus at Colonus*, Polynices states, "My younger brother, Eteocles, expelled me." Sophocles, *The Theban Plays*, 1294.

5. Gail Schwab, in "Mothers, Sisters, and Daughters" (83–84, 89–90), for example, sees *Antigone* as representing the erasure of sexual difference.

6. Compare with Jacques Lacan, who argues that Antigone incarnates the desire of death, in *The Seminar of Jacques Lacan, Book VII* (282).

7. The numbers for *Antigone* refer to the line of the play.

8. Antigone's self-sacrifice is different from rituals of sacrifice usually performed by men, analyzed by Irigaray (SG, 75–88).

9. Mary C. Rawlinson argues that Ismene is a better model of feminist agency than Antigone in "Beyond Antigone" (101–121). Tina Chanter argues that she is an alternative model in "Antigone's Exemplarity" (276), whereas Bonnie Honig argues that we need to interpret the play to consider Ismene's agency beside Antigone's in "Ismene's Forced Choice" (64).

10. This conversation uses the Greek middle voice, showing the sisters as having a part in the same tradition, but the middle voice is abandoned after they follow different courses of action, Irigaray observes (IB, 128). The middle voice can be partially or indirectly reflexive: "I marry," or can express reciprocity: "They love each other" (IB, 147).

11. Similarly, in *Sexes and Genealogies*, Irigaray says Oedipus demonstrated his failure to recognize gender identity in returning to his mother as if there

were no other woman (SG, 134). Nevertheless, we should recall that Oedipus did not *know* she was his mother. Irigaray's view that there is nothing incestuous in Antigone's actions conflicts with that of Isabelle Torrance, who cites ancient sources suggesting Antigone's love for her brother Polynices is near-incestuous. Torrance, "Antigone and Her Brother," 246.

12. See Bonnie Honig "Antigone's Laments," 31. However, Watling argues that Antigone's words here are "inconsistent and even unworthy" but "dramatically right," given how desperate she must be feeling. See Sophocles, *The Theban Plays*, 167.

13. See Mary Beth Mader for a discussion of criticisms of Antigone's argument in "Antigon and Ethics of Kinship," 94.

14. See Marguerite La Caze, *Wonder and Generosity*.

15. See also Elizabeth Grosz, "The Nature of Sexual Difference."

References

Butler, Judith. 2000. *Antigone's Claim: Kinship Between Life and Death*. Columbia University Press.

Chanter, Tina. 2011. "Antigone's Exemplarity: Irigaray, Hegel, and Excluded Grounds as Constitutive of Feminist Theory." In *Thinking with Irigaray*, edited by Mary C. Rawlinson, Sabrina L. Hom, and Serene J. Khader. State University of New York Press.

Grosz, Elizabeth. 2012. "The Nature of Sexual Difference." *Angelaki: Journal of the Theoretical Humanities* 17, no. 2: 69–93.

Hegel, G. W. F. 1962. *Hegel on Tragedy*. Edited by Anne Paolucci and Henry Paolucci. Harper & Row.

Hegel, G. W. F. (1807) 1977. *Phenomenology of Spirit*. Translated by A. V. Miller. Oxford University Press.

Hom, Sabrina L. 2008. "Disinterring the Divine Law." In *Teaching*, edited by Luce Irigaray and Mary Green. Continuum.

Honig, Bonnie. 2011. "Ismene's Forced Choice: Sacrifice and Sorority in Sophocles' *Antigone*." *Arethusa* 44, no. 1: 29–68.

Honig, Bonnie. 2014. "Antigone's Laments—Creon's Grief." In *The Returns of Antigone: Interdisciplinary Essays*, edited by Tina Chanter and Sean D. Kirkland. State University of New York Press.

Jones, Rachel. 2011. *Irigaray*. Polity.

La Caze, Marguerite. 2013. *Wonder and Generosity: Their Role in Ethics and Politics*. State University of New York Press.

Lacan, Jacques. 1992. *The Seminar of Jacques Lacan, Book VII: The Ethics of Psychoanalysis 1959–1960*. Translated by Dennis Porter. Norton.

Mader, Mary Beth. 2010. "Antigone and the Ethics of Kinship." In *Rewriting Difference: Luce Irigaray and "the Greeks,"* edited by Elena Tzelepis and Athena Athanasiou. State University of New York Press.

Rawlinson, Mary C. 2014. "Beyond Antigone: Ismene, Gender, and the Right to Life." In *The Returns of Antigone: Interdisciplinary Essays*, edited by Tina Chanter and Sean D. Kirkland. State University of New York Press.

Schwab, Gail. 2010. "Mothers, Sisters, and Daughters: Luce Irigaray and the Female Genealogical Line in the Stories of the Greeks." In *Rewriting Difference: Luce Irigaray and "The Greeks,"* edited by Elena Tzelepis and Athena Athanasiou. State University of New York Press.

Seely, Stephen D. 2016. "Does Life Have a Sex? Thinking Ontology and Sexual Difference with Irigaray and Simondon." In *Feminist Philosophies of Difference*, edited by Hasana Sharp and Chloë Taylor. McGill-Queen's University Press.

Sophocles. (c. 441 BCE) 1947. *The Theban Plays*. Translated by E.F. Watling. Penguin.

Torrance, Isabelle. 2010. "Antigone and Her Brother: What Sort of Special Relationship?" In *Interrogating Antigone in Postmodern Philosophy and Criticism*, edited by S. E. Wilmer and A. Audroné Žukauskaité. Oxford University Press.

Wilmer, S. E., and A. Audroné Žukauskaité, eds. 2010. *Interrogating Antigone in Postmodern Philosophy and Criticism*. Oxford University Press.

Chapter Ten

Intertwinements of Pictorial Research and Speculative Effort

The Noetic Dance Between Barbara and Luce

Francesca Brezzi, translated by
Edoardo Bellando and Tamara Lee

Introduction, by Louise Burchill

In 1982, the Italian artist Barbara—best known for her participation in the Futurist movement between 1938 and 1942—was to open Irigaray's *Elemental Passions* and find herself literally transported.[1] "I didn't simply read the book: I entered into a mysterious harmony with Luce, with her experience, her thought; between her words-thought-life and my painting-thought-life, a truly fruitful union came to be created. And so these words entered into my paintings, they themselves became sign and colour" (Biglieri Scurto 1998, 370; cited by Brezzi 2009, 64).[2] As related in her autobiography, Barbara was most acutely aware of being on the "same wavelength" as Irigaray, in a reverberation of pictorial research and speculative effort, when she discovered—"flabbergasted"—that the fluid, manifold and infinitely open expansion that she was seeking to express in her painting was, likewise, for Irigaray a characteristic of women's corporeal and subjective specificity. That a woman artist would give expression to an imaginary distinct from that of men—were she able to free herself from the forms fashioned for her from a strictly masculine perspective parading as representative of humanity—is a conviction Barbara had arrived at before her encounter with Irigaray. Indeed, from the 1970s on, the main thrust of Barbara's pictorial research had centered precisely on the elaboration of an "art in the feminine," the most eloquent example of which is the series of "placental paintings" she initiated in 1979, after the death of her mother. These abstract renderings of fluid, seething expanses from which emerge schematic helical forms as representations of "the germs of new life" were, for the artist, both the expression of her innermost being, with color and the play of volume conveying sensations unable to be encompassed by words, and meditations on the complex interrelationality of self-other, life-death, and body-culture. Celebrating the conjointly spiritual and biological creativity of female being, these placental paintings just as adamantly affirm the irreducibly sexuate nature of artistic production itself, Barbara explicitly designating them as works that only a woman could have painted.

The text we are introducing here, "Intertwinements of Pictorial Research and Speculative Effort: The Noetic Dance Between Barbara and Luce," by the Italian philosopher Francesca Brezzi, first focuses precisely on the placental period of Barbara's pictorial activity before then addressing the cycle of paintings—baptized "noetic"—that the artist commenced immediately afterward, under the impulsion in part of her encounter with the thought of Irigaray. Although presented here as a single unified chapter, Brezzi's analyses of these two periods of Barbara's activity comprise, in fact, two distinct sections of the monograph she published in 2009, "When Futurism is a Woman: Barbara of Colors."[3] As its title indicates, Brezzi's monograph frames the consideration of Barbara's Irigarayan inspiration within an overarching review of women artists' participation in Futurism—a participation singularly permeated, to say the least, with paradox and contradiction. To elucidate these ambiguities of women's adherence to a movement often qualified as the "most misogynistic of the avant-gardes," Brezzi deploys a number of crucial motifs that equally resonate, re-embroidered, within her analyses of Barbara's later artistic evolution. We have judged it useful, for this reason, to outline for the reader in what follows certain salient aspects of Brezzi's general argument as this pertains to the particular trajectory of Barbara. In accordance with the motif found throughout Brezzi's monograph of the "new birth" undergone by women engaged in artistic/symbolic creation, we shall begin by recalling Barbara's biography—in specifying from the start that she was to encapsulate her "multiple lives" in the epithet: "a woman born of herself" (Brezzi 2009, 36).

In 1938, after having entered into contact with the group of Futurist artists based in Verona, the young Olga Biglieri created (at the age of twenty-three) her first aeropainting—a subgenre of predilection for Futurists in the 1930s—and signed it as "Barbara," the artist name she had chosen for its consonance with "barbarity" and evocation of the Amazons.[4] She was promptly invited by the poet and writer F. T. Marinetti, who had launched the Futurist movement in 1909 with his *Manifesto del Futurismo* and then revived it post–World War I, to show in the Venice Biennale of the same year (1938), and on this occasion, the painting she exhibited there—*The Airport Grabs the Airplane*—was signed not just "Barbara" but "Barbara, Futurist aviatrix." This was a proclamation of rebirth: an artist had come into being, and this artist was indeed an aviatrix—flight representing for her an unparalleled source of intense sensations and inner freedom. Barbara/Olga had, in fact, obtained her pilot's license five years earlier, at the age of just eighteen, and it was, therefore, with a certain justified hubris that she could later write in her autobiography, when reflecting on Marinetti's invitation, that she had known at that moment that she would have her "own glory" and not a glory through association with a man or men: "A woman had emerged from the group of men and left them all behind on the ground, flying now in a dimension that plunged each and every one of them into stupor and incredulity (Biglieri Scurto 1998, 67; cited by Brezzi 2009, 37–38). As foreseen, Barbara's adhesion to Futurism did assure her fame. She participated in a number of major exhibitions, including the Venice Biennale three times in all, as well as the Rome Quadrenniale in 1939 and 1943, with the works she presented there consecrating her as an important representative of Italian Futurism: the "last Futurist painter." Italy's entry into World War II led Barbara, however, to become increasingly critical of the bellicism that was a defining characteristic of Futurism, as it was, of course, of Fascism with which Futurism had become intrinsically intertwined from 1919 when the Futurist Political Party that Marinetti had helped create a year earlier formed a coalition with Mussolini's Fasci Italiani di Combattimento (Italian Fasces of Combat), itself reorganized in 1921 as the National Fascist Party.[5] By 1942, Barbara had dissociated herself from the movement, judged "too macho and dictatorial." Her last painting of this period, *Aerial Battle*, reflects this rejection of the Futurist credo of war as "the only hygiene of the world"[6]: the canvas depicts two planes that collide in midflight and a third plummeting to the ground with a long trail of black smoke behind it, while, in the painting's lower right-hand corner, there is the profile of a woman who observes the scene from below. For the woman having painted this, "The plane here is no longer the symbol of force and the joy of flying—the values and sensations for which I became a Futurist. It is a machine man launches towards destruction and death" (Biglieri Scurto 1998, 92; cited by Brezzi 2009, 39). The end of the war only reinforced Barbara's loathing for Futurist/Fascist bellicist ideology. Her husband, the Futurist poet Ignazio Scurto—whose earlier "aeropoetic" compositions had included celebrations of Italian aviation and dramatizations of Italy's "right" to occupy former territories (Bohn 2004, 141–152)—returned from the front a man broken in body and spirit. His death in 1954 left Barbara devastated. She had abandoned painting in 1943, when Scurto was drafted, and she was left to care for their two daughters on her own, in favor of the more remunerative activity of authoring romantic novels, but she now found work as a fashion journalist, a profession at which she excelled, before then working in public relations for several large Italian textile companies. Later, in the early 1960s, she hosted a popular radio show, *Stella Polare*, on which she gave fashion tips, and she subsequently founded a press agency in Rome.[7]

Not until the end of the 1950s would Barbara resume painting, seeking to "draw out of herself," as she put it, "the sensations that words couldn't contain" (Brezzi 2009, 46). This aspiration was to give rise to the series *Visions* (1958–1974), in respect of which the painter later specified "the goal of the sign immersed in colour is emotion, but when the emotion is captured, you must forget the sign in order to hold on to it" (*Barbara dal futurismo* 2001, 62). While working on *Visions*, the painter equally executed the two series *Cosmic Genesis* (influenced by her interest in Eastern philosophies) and *Robot* (reflecting her reading of Marx, Freud, Jung, and Fromm), but it was only in the mid-1970s that she would again totally immerse herself in art making, her work from then on unfailingly imbued with a strong spiritual tension and a no less intense social and political passion. Feminism was—as Brezzi precisely details in the chapter that follows here—absolutely determining for Barbara's artistic evolution. Yet some of the painter's most striking artistic and cultural initiatives from the 1980s on were also fueled by her pacifist convictions. Exemplary in this respect is her work, *The Tree of Peace*, a ten-meter-long canvas bearing the imprint, seeped in color, of the hands of a "harmonious collectivity" (comprised of pacifist militants, survivors of the Hiroshima atomic bombing, intellectuals, and Italian political figures, among others), which Barbara donated, in 1986, to the Hiroshima Peace Memorial Museum. In the same period, the painter founded the group Women and Culture, bringing together women artists from different regions in Italy in the express aim of "elaborating a culture of peace between women and expressing it through art" (Brezzi 2009, 48). As this imbrication of her twin passions of feminism and pacifism indicates, Barbara's project of elaborating "an art in the feminine" encompassed all aspects of her existence. Indeed, in the context of an exhibition in 1980 tracing the history of the female avant-garde, she would declare that her militant involvement in the women's movement and association with other women artists had made it possible for her "to reconcile art and life" (49)—the very fusion of art and existence that the Futurists had aspired to, just as had all the avant-garde movements of the early twentieth century. That she "had never abandoned the idea of such a reconciliation" certainly underlines the continuity of her trajectory from its Futurist beginnings, but it no less signals that it was not Futurism per se to which Barbara had remained faithful but the aspirations having motivated her participation in this movement, as they had everything she was to undertake from thereon. She would reaffirm this, some twenty years later, when again reflecting publicly on her trajectory: the totality of her artistic and cultural activity, she then specified, had its source in the pressing need she felt to work on her inner life so as to give form to forces demanding an expression and to dissipate blockages, thereby opening up paths fostering her desire to live, to know, and to grow (8). The reason why feminism had rendered this possible, in contrast to her adherence to Futurism, is simple: the reconciliation of art and life so attained was specifically that articulated between "being a woman" and "being an artist"—two aspects of Barbara's existence that had always been in conflict during her Futurist past.

The complex inflexions of the conflict between "woman" and "artist," as this played out throughout the history of Futurism, forms, as we've indicated, the focus of the first half of Brezzi's monograph. The question Brezzi sets out to explore is why not only Barbara but also a myriad of women—artists, writers, poets, musicians, and dancers—adhered to an artistic courant of such an aggressively—if equivocally, at times—misogynistic complexion. Brezzi's proposed answer is actually fairly straightforward, even if the discursive constellation around Futurism and women that constitutes her corpus is characterized by an almost bewildering profusion of paradoxical positions, contradictions, and ambiguities, accentuated moreover by the sharp ideological shifts demarcating the movement's different chronological periods. Succinctly put, whatever Marinetti or other Futurist protagonists may have declared concerning "women's intellectual inferiority" or the "disdain" women inspired as representatives of sentimentality and other traditional ideals (or institutions) that needed to be destroyed, whatever the Futurists' denigration of women's childbearing capacity or their exaltation of virile virtues such as hypermasculinity, power, the love of danger, and the glorification of war, women chose to belong to this movement because the radical transformations of social, political, intimate, and artistic practices it promoted offered an alternative to the roles traditionally assigned to women and represented, thereby, the possibility for them of forging a new identity. "The adhesion to Futurism represented for these women an act of defiance bent on destruction and dismantlement, a challenge to the spirit of selflessness and sacrifice considered to be the purpose of women's lives" that amounted, in short, to "a demolition of feminine stereotypes" undertaken in the name of an exalting "interpenetration of the aesthetic sphere and life" (Brezzi 2009, 13).

Should it seem paradoxical for women to seek to demolish feminine stereotypes through an adhesion to a movement exalting virile virtues, then this but mirrors the internal contradictions and ambiguities of Futurism itself. Even Marinetti recognized at times that the proclaimed inferiority of women was a product of history and not a biological given, just as the Futurists' condemnation of women as representatives of sentimentalism and bourgeois values morphed intermittently into a promotion of women's social and political emancipation, viewed as a means of destroying the family and parliamentary democracy in accordance with the Futurist credo. Brezzi stresses, however, that the emancipatory ethos espoused by Futurism and acclaimed by the women who participated in the movement was emancipatory only in appearance for it remained fundamentally framed within a hierarchization of values giving preeminence to canonically masculinist attributions. In this sense, the imbrication, defining its final period, of Futurism with Fascism—a movement sharing, of course, these hypermasculine values—can be seen as the logical endpoint of its ideology of woman insofar as all the diverse, contradictory positions espoused therein were subordinated to "the essential category of virilism" (Brezzi 2009, 30). Brezzi particularly emphasizes in this respect the ambiguities of the Futurist positions on maternity: reviled and rejected in the movement's first—"heroic"—period (up to World War I)—motherhood would be exalted in the 1930s as the real (and resoundingly patriotic) reason of women's existence, in alignment with the Fascist tenets on childbearing as a duty toward the State and its commendation of "exemplary mothers." However opposed these positions may be, they cohere in their patriarchal perspective—a far cry from the sexuate specificity Barbara would attempt to give expression to in her placental and noetic paintings.

Figure 10.1 Barbara, *Placenta 1*, 1979, tempera on faesite. *Source*: Courtesy of Mimesis Edizioni. Used with permission.

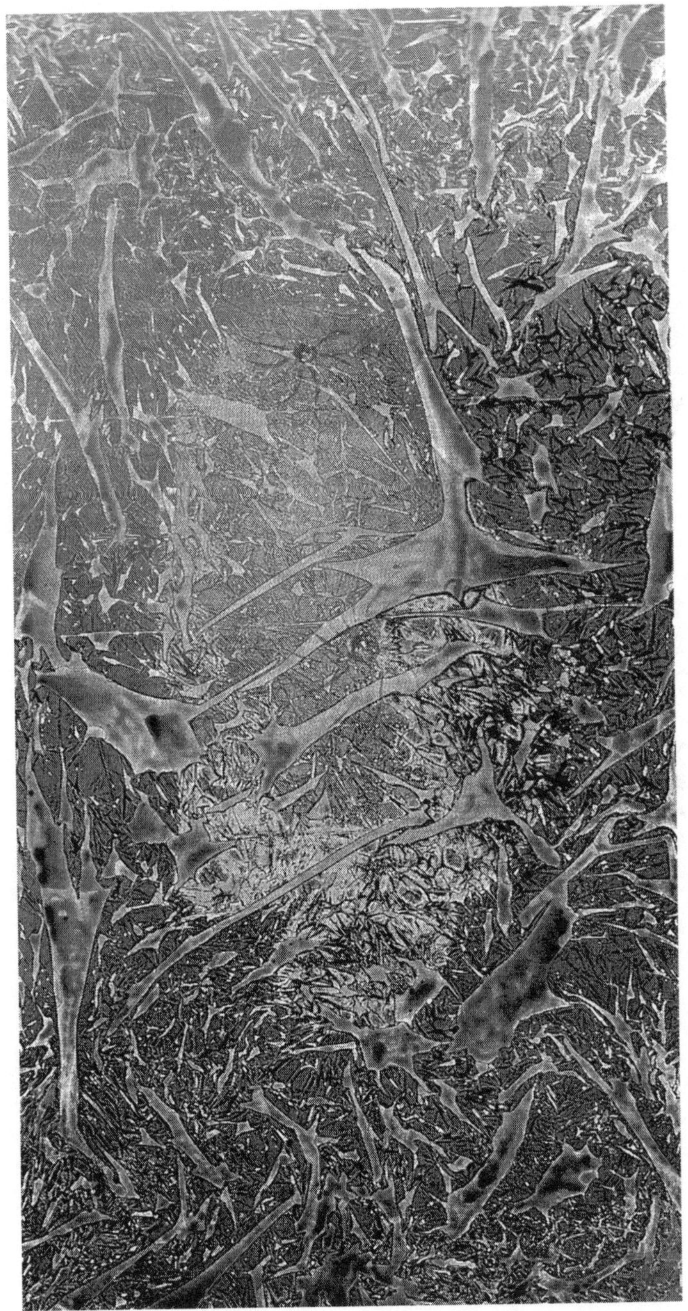

For all Futurism's multifarious contradictions and manifest machismo, these do not, Brezzi concludes, invalidate the quest by the women who adhered to it for a new identity, a new birth. It is not a coincidence, she states, that almost all these women adopted a pseudonym, thus signaling their intention to fashion their existence free of the traditional determinations of gender. Olga Biglieri, on becoming a Futurist painter, was born anew as Barbara. The artist would be reborn again, though, several decades later through her involvement with feminism—with Barbara then becoming, she claims, integrally herself. Such a reconciliation of woman and artist might just qualify as what Irigaray would name "self-affection."[8] Be this as it may, the encounter with Luce—their "noetic dance"—is the post-Futurism future embraced by Barbara in the 1980s. It is to this encounter that Brezzi turns in the chapter that follows.

Intertwinements of Pictorial Research and Speculative Effort: The Noetic Dance Between Barbara and Luce

We are unable to continue tracing the complex weave of Barbara's life any further, but we would like to highlight the way in which the theme of intertwined art and life reappears in the second part of her life, where, with a greater self-awareness perhaps, it takes the form of a harmonious cross-fertilization between individual research and intense, absorbing feminist engagement.[9] The conflict between being a woman and being an artist then morphs into a different type of union of art and life, which is to be sought above all by freeing human beings from society's spiritual and social conditioning and pursued by fighting against all forms of alienation. "And for me, as a woman, this means fighting for liberation from the specific social and cultural subalternity that male society has imposed on the other half of the human race" (Biglieri Scurto 1998).[10]

We propose, therefore, to focus on what we consider the core of the pictorial activity of an artist who, born with Futurism, was to arrive at far distant shores. We start with the placental period, followed by that of noetic creation, both of which are underpinned by a theoretical elaboration that is traceable to and closely intertwined with a philosophical reflection under the rubric of "woman." Here, as earlier, it is not the aesthetic aspect of Barbara's work that will concern us, but rather, by way of the author's own words, the reasons, the content, and the underlying symbolic imaginary of her endeavor.

The series of paintings Barbara defined as *placental* represent in a certain sense the preparation for the noetic period, which blossomed immediately thereafter. Significantly, the first series, dating from the years 1979 to 1981, was created after the death of her mother, at the same time as the issue of abortion was being debated in Italy.[11] If what these paintings expressed on a rational level was a journey related to womanhood, and thus to sexual difference, which is to say the journey of giving birth, on a symbolic level "they were inextricably linked to my relationship with my mother: indeed to a dramatic moment in that relationship, . . . to the intimate, mysterious, poignant bonds that bind a daughter to her mother" since "my mother's death touched me to the quick, viscerally calling into question my roots and my deepest affective ties" (Biglieri Scurto 1998, 314 and 312). It was while she was busy closing up and emptying her mother's old home, a place full of memories, that Barbara happened, almost inadvertently, to trace a few colorful strokes with poster paint once belonging to her daughters: "and it was from those colors that my hand and my brush gave shape to the first placenta, visualizing both the great promise and the drama of femininity, in which life is generated in the knowledge that it is destined to die" (312).

At the Venice Women's Festival held in July, Barbara no longer exhibited "old Futurist stuff" but the fruits of her most recent research: "with those two placentas I was really exposing my entrails, the most intimate and painful layer of myself, of my life. . . . This flurry of works, playing on different color ranges (from black to bright red, green and yellow ocher), immediately attracted attention. They were all variations on the same theme: the emergence of one or more placentas, amoebic and diaphanous in form, from a seething liquid mass, . . . each placenta was 'pregnant,' it held within itself the germs of a new life represented as elemental, fringed, almost flower-like corpuscles" (Biglieri Scurto 1998, 357; 2001, 76).

Yet, the paintings were also, as Barbara herself declared with her usual verve, the expression of an imaginary that no male could understand, and she was to speak more insistently from then on of a women's painting that had to come into being. Indeed, it was in these terms that Barbara, on returning to painting after years of silence, characterized what she had set as her goal, in speaking in the first person: "I wanted to express myself, to draw out of myself sensations that words could not contain. I substituted heart for words" (Biglieri Scurto 2001, 15). The placental paintings sought to express the dual, biological and historical, roots of female specificity, but not that alone. They also sought to make manifest that the imaginary, emotions, and personal sentiment, in their intertwining with conceptual research, are all part of artistic production, which comprises in this way a new relationship between subjectivity, idea, and reality. "The placental," Barbara further states, "exalts the fulcrum of woman's body, the envelope of biological creativity. Seeing with imagination to find the divine, illustrating it with colors and marking new life with the imprint of a flower . . . here the aim of the research is to discover the joy, the pain, the acceptance surrounding the nuclei of new lives. The magical body of the woman is probed internally, in its most secret and precious part" (76).

How far we have come from Futurism's gloomy and fanatical thought on motherhood! Barbara in her autobiography, moreover, views her adherence to Futurism as an incomplete path, interrupted by necessity; the numerous women artists having embarked on this path had failed to affirm their feminine specificity and, despite appearances, had continued to equate diversity with inferiority. "For years and years, I had considered my Futurist episode as simply a glorious season of my life. And it wasn't until I undertook the journey of self-awareness with other women in recent years that I faced up to reality, recognizing in that 'glory' signs of my dependence and my self-denial as a woman" (Biglieri Scurto 1998, 317–318).

The artist's thinking on female specificity in art and culture was to attain its acme in these moments, without being detached, however, from the concrete, whirlwind activity that allowed her to engage on new paths—the fertility of which she attributed to the continual interaction, communication, and striving with other women. Later, she would emphatically insist, in various public interventions, on the way forward for women artists who would until now—minoritized and obscure presences—have disavowed themselves as women, perpetuating thereby their subordinate condition "by letting themselves be dispossessed of liberating fecundity, de-sexualizing themselves in their own art, [and] losing all sense of value as a woman": all concepts Barbara herself had mastered at great cost.

We shall soon consider her relationship with the important philosopher Luce Irigaray, but I would first like, for my part, to situate this period during which Barbara's feminist reflections already impact, consciously or not, her lived experience and her painting as preparing the way for that ideal encounter.

The connection between the two can be made if we take into consideration that Irigaray, in *Je, Tu, Nous: Toward a Culture of Difference*, outlines a "placental relation" in which she focuses on the felicitous complexity characterizing the body: on the one hand, the essential physical imprint, the relationship with the material processes of biology, and on the other hand, the symbolic, cultural-spiritual element (JTN, 39).[12] Feminism itself highlighted this complexity (and it was the first theoretical movement to do so), reflecting on the profound issues implicit in the ambiguities of the body and of life—birth, death, illness—which themselves derive from these two roots. Both body and life are, that is, related to material biological processes and inscribed, at the same time, in cultural developments.

Let us examine this in more detail. Feminism, as well as contemporary reflection as a whole, has addressed the question of life and birth with reference to the psychophysical connection. Edmund Husserl spoke, as is well known, of *Leib* (own or living body), and his most brilliant pupil, Edith Stein, was to grasp in the dynamic development of the body the progression of the lives of living beings, from plants to animals to humans, the latter being composed of soul or psyche (*Seele*), spirit (*Geist*), and body (*Leib*). From the foundation of lived experience, it is possible to proceed to an understanding of human complexity and from there to venture on the paths of ethics and, perhaps, religious experience.

The danger exists, as the scholar Barbara Duden[13] has recently highlighted, of thinking the genesis of the human being without reference to the female body, that is, the mother, such that the maternal body would become, as it were, transparent. Irigaray contributes to countering this danger, as do other female thinkers (including some theologians) in that they all deem it imperative in their work—reflected, in my opinion, in Barbara's placental paintings—to investigate woman's specificity. Taking female corporeality into consideration entails an awareness of woman's being potentially two and, as such, her having always been in relationship. This awareness must become the common heritage of men and women, as many philosophers (Emmanuel Lévinas and Paul Ricoeur, among others) have shown, since life is bound, through the body, to the insubstituable materiality of the individual, to her or his joys and sorrows, and this will allow the introduction of a disruptive, inevitably *critical* element within the aseptic incorporeality that—paradoxically—surrounds us with the development of modern technologies. Women's being as the potentiality of duality, as recognition of, or passion for, the other, as life that thus becomes living and spiritual flesh, and consequently ineradicable relationality: "this stage," maintains Irigaray, "is not just necessary for their [women's] divine becoming, but also for that of men" (AB, 151).

Irigaray identifies in respiration, understood as breathing, breath, spirit (*ruah*), the sign of new life: breathing is the first autonomous gesture of the living; for women, therefore, it is the cipher of their being born to themselves, through which they can access the spiritual, discover an incarnation of their own. "The feminine breath seems at once more linked with the life of the universe and more interior. It seems to unite the subtlest real of the cosmos with the deepest spiritual real of the soul" (KW, 166).

Unlike relationships derived from the Darwinian model of living to survive, and thus living "against others," or from the Pavlovian model of mechanical repetition, of "acting alike," which are subject to static social rules, the bond between mother and child is the mark of a relationship that is not fusional but respects the life of both. The placenta is tissue connected to, yet separate from, the uterus and while formed by the embryo, it is nonetheless quasi-independent of this. It plays a mediating role between the two bodies at both the spatial level and the level of relational exchange between different organisms: the fetus grows, but the mother is not depleted; hence, the relationship between the two living beings, mediated by the placenta, cannot be ascribed to mechanisms of either assimilation or aggression.

Biological reality proves to be articulated and meaningful because it permits peaceful and respectful coexistence. The mother seems to know that the embryo is other than herself, and she accepts it as such; hence, as Irigaray underlines, the exemplary, almost ethical character of her relationship to the fetus as the recognition of otherness (JTN, 41). Instead of perceiving the new life as an invasion, the woman reshapes the boundaries of her body and mind, her perception of herself and the other. This, however, does not happen naturally or passively but constitutes a crisis in the woman's existence, in her body, her psyche, and conceptual elaboration; existing equilibria are thrown into disarray and gradually revised and readjusted, which might well give rise to new questions for philosophical and theological reflection.[14]

Barbara's words ring out: "The placental exalts the fulcrum of woman's body, the envelope of biological creativity. Seeing with imagination to find the divine, illustrating it with colors and marking new life with the imprint of a flower" (Biglieri Scurto 2001, 76).

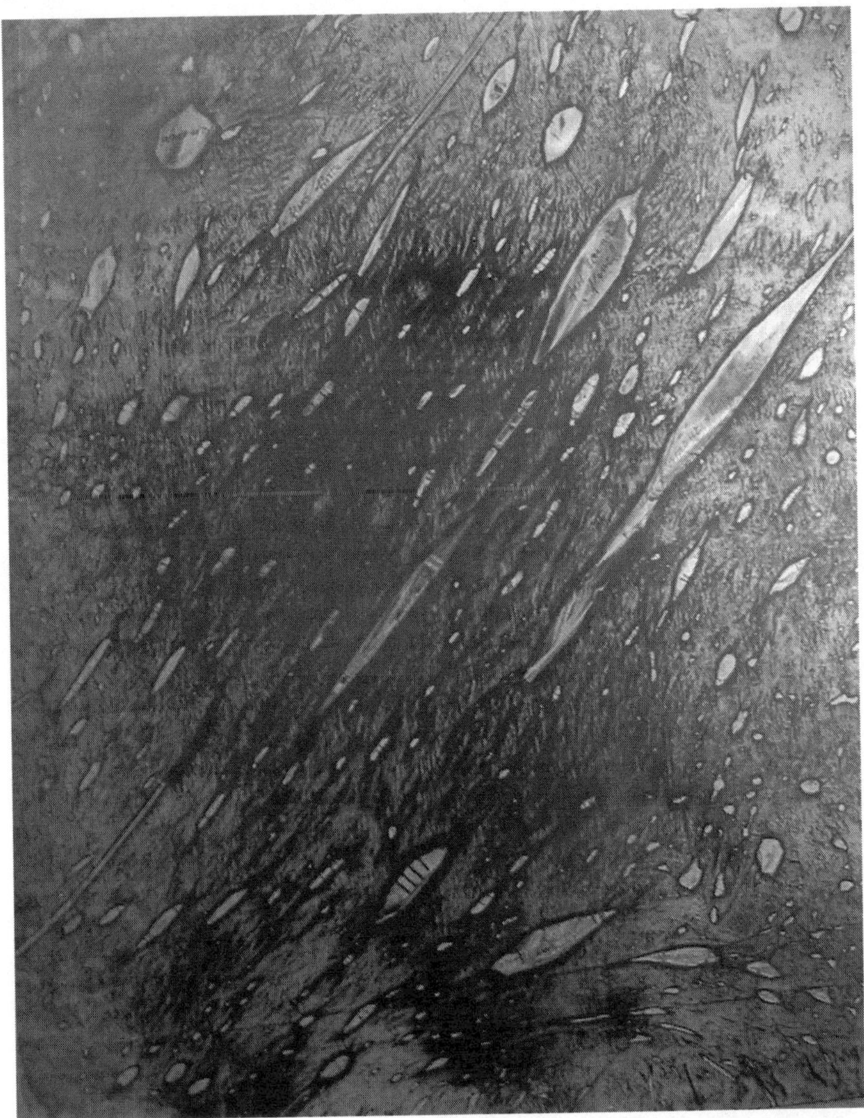

Figure 10.3. Barbara, *Noetico*, 1982–1983, acrylic on rhodoid. *Source*: Courtesy of Mimesis Edizioni. Used with permission.

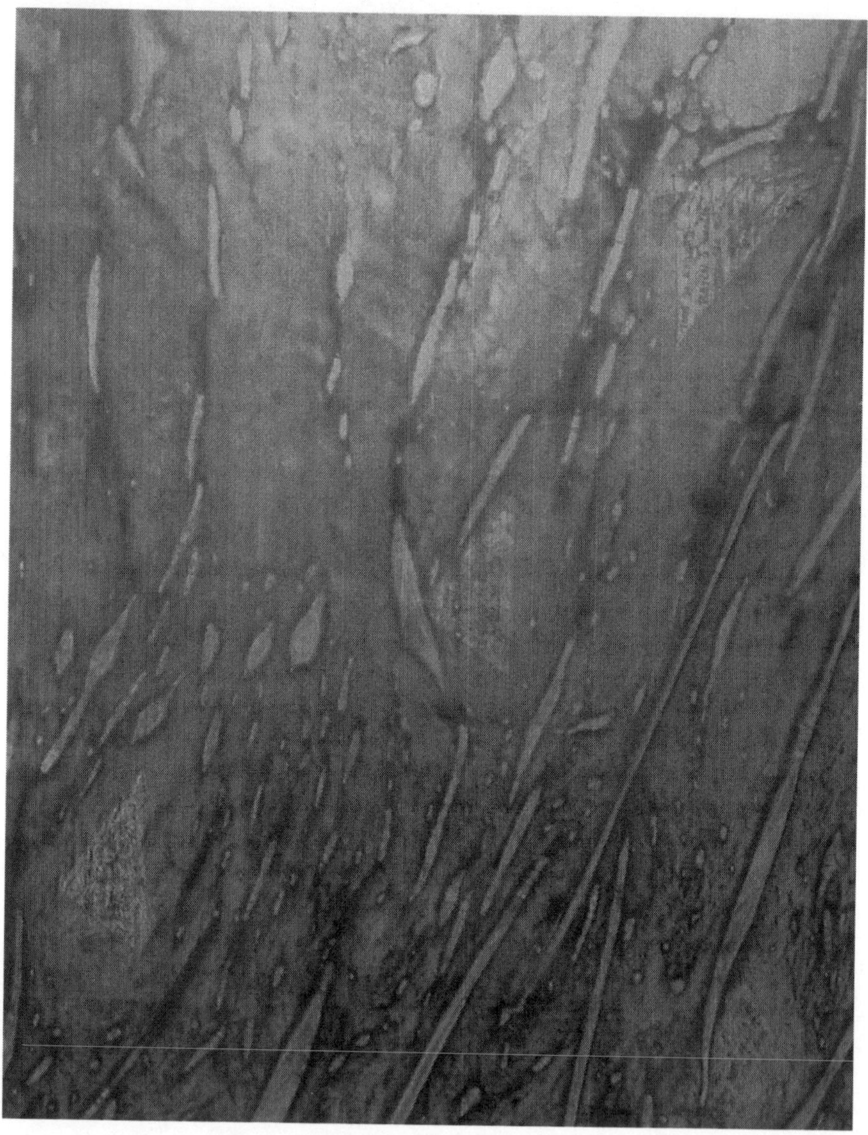

A Grand Noetic Dance Between
Barbara and Luce, An Infinite Dance

The noetic paintings are, as mentioned, the culmination of this line of thought, which Barbara continued to express in close association with other women as well as in her newly discovered empathetic affinity with the writings of the philosopher Luce Irigaray.[15]

This multifaceted association was significant and singular from its very inception: from exchanges, meetings, discussions, and dialogues among women artists, "little by little we found ourselves becoming a 'we.' And we gave ourselves direction, a project . . . and this melding was one of the qualities that made those meetings rare and splendid" (Biglieri Scurto 1998, 360).[16] They immediately became aware that theirs was a new path, perhaps a journey, or further still, a struggle against consolidated resistance necessary to wage if they were to embark on this adventure. Free from ideological affiliations (we shall discuss later the rejection of memory), these "piratical" or "undisciplined" women (according to the categories proposed initially) grasped the importance of this experimentation through which they sought something akin to a *new birth*—a theme equally common to the female Futurists. Barbara defines herself more than once, after all, as "being born of herself" (Biglieri Scurto 2001, 29).

Such then are the motivations, while the content strikes one as remarkable: the elaboration of a women's painting, which the term *noetic* summarizes with deliberate hermetism; "woman's route to creative expression, to art, is not technical or rationalistic; it does not arise from abstract and well-organized thought . . . ; woman reunites mind and body, art and life, thought and action. She moves forward through intuitive knowledge, precisely through *noesis*" (Biglieri Scurto 1998, 360).

Readings from the past, such as Bachofen's *Mother Right* or Greek myths, with their rich cortege of female figures—analyzed so acutely by Vernant, for example—formed the backdrop against which the inception of an era of "woman art" could be substantiated: "painting, sculpture, poetry, music, literature by women with women" (Biglieri Scurto 1998, 360). It was the encounter with a text, though, by Irigaray, *Elemental Passions*, that was to be of paramount importance for Barbara and her personal trajectory: "It was love at first sight: that book, imbued with a sexuality conceived and lived in the feminine, full of poetry and warmth, evolved, in a truly astonishing manner, on the same wavelength as my, as our, noetic research" (360). Barbara, as she herself recognizes, was "transported" by Irigaray's text: "I didn't simply read the book: I entered into a mysterious harmony with Luce, with her experience, her thought . . . ; between her words-thought-life and my painting-thought-life, a truly fruitful union came to be created. And so these words entered into my paintings; they themselves became sign and color" (370). A fundamental harmony, born of the meeting of two female emotions, in the merging of pictorial research and speculative effort—such was the impression felt by the artist.

What we propose, then, is to read some of Irigaray's texts[17] in parallel with Barbara's paintings so as to grasp the extraordinary correspondences between them or, rather, to highlight how a possible illustration of the theses of one can be found in the work of the other.

It is well known that Irigaray is today one of the most authoritative representatives of the thought of sexual difference, that strand of contemporary philosophy conscious of the downfall of systematic philosophies and witness to the collapse of "worldviews"—a collapse it would, in a certain sense, have provoked by its rejection in a time of crisis such as ours of universal knowledge and, in particular, of reason itself, the very instrument of the latter. It has opened a new avenue, initiated yet another journey, and brings to fruition that "thinking without a banister" advanced by Hannah Arendt, which is to say, the critique of the Western *ratio* that, although portrayed as neutral and universal speculation, is, in fact, masculine. Countering the totalitarian and unifying *logos*, a fragmentary, restless reason has gained ground, stuttering, critical, and discontinuous, long relegated to silence or to the hidden folds of knowledge but present in myth, metaphor, and artistic imagination. This is a reason that speaks of women and poses disturbing questions, a reason engaging with a range of contexts, from the speculative to the ethical, from political thought to religious reflection, and, in our case, with art.

The style in which Irigaray tackles these themes is unconventional, replete with such weighty philosophical questions as: Where do we come from? To whom are we speaking? Who am I? Who are you? And finally, How can the subject find herself when she is an expatriate in the context of discourse (ESD, 74)? To which we must add, because they are the same questions as Barbara's: How do you speak of the other without submitting to the one since the feminine has not yet given itself a language, despite its being a reserve of meaning and the madness of discourse?

Irigaray seeks to dig deeply into the history of philosophy, just as Barbara retraced the history of art. Both came to recognize the sexed nature of so-called neutrality, which, under the guise of a universal, conceals the arbitrary "a priori" assumption—and fundamental blind spot—that the male perspective is representative of humankind. Irigaray's diagnosis is concise and radical: "We can assume that any theory of the subject has always been appropriated by the 'masculine.' When she submits to (such a) theory, woman . . . subjects herself to objectification in discourse—by being female. Re-objectivizing her own self whenever she claims to identify herself 'as' a masculine subject" (S, 137).

In much the same way, Barbara, as we have seen, was convinced that the marginalization of women in art must end because the assumption that led to it is unacceptable: "for a long time the diversity between the sexes has been thought as our inferiority . . . , in the field of visual arts this position has led to women (considered instinctive and irrational) being judged as capable of merely a simplistic, decorative creativity that is in no way comparable to the aesthetic genius of the male, the creator and coordinator of beauty" (Biglieri Scurto 1998, 315).

Both repeat with conviction that it is naïve not to recognize the great "forgetting" of the feminine wrought in favor of masculine truth. This is the visible dimension of the "truth of the one"—the logic of identity that condemns any attempt to change this monadic, compact construction as subversive and disruptive, ultimately marginalizing any difference as deviant behavior. Irigaray considers this construction to have begun with Plato, from whom the entire Western tradition has inherited a kind of eidetic architecture as the operational structure of truth: the universal dominates and subjugates every singular approach, which is only acceptable if it can be traced back to a general concept; the categorial discursive guides and nullifies the sensible immediate; when not abolished, "nature" and the body are forgotten.[18]

Fearful of any fluidity, of any unmeasurable nondifferentiation, the *logos* has come to enclose itself in this progressive crystallization. Not only that, but the empire of the solid has also taken hold of the human sciences, for instance of psychoanalysis, which remains imprisoned in classical rationalism: an "interpretive model for the already past, psychoanalysis refuses to listen to what, in that past, was not yet able to speak" (SN, 234).[19]

Barbara, in turn, stresses the consequences of this privileging of the solid in art and concurs with Irigaray on the need for a fluid expansion: "I was flabbergasted: this fluid, manifold and infinitely open expansion was the same as that I was looking for at that time in my rhodoidal paintings" (Biglieri Scurto 1998, 371).[20]

Having grasped the original flaw, Irigaray ponders: What truth, what enigmatic word will emerge then, if there is a meaning beyond identity? A revolution in thought is needed, a new creativity and new poetics that will shake up that which is ostensibly secure and fixed, to make room not only for an innovative way of speaking or a women's language but also a different way of thinking.

The awareness of setting out on a difficult terrain is patent, there being no possibility of making use of that which is already given and known. This is not an easy undertaking: what one has to do, as a result, is lift that sort of veil of Maya that masks reality, or rather, in keeping with Irigaray's invitation, one must "cross back through the mirror" (*speculum*) that subtends all speculation, a blind mirror that conceals and in which differences and contradictions have so far been nullified, in order to make the repressed reappear, thus allowing women to rediscover the place of their self-affection.

When will we see the dawn of a new way of speaking? Both authors ask this in different ways. When women work toward *assuming the word*, a unique and irreplaceable word that arises, unlike the abstract *logos*, from lived experience and is rooted in the carnal, concrete, and corporeal existence of this world, having thus left the solitude of unitary reason—and the motif of resemanticizing the body returns. Irigaray defines this *novum* as ethics versus ontology, an ethics that will determine different relationships between subjects and between the subject and the world (ESD, 5). Barbara, for her part, identifies, as we shall see, noetic painting as painting that changes all memory.

More particularly, the harmony between Barbara and Irigaray originates precisely in the characterization of the female subject as an identity consisting not only of *logos* but also of "primal" categories—passions such as wonder, desire, the caress—which represent the fundamental stages of this journey of identity. To counter the Platonism of our metaphysical tradition, it is essential to recover the vital sap that circulates in the veins of men and women, essential to recover what the early philosophers and ancient sages understood and accepted naturally: the indivisibility of body and reason—whose splitting threatens thought. Barbara echoes the words of Irigaray when she emphasizes that women's contribution to art is situated "at a crucial point for the development of humanity: biological reproduction and its daily conditions, sexuality and affectivity, the relationship between the personal and the political . . . it is the great theme of subjectivity, of the concrete development of human faculties" (Biglieri Scurto 1998, 315).

The ultimate goal, according to the philosopher, is the establishment of an ethics that, by setting as its cornerstone the hitherto always repressed, suffocated, and unexpressed passions, will represent a new ethics, the ethics of sexual difference, and a new religion—outlined by Irigaray with bold, suggestive, and sumptuous metaphors. The passions must be returned to their proper place, between man and woman: "into this place came attraction, greed, possession, consummation, disgust, and so on. Not that wonder which beholds what it sees always as if for the first time, never taking hold of the other as its object. It does not try to seize, possess, or reduce this object, but leaves it subjective, still free" (ESD, 13).

Barbara keenly grasps the resignifications of meaning that derive from this progressive immersion in the uncharted terrain of the passions: *desire*, *wonder*, the *caress* are paradigmatic expressions of difference, at once a place of interval and the sign of a new alliance. Indeed, desire, in contrast to knowledge that assimilates, expresses the path toward the other, and the richness this entails can be seen more clearly by associating it with wonder, the first of all the passions according to Descartes, which is born from astonishment (as is philosophy), from the unprecedented or the novel, and which initiates movement. Avoiding any identification, this passion opens toward a "where," toward an unknown land, into which expedience and interest do not enter; rather, it is a place of freedom between the subject and the world.

Wonder—attracting me toward—is bereavement for the self as an autarchic entity and the advent of the other, the beginning of a new history, marked by the question, "Who art thou? I am and I become thanks to this question. Wonder goes beyond that which is or is not suitable for us" (ESD, 74).[21] An even more profound way to describe wonder, counter to a certain common cerebralism, is as a third dimension (such as an artistic experience can be), which leaves the path open between the physical and the metaphysical, between the empirical and the transcendental, between heaven and earth. Wonder, then, appears as a kind of contemplative illumination (and the reference to the classic terms of mystical vision is strong) arising from the amazement experienced before objects that are rare, extraordinary, and different: "The passion that inaugurates love and art. And thought. Is it the place of man's second birth? And of woman's? A birth into a transcendence, that of the other, still in the world of the senses ('sensible'), still physical and carnal, and already spiritual" (ESD, 81–82).[22]

The last of the original categories of ethics taken up by the philosopher is the caress, also considered a preliminary gesture and one that avoids assimilation and respects differences.[23] If at first glance a correlate does not seem to present itself in Barbara's paintings, upon closer examination we are inclined to associate the caress with the Tree of Peace that we referred to earlier as a significant paradigm of the *union of body and language* in which the handprints express the desire for peace.[24] Barbara herself underlines the great emotion that the work sought to communicate: "that long and slender plant formed by the union of many hands having chosen and supported universal pacifist thought" (Biglieri Scurto 1998, 384). Moreover, for Irigaray, the caress is also *remembrance of the other* and therefore ethical fidelity, *waiting* and *hope*, and the thinker underscores the evanescence of the caress as opening up a *future* that grants access to the mystery of the other—all terms more or less consciously present in Barbara's commitment to the Tree of Peace.

Finally, while for her part Irigaray adds that in the caress lovers are "like sculptors (as Barbara will be) who are going to introduce themselves, entrust themselves to one another for a new delivery into the world" (ESD, 193), the painter equally finds her placental theme in the pages of the French philosopher and declares in her turn: "we are placental, we share that unity of the first dwelling without having to tear it, cut it, divide it into pieces" (Biglieri Scurto 1998, 371; quoting EP, 67).

Let us return now to noetic painting to illustrate symptomatically its characteristics, again from a theoretical point of view: in November 1983 the artists drew up a *Noetic Manifesto* that was displayed in an exhibition-performance in which they publicly introduced themselves in Rome the following February, in the atypical venue of Cinecittà.[25]

The first line of the *Manifesto*, "the noetic determines a constitutive aspect of thought," succinctly expresses all that has just been elaborated in a decanted and purified manner, as shown by its resonance with the statements of Irigaray found above. But for clarification and elucidation, we can turn to Barbara herself, who specifies: "the rationality that dominates is not the only way to achieve thought or knowledge . . . not only is noesis, knowledge by means of the intuition, not inferior or less reliable, but it is the sole capable of giving us full knowledge, a knowledge that is able to grasp reality in all of its various dimensions: material, mental, spiritual" (Biglieri Scurto 1998, 366).

Yet one must read beyond the triumphal and sometimes didactic phrases of the *Manifesto* to appreciate the strength of the movement, which "dares that which has never been dared, opens not a new avenue but a new horizon in which women were alone able to move and express themselves freely." This knowledge allows women not only to speak in the first person but also to engage with their whole being given that the body is a compass, and it continuously creates and recreates: "a magical, sexed body, within which is concealed the secret of the generation of life. Not only generation of that specific dimension of life that consists in bringing children into the world, but cosmic generation. In this sense, ours is a total, spherical sexuality." And noesis, Barbara concludes, recalling Irigaray, is intuition, an enchanted, mad, and magical vision (Biglieri Scurto 1998, 361; 2001, 98).

Equally significant is the concept of the return of time: no longer the Bergsonian time, which had fascinated Barbara at the time of her participation in Futurism, but the "madness of the moment, where at every single instant all futures are possible." A time without memory, which represents baggage that is too heavy for women to bear, memory of bondage, dependency, marginalization, a time that rejects repetition but goes beyond this "to generate and regenerate thought, action and reality in their otherwise elusive fullness."

The Manifesto concludes thus "Snapshot of the moment—without memory. Madness of the moment—without memory. Multidirectional dimension—without memory. Different emotionality—without memory. Total spherical sexuality—without memory" (Biglieri,1998, 361).[26]

For the first exhibition in which the artists introduced themselves, Barbara composed an innovative work, entitled *Organ of Light and Color*, which she describes in detail: "Interactive mixed-media work; more sculpture than painting . . . five rhodoid tubes . . . expression of liquid, enveloping painting, offering intriguing transparencies" (Biglieri 1998, 365).[27]

In a subsequent exhibition in Brussels, Barbara enhanced her work to better express its mirroring the text by Irigaray referred to earlier—indeed, *Contact placental avec Luce* is the work's title—by inserting in the rhodoids small white fragments on which she wrote in black marker sentences taken from the philosopher's texts: "the game didn't consist in being able to read these sentences, which were nearly always immersed in liquid color. The game was completely symbolic: it was a grand noetic dance between Barbara and Luce; an infinite dance" (Biglieri 1998, 372).

Notes

1. I thank Rebecca Hill for her comments and suggestions concerning this text.

2. "Barbara" is, as we shall soon see, the artist name adopted by Olga Biglieri, who published her autobiography *Barbara dei colori* under her legal (married) name. All references to Barbara's autobiography will, therefore, take the form "Biglieri Scurto 1998" followed by the page or pages referred to.

3. Brezzi's monograph has not been published in English translation. Its title in Italian is *Quand il futurismo è donna. Barbara dei colori.*

4. "Barbara" and "barbarity" share, in fact, a common etymology, both being derived from the Greek βάρβαρος, "foreign, strange; ignorant," from the Proto-Indo-European root *barbar,* echoic of the unintelligible speech of foreigners. What determined, though, Olga Biglieri's choice of Barbara as her artist name was barbarity's being opposed to gracefulness and affectedness—qualities rejected by the Futurists as "passéist." Biglieri also liked the fact that Saint Barbara is the patron saint of firefighters. See Mirella Bentivoglio and Franca Zoccoli, *The Women Artists of Italian Futurism*, 190, note 41.

5. On the relationship between Futurism and Fascism, see Gunter Berghaus *Futurism and Politics* and "The Futurist Political Party;" Emily Braun, "Shock and Awe;" and Susan Thompson, "Futurism, Fascism, and Mino Somenzi's Journals of the 1930s."

6. This expression appears in Marinetti's *Manifesto of Futurism* of 1909. Here is the sentence in its entirety: "We intend to glorify war—the only hygiene of the world—militarism, patriotism, the destructive gesture of anarchists, beautiful ideas worth dying for, and contempt for women." In Rainey, Poggi et al., *Futurism: An Anthology*, 51.

7. In addition to the biographical details provided by Brezzi, the other sources on which I've drawn for this succinct overview of Barbara's life between the late 1930s and early 1960s are, essentially, the following:

https://vitaminevaganti.com/2022/01/08/olga-biglieri-barbara-dei-colori/

https://www.futurismo.org/barbara-olga-biglieri/

https://www.buongiornonovara.com/tutti-gli-artisti-che-vissero-ed-animarono-casa-bossi/

8. In an essay on two women artists, Irigaray defines self-affection in the following terms:

"Self-affection does not amount to a mere auto-eroticism or narcissism. It rather signifies a perception of one's whole being: as much body as spirit or soul, as much matter as language and forms, as much separate as being in relation. In self-affecting, both the way of perceiving and the 'object' of perception are specific to a masculine and a feminine subjectivity" (HM, 37–38).

That said, Barbara's insistence on the harmony she achieves as woman and artist is not, arguably, an insistence that Irigaray would echo given her commitment to a philosophy of sexual difference in which feminine subjectivity necessarily implies self-differing.

9. This chapter is a translation of chapters 3 and 4 of Francesca Brezzi's *Quando il futurismo è donna* (Mimesis Edizioni 2009). Chapter 3 of Brezzi's book is entitled "Woman's Magical Body: The Placental Paintings." Chapter 4's title, "A Grand Noetic Dance between Barbara and Luce, An Infinite Dance," figures in this translation as a section heading, thus marking the division of the two original chapters. The translation was undertaken by Edoardo Bellando and Tamara Lee and revised by Caroline Petricola, with a final revision done by Louise Burchill.—Editors' note.

10. Although Olga Biglieri adopted "Barbara" as her artist name, she published her autobiography *Barbara dei colori* under her legal (married) name. Henceforth, all references to "Barbara's" autobiography—which will be placed in-text—will, therefore, take the form "Biglieri Scurto 1998," followed by the page or pages referred to. That said, wherever it is evident that the autobiography is being cited, only the page reference will be given.—Editors' note.

11. Two referendums were held in 1981 on the recent law legalizing abortion, which had been adopted in 1978.—Editors' note.

12. I cannot dwell on the question I have addressed elsewhere and that can be formulated as follows: Could the placental relationship be used—as a metaphor—by extending it to the whole human context and to the finite-infinite relationship?

13. Barbara Duden has long devoted herself to a reflection on the history of the body. Let us recall simply her best-known and most recent works, such as *Der Frauenleib als öffentlicher Ort: Vom Mißbrauch des Begriffs Leben* (English translation: *Disembodying Women. Perspectives on Pregnancy and the Unborn*), and *Die Gene im Kopf—der Fötus im Bauch: Historisches zum Frauenkörper.*

[There also exists in English translation: *The Woman Beneath the Skin: A Doctor's Patients in Eighteenth-Century Germany*—Editors' note.]

14. Genevieve Vaugham's book *For-Giving: A Feminist Critique of Exchange* (1997) has interesting passages in which the author refers to what is known about the heart and the unimpeded circulation of blood between mother and child in the uterus as an example of a healthy society, of a life-giving partnership in which both hearts pump the same blood and nourishment is shared, life being transmitted freely in various forms from mother to child (chapter 19).

15. The heading of this section of the translation marks the beginning of chapter 4 of Brezzi's *Quando il futurismo è donna. Barbara dei colori*—Editors' note.

16. Again, significantly, "rarely, in my long experience, have I happened to encounter such a focusing of creative energies capable of melding, acting in unison. When we had finished and compared the notes that one or the other

of us had taken, it was almost impossible to distinguish where the thought of one ended and that of the other began" (Biglieri Scurto 1998, 360). The original group, which was later augmented by other women artists, consisted of Felicitas Nusselein, a Belgian painter transplanted to Italy; Loredana Baldin, a painter and jewelry designer; and, of course, Barbara.

17. The thought of Luce Irigaray is by now well known, and while we are unable to address it here with the thoroughness it merits, we hope to bring out its imbrication with Barbara's pictorial elaboration. Let us nevertheless recall, very succinctly, that Irigaray, setting off from a critique of the language and the methodology of science having created a domain without a subject, proposes to recover the forgotten subject—in this case, the feminine—from behind the theoretical *speculum* that has hidden it for millennia and within which differences have up to now been nullified. What Irigaray arrives at is a different way of saying, another language, substantiated by new or original categories that are the passions of the soul (see below). In limiting ourselves to the main works of the French philosopher related to our theme, we would mention, in addition to *Elemental Passions*, the texts *Speculum of the Other Woman, An Ethics of Sexual Difference, To Speak Is Never Neutral*, and *I Love to You: Sketch of a Possible Felicity in History.*

18. The subject of which science speaks stands before the world oblivious to its being also inside the world: "an encoding of the world from which subjectivity is removed, and which is subordinated, under cover of the universal, to one single subject, or to several subjects. No feelings apparently. . . . A language divested of all *pathos*, absolutely neutral and detached, is transmitted by someone to someone else, who has not acknowledged origin or source either" (SN, 1). This situation, encountered not only in the exact sciences, is more serious in the human sciences, such as psychology and psychoanalysis, which originated as sciences of the subject but have contributed instead to the loss of the subject by locking it up in a cage (Irigaray says a net), that of universality, thereby stripping it of its own identity and engulfing it in repetitive, neutral or dead formulas.

19. In addition: "(psychoanalysis) maintains, indeed confirms, man in his destiny, his perennial discourse. It does not go so far as to question the sexualization of discourse itself, of theory in general. It is a theory of sexuality that misses its own sexual determinations, and it remains naively metaphysical in that way. [. . .] It claims to be indifferent to sex: Truth" (SN, 230).

20. Just as pressing are the questions Irigaray addresses to philosophy: "Where and how does [nature] appear in the forms of discourse? What remainder of silence resists such formations? What does truth—or the *logos*—say or do about the sensible immediate?" (SN, 229; trans. modified).

21. "The other never suits us simply. We would in some way have reduced the other to ourselves if he or she suited us completely. An *excess* resists: the other's existence and becoming as a place that permits union and/through resistance to assimilation or reduction to sameness" (ESD, 74–75).

22. "It constitutes an *opening* prior to and following that which what surrounds, enlaces. . . . Outside of repetition. It is the passion of the first encounter. And of perpetual rebirth?" Later on Irigaray concludes about wonder: "A third dimension. An intermediary. Neither the one nor the other. Which is not to say neutral or neuter. The forgotten ground of our condition between mortal and immortal, men and gods, creatures and creators. In us and among us" (ESD, 82).

23. "Primary Eros, the caress comes to represent a new birth, for both the man and the woman: to her in fact, lover and not only loved one, is given a space of identity, a new incarnation, a becoming other with no return to self" (ESD, 197).

24. See The introduction we have provided to Francesca Brezzi's chapter, supra.—Editors' note.

25. It was a multimedia event, with the three signatory artists of the *Manifesto* being joined by a painter and poet, Rosanna Fiocchetto, who composed a poem for Barbara, a musician, Fiorella Petronici, and a dancer, Alma Falkenberg, all of whom performed during the exhibition. The critics neglected the event, with the exception of Claudia Salaris, whose review appeared in the journal *Rinascita*.

26. And again "the noetic wants to free expression from messages that try to push it in a single direction, in a horizontal economy that intentionally seeks to make creativity complicit with the system." Biglieri Scurto 2001, 99.

27. An interactive work in that the visitors could use a keyboard to turn the colors on and off.

References

Barbara dal futurismo al 2001. 2001. Centro Internazionale Antinoo per l'Arte, 2001. Catalogue of an exhibition of Barbara's works held in Rome, in April 2001.

Bentivoglio, Mirella, and Franca Zoccoli. 1997. *The Women Artists of Italian Futurism: Almost Lost to History*. Midmarch.

Berghaus, Gunter. 1996. *Futurism and Politics: Between Anarchist Rebellion and Fascist Reaction 1909–1944*. Berghahn Books.

Berghaus, Gunter. 2006. "The Futurist Political Party." In *The invention of Politics in the European Avant-Garde*, edited by Sacha Bru and Gunther Martens. Brill.

Biglieri Scurto, Olga (Barbara). 1998. *Barbara dei colori*. Centro Internazionale Antinoo per l'Arte.

Biglieri Scurto, Olga (Barbara). 2001. "Barbara parla di Barbara." In *Barbara dal futurismo al 2001*. Catalogue published on the occasion of the exhibition held in Rome in April 2001. Centro Internazionale Antinoo per l'Arte.

Bohn, Williard. 2004. *The Other Futurism: Futurist Activity in Venice, Padua and Verona*. University of Toronto Press.

Braun, Emily. 2014. "Shock and Awe: Futurist *Aeropittura* and the Theories of Giulio Douhet." In *Italian Futurism 1909–1944: Reconstructing the Universe*, edited by Vivien Green. Guggenheim Museum Publications.

Brezzi, Francesca. 2009. *Quand il futurismo è donna. Barbara dei colori*. Mimesis.

Duden, Barbara. 1991. *Der Frauenleib als öffentlicher Ort: Vom Mißbrauch des Begriffs Leben*. Luchterhand Literaturverlag.

Duden, Barbara. 1993. *Disembodying Women: Perspectives on Pregnancy and the Unborn*. Harvard University Press.

Duden, Barbara. 1998. *The Woman Beneath the Skin: A Doctor's Patients in Eighteenth-Century Germany*. Harvard University Press.

Duden, Barbara. 2002. *Die Gene im Kopf—der Fötus im Bauch: Historisches zum Frauenkörper*. Offizin.

Marinetti, Filippo Tommaso. (1909) 2009 "The Futurist Manifesto." In *Futurism: An Anthology*, edited by Lawrence Rainey, Christine Poggi and Laura Wittman. Yale University Press.

Thompson, Susan. 2014. "Futurism, Fascism, and Mino Somenzi's Journals of the 1930s: *Futurismo, Sant'Elia* and *Artecrazia*." In *Italian Futurism 1909–1944: Reconstructing the Universe*, edited by Vivien Green. Guggenheim Museum Publications.

Vaugham, Genevieve. 1997. *For-Giving: A Feminist Critique of Exchange*. Plain View Press.

Part Four

Sexuate Art in the Making

Figure 11.1. Jacqueline Taylor, *My Language is a Skin*, 2015, oil and acrylic on canvas. *Source*: Courtesy of the artist. Used with permission.

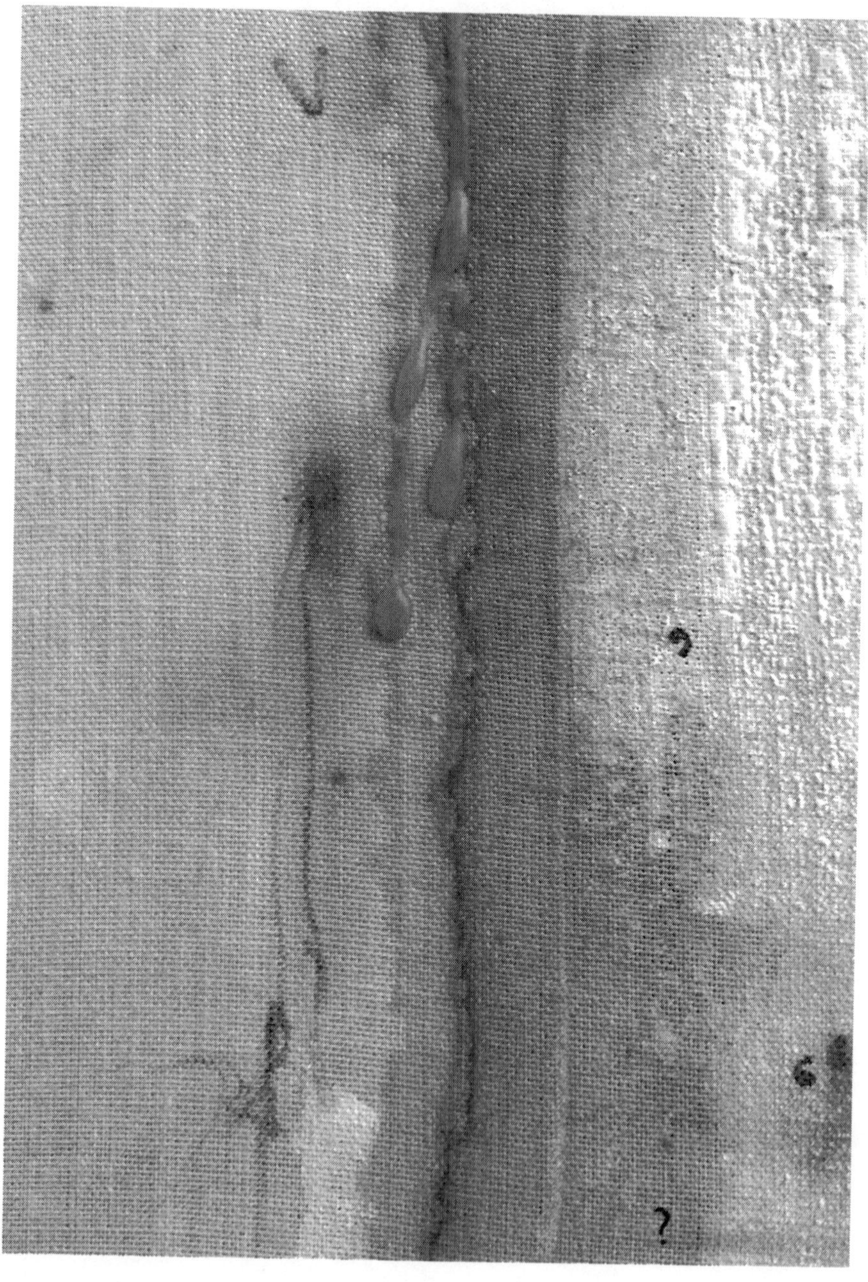

Chapter Eleven

Painterly Poetics and Difference in the Making

Jacqueline Taylor

The work of Luce Irigaray has proven instrumental in opening up possibilities for feminist and women artists from the 1970s onward. It has provided ways to articulate and visualize feminist issues and to critique power structures that marginalize women, be they social, cultural, political, visual, linguistic, or otherwise. Crucially, feminist art practice has provided a platform to problematize the status that Western art history accords to painting, understood as a socially constructed, masculinist discourse (Pollock 1988, 9). Indeed, as a historically privileged medium, painting's position within Western art history has depended on gendered power relations and patriarchal representational structures. These relations and structures have not only marginalized women artists from most art historical narratives but also reinforced women as passive objects under the "male gaze."[1] Irigaray's oeuvre is useful as it charts a critique of phallocentrism and patriarchal systems through the promotion of a "feminine" language counter to the veiled masculine bias (the nonneutrality, nonuniversality) of the existing economy of language.

Painting, like language, is heavily coded and conventionalized, subject to selective canons determined by, and reinvested in, social, political, and economic values (Deepwell 1994, 14). Historically, the canon of painting has established a "monocentric hegemony" centered on white male supremacy (Buchloch 1987, 66). As a voice for difference, painting can be recognized as "a gendered and an *en-gendering* discourse" (Pollock 1999, 26). While modernist art practice proclaimed itself avant-garde and in rupture with the Western tradition of representation, abstract painting emerged as the dominant paradigm of nineteenth and twentieth century art (Pollock 1988; Harrison and Wood 1993)[2] in part due to its framing by the critic Clement Greenberg. Renowned for its inflexibility, modernist abstraction has been described as "the most resistant and decisive discourse within modernism" (Kaneda 1991, 58) and as forming a critical orthodoxy centered on exclusion and privilege.[3]

As an artist concerned with articulating sexual difference and whose practice is engaged in abstract painting, I have inevitably been led to dialogue with and rethink the embedded conventions and hierarchies in painting and modernist abstraction. This has entailed thinking extensively about modalities of signification by the means of which one may articulate difference in nonrepresentational art practice. This chapter elaborates this dialogue in which, drawing on elements of Irigaray's thinking, I propose a poetic understanding of abstract painting that explores the ways that difference may be manifest through art-making processes. I refer to feminist and women artists as they have historically primarily engaged with Irigaray's thinking in artistic practice. However, this project is not feminist per se but rather seeks to open up sites of difference for marginalized subjectivities. While this discussion is rooted in painting and aesthetic practice, it is my hope that such a rethinking of representational structures is of interest to those across the many disciplines and discourses engaged with feminism and developing topologies of sexual difference.

The "Problem" of Painting

I will briefly consider some of the orthodoxies and conventions embedded in painting, foremost to provide a context for those unfamiliar with the discourse of modernist abstraction and Western art history and, secondly, because in a book focused on Irigaray's thought, the ways in which women and feminist artists have sought to reconceptualize these conventions and develop their own visual languages may have implications for others who share Irigaray's critique of dominant sociocultural structures.

Modernist abstraction's ideal of "medium specificity," as defined by critic Clement Greenberg, promoted nonrepresentational painting as superior to all other art forms. Said to be the autocratic voice of abstraction (Rosler 2006, 99), Greenberg's views became deeply entrenched across art practice, art criticism, curatorial practice, and visual culture, cementing abstraction as a hegemonic force. The purported superiority of abstract painting was said to lie in its medium specificity—its unique and pure essence of "flatness." This flatness referred to abstract painting's two-dimensionality, whereby entirely aesthetic values such as pure visuality and nontactility took precedence over any representational function in the artwork (Greenberg [1965] 2001, 755). Problematically, through its supposed purely aesthetic qualities, abstract painting was said to be asocial and apolitical, communicating nothing outside its specific materiality but instead functioning autonomously and transcendentally as an unmediated expression of the artist's psyche. However, while such work was theorized as disembodied, it was at the same time embodied via narratives that privileged terms traditionally associated with masculinity, such as "virile," "strong," "vigorous," and "assertive." In describing the artwork in these terms and championing selected male artists as "heroic" or "genius" representatives of creative identity, critics, curators, and artists established a criterion of greatness that was exclusively defined as white, heteronormative, and male, at the expense of female and other marginalized counterparts.

The iconic photographs by Hans Namuth of Jackson Pollock creating his drip paintings exemplify this assertive masculinity. The photographs emphasize the corporeal presence of Pollock's body and its traces, physically manifest on canvas, and in so doing affirm the active (male) artistic subject. This assertion of masculinity is enhanced by the presence of Pollock's wife Lee Krasner (an artist in her own right but largely omitted from contemporaneous art narratives), who often figured in the photographs as a passive viewer while Pollock actively assumed his role as "heroic" creator. Paradoxically, while Pollock's work was categorized as disembodied and devoid of any social or political meaning or subjectivity, it simultaneously implicitly coded the artist as (masculine) subject (Brennan 2004, 139). As a result, modernist abstraction and its conventions have been perceived as "masculine," "masculinist," "patriarchal," and "phallocentric" and subsequently positioned in opposition to feminist art practice. That abstraction should be deemed of little use for artists concerned with feminist politics of representation and signification is, to my mind, proof of the longstanding detriment wrought to painting's reputation by Greenberg's framing of modernist abstraction.

Alternative Visual Languages

Feminist art practice that engaged with Irigaray's thinking from the 1970s to 1990s has been pivotal in problematizing the masculinist presuppositions and hegemonic pretensions of modernist abstraction. For artists wishing to challenge these issues and develop alternative, feminine, painterly languages, Irigaray's notions of *parler femme* and the feminine imaginary offered a conceptualization of the tactility and materiality of writing wrought by, and through, a feminine subject that directly countered modernism's privileging of pure visuality and nontactility. In Irigaray's critique of the specular logic of patriarchy, whereby the feminine is unrepresentable and woman is caught up in and can only return as man's specularized other in patriarchal culture, artists were to find "the most powerful critique of the primacy of vision as a model for comprehending the female body" (Betterton 1996, 13). Indeed, Irigaray's critique of this patriarchal form of specularization challenged Western systems of representation and constructs of looking as phallocularcentric,[4] discerning conceptions of the female body and "being" throughout history to be the projection of male desires, such that "femininity" is a mirror image of the masculine, and the feminine subject is unrepresentable in Symbolic discourse. This radical reconceptualization of the visual thus provided a means for artists to rethink the pure visuality and singular authoritarian logic associated with modernist abstraction.

In a similar manner, Irigaray's *parler femme* promoted an alternative syntax appropriate to women as equal but different subjects (JTN, 13). The strategies developed by Irigaray—such as specularization and mimesis—made it possible to challenge the position attributed to "woman" and the "feminine" (qua the specularized site of male projections) within the symbolic order as a whole and, more specifically, within cultural and visual languages. For feminist artists, this enabled ways for the female body to be revisualized and reinserted into discourse as an active subject no longer fashioned by phallocentrism.

Although feminist art practice that engaged with Irigaray's ideas from the 1970s to 1990s offered multiple strategies for disrupting patriarchy, the medium of painting was seen as having little value and marginalized by feminist artists. Indeed, as Betterton states, "painting as a medium was rejected in favour of photo-text, performance and scripto-visual media" (1996, 10). Many feminist artists dismissed painting altogether, understanding it to uphold "the patriarchal reign of the painted masterpiece

[. . .] [as the] traditional medium of heroic self-expression" (Nochlin 2007, 49). Work such as Mary Kelly's iconic *Post-Partum Document*,[5] deploying text, photography, and material objects, including nappies soiled with fecal marks akin to the painterly gesture privileged in modernist abstraction, could be seen as a parodic rejection of painting itself. Such alternative media were considered more appropriate for feminist art practice precisely because they were not bound up with the tradition of painting as a privileged medium and its perceived masculinist and patriarchal conventions. In the (then contemporary) context of postmodern debate, there was, as such, a "problematic relationship between feminism and the practice of painting" (Lee 1987, 5).

There have been, and still are, notable painters engaged in feminism and the articulation of sexual difference. Such artists like Jenny Saville and Cynthia Mailman have, however, focused primarily on figurative (or partially figurative) strategies to raise sociopolitical questions about the female body through representational means. "[T]he images in a feminist painting have to be socially legible, that is, recognisable. Figurative," Marjorie Kramer was to argue, for example, disqualifying *any* possibility of a feminist abstract painting practice ([1971] 2001, 293). Moreover, this disqualification of abstract painting has been reiterated more recently, with Katy Deepwell focusing only on figuration as providing feminist possibilities in painting (2010, 156). In short, while feminist artists have drawn widely on Irigaray's ideas, they have rarely utilized the latter in relation to abstract painting. As Betterton notes: " 'Abstract' or 'non-representational' painting has been one of the most ignored areas of feminist intervention [. . .] decisively dismissed by a generation in the 1970s and [. . .] [largely] dismissed within feminist art practice ever since" (1996, 79).

On an artistic and theoretical level, I have always been drawn toward the aspects of Irigaray's work, along with those of Julia Kristeva, concerned with the nonrepresentational potential of "poetic" language, capable of conjointly articulating the "feminine" and challenging the Symbolic. It is precisely these aspects of Irigaray's thought that I contend are most suggestive of articulating sexual difference in abstract painting practice and of developing alternative modalities of signification not bound by the codes and conventions of modernist abstraction. This appreciation of Irigaray's thought was shared by other abstract painters, especially in the period from the 1970s to 1990s (for example, Rosa Lee, Eve Muske, and Beth Harland). Notably, such artists drew on textual qualities—such as heterogeneity, fluidity, plurality, and amorphousness—interpreted via readings of *parler femme* and the wider rubric of *l'écriture féminine* (which homogenized Irigaray, Cixous, and Kristeva's work on "feminine" language).

There are multiple manifestations of these textual qualities in Irigaray's writing, in her conceptualization of the feminine and her use of poetic language. For instance, in *This Sex Which Is Not One*, Irigaray writes: "Her sexuality, always at least double, goes even further: it is *plural* [. . .] *Woman has sex organs more or less everywhere*. She finds pleasure almost anywhere. [. . .] The geography of her pleasure is far more diversified, more multiple in its differences" (TS, 28; emphasis in original). Repeatedly referring to the qualities of plurality, multiplicity, and heterogeneity throughout her corpus, Irigaray often links these to those of excess, fluidity, materiality, tactility, boundlessness and flux in her theoretico-poetical explorations of autoeroticism and self-touching (TS, 30). Irigaray also emphasizes, in *Speculum of the Other Woman*, qualities of movement, rhythm, and volume when she notes that the feminine "has to be rethought in terms of curve(s), helix(es), diagonal(s), spiral(s), roll(s), twirl(s), revolution(s), pirouette(s). Speculation whirls around faster and faster as it pierces, bores, drills into a volume that is supposed to be *solid* still . . . whipped along, spinning, twirling faster and faster until matter shatters into pieces" (S, 238; emphasis in original). This particular passage enacts rhythmicity through a multiplicity of commas and the juxtaposition of short and long clauses. Irigaray incorporates an excess of verbal adjectives, each with multiple syllables that resonates with the "quickness" of the movement to which she refers. Similarly, her use of multiple parentheses visually and otherwise plays on the singular and plural to elicit the material dimensions of language. In this way, Irigaray also highlights the challenge presented to the fixity and linearity of patriarchal optics by the feminine and its gradations, curves, and "anexactitudes."

Qualities such as those discussed have been translated by feminist artists into abstract painting, forming a painterly language and aesthetic that utilizes flux, flow, plurality, and tactility in its form and materiality. Such "feminine" painting has been argued to be nonlinear, intuitive, and "structurally unprincipled" (Kaneda 1991, 63) in virtue of its being characterized by the incorporation of fragile elements such as swirls and the "abstract sexuality inherent in circles, domes, eggs, spheres and biomorphic shapes" (Heartney et al. 2007, 14).[6] As such, these painterly qualities pose a direct challenge to the "Masculine panoptics" of modernist abstraction (Kaneda 1991, 63), whose qualities are visually and conceptually defined as rigid, angular, geometric, objective, uniform, and controlled and whose harsh lines and angles have been labeled as "masculine" (Battersby 1995, 133). Furthermore, synesthetic qualities such as touch that Irigaray attributes to the feminine imaginary and the qualities of fluidity, mobility, and flux she associates with the prelinguistic drives are represented in artists' exploration of the material properties of paint as viscous, fluid, tactile, and overflowing. Strategies of embodiment have also been used to highlight equivalencies between the materiality of paint and painterly surfaces and the gendered corporeal "feminine" body. Such works refer to fleshy skin and often incorporate pinkish or pastel colors, evoking the feminine through formal properties (Betterton 1996, 96). This strategy can be seen in the work of Mira Schor and Laura Godfrey-Isaacs, for example, who often incorporate the fluid and oozing nature of paint into the painted surface in the ways Betterton describes above.

While the development of an alternative "feminine" visual language has indeed provided possibilities for articulating topologies of difference in abstract painting, this engagement is problematic and raises certain questions. Foremost, attempts to translate the textual qualities and thinking underpinning Irigaray's *parler femme* (and so-called *l'écriture féminine*) into paint and painting literally, metaphorically, formally, and visually have resulted in the feminine being reduced to a visual aesthetic. Moreover, this aesthetic is one that *represents* the feminine through nonrepresentational means. As well as risking essentialism and universalism, this paradox highlights that visual language is a very distinct signifying system to that of the textual. For example, modes of affect, sense, color, form, materiality, and composition are performed in writing in a very different way than they are in painting. This raises two questions: Can subjectivity be *represented* visually through nonrepresentational means and to what extent can we really *represent* subjectivity at all?

I would argue that such "translation" or interpretation has created a "feminine" aesthetic defined by visual characteristics that *represent* the feminine and sexual difference formally and visually but do not problematize phallocentrism on a deeper, structural level or consider the subject as in process relative to the complexities of art practice. Additionally, the development of a "feminine" painterly language has been positioned in opposition to the perceived "masculine" and "masculinist" conventions of modernist abstraction. A plethora of binary oppositions has resulted, which are presented as analogous both to "patriarchal/feminist" and the "masculine/feminine" dualistic relations identified by Irigaray as underpinning Western thought and its associated patriarchal power structures.

For example, the nontactility privileged in the dominant Greenbergian narrative of modernist abstraction has been set up in opposition to the tactility and haptic visuality celebrated in "feminine" painting, alongside binaries such as pure visuality/materiality, linearity/nonlinearity, rigidity/fluidity, homogeneity/heterogeneity, disembodiment/embodiment, singularity/multiplicity, and so on. While this oppositional strategy equally challenges modernist abstraction on a formal and visual level, it maintains binary thinking, therefore undermining Irigaray's goal to rewrite binary logic "*qua different*" (JTN, 13).

Difference in the Making: Space-Time Poetics

Artists' engagement with Irigaray's work has, as just seen, been explored in visual and formal terms. Yet, the materiality of an artwork is a vital epistemological dimension of art practice and aesthetic experience that can be transformative for the subject (Barrett 2013). As an artist engaged with painting, I am invariably interested in the materiality of paint; however, my exploration of difference also extends to the materialities of the self, language, and knowledge. With respect to the relation between such materialities and the *process* of making, I have found Irigaray and Kristeva to be of vital resource for considering artmaking and encountering art as a generative site of material subjectivity. For much of the Western philosophical tradition, the nonrepresentational is akin to the sense*less*; there is no meaning or signification to be given to what is beyond the communicative and representative functions of discourse. I would argue, however, that the affective dimension of aesthetic practice, encompassing materiality and process *in addition to* the visual, is also a vector of meaning—one that can allow us to make sense of difference via nonrepresentational means. I conceive of this as "difference in the making." What I call a "poetic understanding" of abstract painting presupposes a crucial shift away from *representing* the feminine in abstract painting toward difference as *becoming*, manifested through the processes of making.

Such a poetics of abstract painting and difference in the making is grounded in Irigaray's reformulation of space-time relations. The traditional Western conceptions of time as referring to the interiority of the subject (historically referenced as "masculine") and space as referring to the subject's exteriority (historically referenced as "feminine") maintain, Irigaray contends, the world's ordering (ESD, 7). In painting, time and space are similarly often correlated with interiority and exteriority. Time is bound up with art-making processes interior to the subject, thereby becoming a privileged sphere of the artistic creator, while space is the realm external to the subject in which the artwork is encountered.

In respect of the categories of space-time, the subject and discourse, Irigaray calls for the creation of a "new poetics" (ESD, 5). Her metaphor of the speculum, for instance, promotes a different space-time and subjectivity. Whereas the Lacanian mirror is flattening with no perspectival space and constructs the self as a unitary subject through reduction, the curved mirror of the speculum allows for a voluminous and multidimensional reality with a rounded view of space-time relations where points merge and blur. The conception of the subject in this spatiotemporal multidimensionality is highlighted in "Volume-Fluidity" in *Speculum* as follows: "woman is neither open nor closed. She is indefinite, in-finite, form is never complete in her. This incompleteness allows her continually to become something else within an extension swelling outward without discernible limits" (S, 229). To this Irigaray adds that the "feminine" occurs as a shapeless flux that can never be fixed or gathered into one space but exists as volume imbued with fluidity—a circularity of movement looping back upon itself (S, 230–240). This stress on the dynamic fluidity of space-time is equally found in her characterization of the interval as an *in-between*, or passage between pairs of opposites, that is never fixed but ever changing.

In abstract painting, "spatiality" usually designates, visually and formally, space *in* painting and painting *as* space. Attempts to develop an alternative "feminine" painterly language have, as a result, focused on rendering space in conformity with what might be called a "female" optics. For example, the abstract painting of Kay Sage has been argued to visually signify the feminine through qualities such as swirls (Battersby 1995, 133). Other artists such as Katharine Grosse have sought to create an alternative spatiality by literally expanding the painting surface, as with work painted directly onto architectural elements that envelop the viewer, thus directly challenging the pure visuality and nontactility associated with modernist abstraction. Similarly, artists such as Angela de la Cruz have physically and formally ruptured the conventions of modernist abstraction in their attempt to create a feminist space of painting. In de la Cruz's case, this has involved dismantling the structure of the canvas frame to transform the painting from a two-dimensional representation into a three-dimensional object. Such practices conceptualize abstract painting as an-*other* practice—a practice or model of painting existing in addition to, and thus separate from, conventional practices. In this sense, while de la Cruz's work exists in a particular physical space denoted by temporal and historical markers, her paintings are situated in a "feminist space" distinct from the historical (patriarchal) space of modernist abstraction. Arguably, the space in which de la Cruz's work exists, along with that of Sage and other alternative "feminine" abstract painters, is a "feminine" space, "othered" from the "masculine" space of abstraction.

Theorizing "feminist" and "feminine" practices as separate (from the masculine) and in opposition to modernist abstraction yet again adheres, however, to a binary structure. While contemporary abstract painting has evolved, the binary conventions inherent in modernist abstraction lurk within and beneath its structures and thus still need to be renegotiated. As art critic Barry Schwabsky notes in acknowledgement to such renegotiation, painters today are "conscious of their production as sharing in an array of practices and conventions with deep roots in history" (2011, 11). I propose that the very entity of abstract painting be reconceptualized as a heterogeneous and multidimensional spatiality in which modernist abstraction has its roots and of which it is an intrinsic part. Modernist abstraction (as a historical project) and abstract painting are not, therefore, in opposition with one another—they are not separate entities—but they do not comprise a singular reality. Rather, they take the form of an infinite and continuous multiplicity always in a state of becoming and renewal. This spatiality is unfixed, shifting, and expanding, characterized by mobility and flux in its internal structure. This resonates with Irigaray's notion of space and time, where she refers to "an other topo-(logy) of jouissance, always already in a state of anamorphosis and an excess never defined" (S, 230).

The binary thinking and conventions of modernist abstraction are continually renegotiated within this prismatic and infinitely mobile space. Indeed, reconceptualizing painting as such a multiplicity enables an opening up, or unfolding, of binary oppositions and conventions. Painting's spatiality could, then, be said to be the place of *terrains vagues*, vague but not vacant areas of liquidity and ambiguity amid oppositions (Schor 1997, 155). This brings to mind the work of Cy Twombly, whose painterly surfaces possess a prismatic and multidimensional spaciousness within them. Littered with material events and a palimpsest of marks oscillating between the visible and barely visible, these surfaces invite a *haptic* exploration of their inside and underneath that destabilizes conventions such as the surface/ground distinction. Instead of abstract painting existing as a pure, autonomous realm of flatness, it can be thought of as having an internal plurality comprising conventions layered into a medium.

Rosalind Krauss refers to plurality as a recursive structure—one always under construction that "produce[s] the rules that generate the structure itself" (2000, 6). For me, this echoes Irigaray's attributing a circularity of movement to the feminine, looping back on itself and then setting off again in all directions at once (TS, 29) as part of a continual process of becoming. From this perspective insisting on painting's internal plurality, the conventions of abstraction are not phallocentric per se but have rather been *interpreted* as masculine because of their association with patriarchal and masculinist power structures and rigid doctrine. Certainly, contemporary abstract painting is still heavily indebted to the history of modernist abstraction, but the latter's structures and conventions must be recognized as malleable and open to change and variation.

Figure 11.2. Jacqueline Taylor, *In-finite*, 2015, oil and acrylic on canvas. *Source*: Courtesy of the artist. Used with permission.

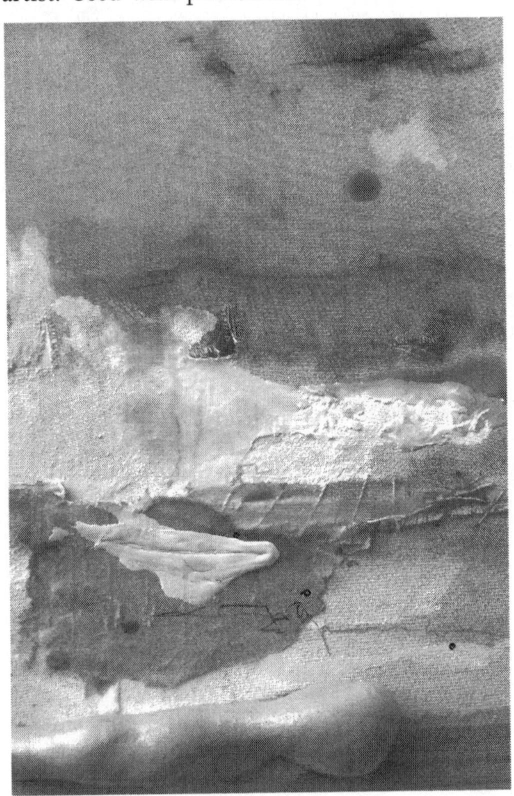

Unfolding and Enfolding Difference

Thinking the feminine as "becoming" in abstract painting calls for a focus on the *practice* of painting. As Irigaray notes in relation to *parler femme*, "it is a question of trying to *practice* the difference" (TS, 159; emphasis added). Here, we need to recall that for Irigaray, as for Kristeva, "the feminine" bears a particular relation to the partial drives that comprise the prelinguistic Imaginary, just as they comprise desire or jouissance, while these drives are evidently not representable as such, they are able to be mobilized and reactivated through the *practice* of poetic writing, as well as certain other aesthetic praxes. Indeed, for Kristeva, the drives are organized through the child's interaction with the mother into a mobile totality she names the "semiotic *chora*," which corresponds to "a precise modality in the signifying process" (1984, 25). Irigaray and Kristeva insist on the disruption of the normative communicative function of language, aligned with the Symbolic, that is wrought by the poetic language privileged in feminine writing. Such disruption takes the form of breaks in structuration in which the sign exceeds itself through the infinite free play of the signifier, escaping the closure of symbolic language and syntax. Textually, this materiality can also manifest as silences, contradictions, vacillations, and collisions in a piece of writing where codes move and come into contact (Barthes 1975, 4–6; Conley 1991, 8).

Painting as a practice—distinct from the production of an object—has too been argued to resonate with "the feminine" understood as the changing configuration of partial drives or heterogenous generative processes able to transgress and renew the Symbolic (Pollock and Rowley 2003, 65). What is involved here is, I would argue, tied up with what Barbara Bolt calls the "heat of making" (2004, 47). This expression refers to the performative potential of painting and the indefinable moment in *process* when a painting takes on a life of its own and something *other* happens outside any signifying chain. I would like to propose that the *unfolding* of abstract painting and its embedded conventions enables at the same time an *enfolding* of difference within the abstract spatiality of which I have spoken above. Here, the heat of making that occurs amid praxis reactivates the partial drives of the subject in process, and this enfolding is a generative site of the subject's renewal. Difference can, then, be understood as a rhythm that insinuates itself within the space-time interval (to follow Irigaray) where the subject is and *becomes*, at the convergence of the bodies, matter, signifying modalities, and creative and psychic strata mobilized by the making process as this engages the multiplicity of elements constituting the internal structuration of abstract painting. The interval can, accordingly, be characterized as a site of becoming and being in which difference manifests itself in the process of making.

As is the case with poetic language, the signified and signifier have an unstable relationship in abstract or nonrepresentational painting and do not always cohere, whence my argument that the performative and material nature of painting resonates with a poetic understanding of abstract painting. As mentioned, the performative potential of painting referred to by Bolt comes into play at the moment in *process* when a painting takes on a life of its own and something "other" happens outside any signifying chain. Bolt highlights the disturbance of signification thereby entailed, specifying that "where materiality insists, the visual language begins to stutter, mumble and whisper" (2004, 47). This is also highlighted by Parveen Adams, who notes that it is in the materiality of the image that the "otherness" of the artwork is rendered manifest—an "otherness" outside the signifying chain, desired and merely dimly glimpsed by the artist, who accedes to it only by way of "accidents" or "chance" effects (1996, 113). Indeed, Kristeva notes that it is the "encounter with chance" in Pollock's drip paintings that bring his work into the space of the semiotic and to the edge of representation (1989, 36). Such "material utterances" and "slippages" occur during the process of an abstract painting's creation and cannot be thought of in advance. They are comparable with the breaks in syntactic structure and the free play of the signifier in poetic language that transgress the rules of normative communication. Examples that come to mind here include Cezanne's "little sensations;" what Yves-Alain Bois calls "the blob" in Twombly's paintings, which appears as a "turd-like handful of paint applied to the canvas and unexpectedly remaining there" (2002, 72), and Frances Bacon's "accidents," described by Adams as "anamorphic" affects that exist as something *other* than representation (1996, 111). Such examples are tied up with the artists' process of creation and are crucial to how one encounters and makes sense of their work, all while they remain fundamentally ambiguous, both resisting and exceeding articulation in any symbolic sense.

Color is also intrinsic to the poetic possibilities of abstract painting. Kristeva helpfully explores color's relation to signification, noting that color is representationally ambiguous and impossible to define or describe because it does not have an equivalent in linguistics (1980, 216). For Kristeva, it is in the case of color that the prelinguistic drives interact most directly with the Symbolic and like "rhythm in language," involve "a shattering of meaning and its subject into a scale of difference" (1980, 221). Irigaray too highlights the possibilities of color in her text "Flesh Colours" in *Sexes and Genealogies*. She notes that color does not obey binaries, rules, and codes and as such does not correspond with communicative language (SG, 157–158). Rather, for Irigaray, color is linked to the realm of sense, affect, and perception. Accordingly, color is inherently connected to a different space-time (SG, 159) and has the capacity to render that which is beyond cultural codes. Color is thus not confined to the pure aestheticism and visuality of "flat" modernist abstraction but is, rather, a crucial component of the performative and material nature of painting, inducing pure sensation and affect. Blue does not, then, necessarily denote the sky or sea as it would in a landscape functioning in a representational capacity in which the signified and signifier yield meaning through form, gesture, or other markers. Rather, in an abstract painting, blue may denote blueness in which form, gesture, composition, and texture are removed from any reference.

The "silences" of poetic language can be seen to be produced in the endless movement of giving and reading and the differences between traces and spaces (Conley 1991, 8). This can also be said of abstract painting in which meaning is potentially open-ended. Such movement resonates with Irigaray's discussion of color and sound, whereby the almost imperceptible transitions between sounds (and indeed color) "must constantly be discovered or recovered" (SG, 158). There is no closure to the interpretation of elements comprising the "material system" of an abstract painting that exceed communicative signification. The poetic realm of abstract painting is, then, ultimately ambiguous, undecipherable, and "undecidable."[7] Its meaning is never stable or singular but relies heavily on the *affect* it creates through sensory means, as the viewer interprets the multiplicity and mobility of the painterly elements they encounter. The silences of poetic language are also comparable to Irigaray's consideration of the "invisible," where she argues that the materiality of painting allows us to perceive that which language does not let us perceive (PI, 395). This can be seen in the work of Twombly where the palimpsest of marks and graphisms on his often-huge painterly surfaces appear to levitate as if, referencing Cixous, they are *approaching* writing in the "happening of an instant" (1991, 104) and incorporate visual silences which one cannot fully grasp. The notion of "intermateriality" can perhaps be useful here in attempting to grasp the material potential of the intertextual nature of the poetic text as a *relation of relations* containing its own internal form of communication that modifies all others. The open-ended play of material differences based on the presence of the signifier and the absence of another signifier through deferral (resonant with Derrida's *différance*) creates a never-ending chain of elements in an artwork. Meaning can only be grasped here by precisely letting it slip through one's fingers in this continuous multiplicity.

Rethinking Difference and Nonrepresentational Aesthetic Practices

The mobility of internal elements and the way structuration comes into being are crucial, then, to the production of meaning within abstract painting. Crucially, while the meaning of such work is never fully graspable and is largely a matter of interpretation and affect, we are still dealing with a signifying process, albeit one different to that of representation. The notion of intermateriality offers us the possibility here of opening up the surface of a painting and understanding its material elements to not just exist on a two-dimensional plane but to shape meaning within the work on a structural level, rather like the materiality and "depth" of textual language Irigaray explores.

Reconceptualizing abstract painting as a heterogeneous spatiality and continuous multiplicity, comprising complex shifting spaces within its internal structuration, has, in short, two major consequences. First, it reveals the embedded structures and binary logic of modernist abstraction as malleable and not phallocentric per se. Secondly, by "unfolding" the surface and conventions of painting, we are directed toward an understanding of the work as produced through an enfolding of drives and creative psychic processes that, effected in the "heat of making," can be traced in the interplay of the poetic and intermaterial strata. This, in turn, opens up new ways of conceptualizing and enacting difference such that, rather than attempting to represent the feminine visually and formally by nonrepresentational means, we are led to conceive the feminine as linked to productivity and creative psychic processes—a "feminine" that becomes manifest through making.

As Estelle Barrett notes, performativity in creative production involves an interaction between the subject as a material process as *being* and the subject as a *signifying process*, resulting in the renewal and alteration between subject and language (2011, 131). Considered in this light, abstract painting as a nonrepresentational entity is indeed a valuable modality of signification capable of articulating difference on a poetic level. Unlike representational practices offering up signs or symbols whose meaning can readily be grasped by a subject, abstract painting practices may be "slippery" to understand; in their presence, however, we come to *experience* difference.

Notes

1. For a fuller discussion of the male gaze, see Laura Mulvey, "Visual Pleasure and Narrative Cinema."

2. While abstract painting can be traced back through the centuries (that is, in Aboriginal and Islamic art), I refer here to the abstract painting that emerged in Western countries during the 1940s and that is aligned more broadly with modernist thinking.

3. This argument has been well-documented through feminist, postmodern, and other critiques of Western art history that problematize the modernist canon as white, heteronormative and male, excluding women and other "nonnormative subjects" such as Black and queer. (For example, see Katy Deepwell, *Women Artists and Modernism*; Rosa Lee, "Resisting Amnesia: Feminism, Painting and Postmodernism"; and Charles Harrison and Paul Wood, "Modernity and Modernism Reconsidered.")

4. The term *phallocularcentrism* refers to *ocularcentrism* as a critique of the privileging of sight over the other senses and *phallocentrism* as a critique of the phallus as transcendental signifier.

5. Mary Kelly's *Post-Partum Document* (1973–1979) explored the mother-child relationship with her infant son over six years. The work includes a mass of material exhibited at different phases that documents her son's development, including linguistic analysis, diary entries, and soiled nappies. The work is claimed not to be autobiographical but a critique of the Lacanian symbolic and of the orthodoxy of painting.

6. There are many examples of how these qualities have been interpreted in "feminine" abstract painting, and I have given just a few here to demonstrate this. This trend was not limited to the 1990s, and more recently, Anne Ring Peterson has argued that the current generation of women painters challenge the canon of 'great' painting by using "a palette of pastels, a girlish pictorial language,

or other visual effects and signs that are readily associated with femininity." Ring Peterson, "Painting Spaces," 17.

7. Derrida's "undecidable" refers to a term or entity that is unable to be reduced to the polarities of a dichotomy, thereby troubling dualisms or revealing the trouble that is already at their core. For example, the figure of a ghost is an "undecidable" insofar as it is neither present nor absent or, alternatively, both present and absent at the same time.

References

Adams, Parveen. 1996. *The Emptiness of the Image*. Routledge.

Barrett, Estelle. 2011. *Kristeva Reframed*. I.B. Tauris.

Barrett, Estelle. 2013. "Materiality, Affect and the Aesthetic Image." In *Carnal Knowledge: Towards a 'New Materialism' through the Arts*, edited by Estelle Barrett and Barbara Bolt. I.B. Tauris.

Barthes, Roland. 1975. *The Pleasure of the Text*. Translated by Richard Miller. Hill and Wang.

Battersby, Christine. 1995. "Just Jamming: Irigaray, Painting and Psychoanalysis." In *New Feminist Art Criticism: Critical Strategies*, edited by Katy Deepwell. Manchester University Press.

Betterton, Rosemary. 1996. *An Intimate Distance: Women, Artists and the Body*. Routledge.

Bois, Yves Alain. 2002. "A Certain Infantile Thing." In *Audible Silence; Cy Twombly at Daros*, edited by Eva Keller and Heiner Bastian. Daros Services.

Bolt, Barbara. 2004. "Painting Is Not a Representational Practice." In *Unframed: Practices and Politics of Women's Contemporary Painting Practice*, edited by Rosemary Betterton. I.B. Tauris.

Brennan, Marcia. 2004. *Modernism's Masculine Subjects: Matisse, the New York School, and Post-Painterly Abstraction*. MIT Press.

Buchloch, Benjamin. 1987. "Theories of Art After Minimalism and Pop." In *Discussions in Contemporary Culture*, edited by Hal Foster. Bay Press.

Cixous, Hélène. 1991. "The Last Painting or the Portrait of God," translated by Sarah Cornell. In *"Coming to Writing" and Other Essays*. Harvard University Press.

Conley, Verena Andermatt. 1991. *Hélène Cixous: Writing the Feminine*. University of Nebraska Press.

Deepwell, Katy. 1994. "Paint-Stripping: Feminist Possibilities in Painting After Modernism." *Women's Art Magazine* 58 no. 1: 14–16.

Deepwell, Katy. 1998. *Women Artists and Modernism*. Manchester University Press.

Deepwell, Katy. 2010. "Claims for a Feminist Politics in Painting." In *Contemporary Painting in Context*, edited by Mikkel Bogh, Hand Dam Christensen, Peter Nørgaard Larsen, and Anne Ring Petersen. Museum Tusculanum Press.

Greenberg, Clement. (1965) 2001. "Modernist Painting." In *Art in Theory 1900–1990: An Anthology of Changing Ideas*, edited by Charles Harrison and Paul Wood. Blackwell Publishers.

Harrison, Charles, and Paul Wood. 1993. "Modernity and Modernism Reconsidered." In *Modernism in Dispute: Art Since the Forties*, edited by Francis Frascina, Jonathan Harris, Charles Harrison, and Paul Wood. Yale University Press.

Heartney, Eleanor, Helaine Posner, Nancy Princenthal, and Sue Scott. 2007. *After the Revolution: Women Who Transformed Contemporary Art*. Prestel Publishing.

Kaneda, Shirley. 1991. "Painting and Its Others: In the Realm of the Feminine." *Arts Magazine* 65, no. 10: 58–64.

Kramer, Marjorie. (1971) 2001. "Some Thoughts on Feminist Art." In *Feminism-Art-Theory: An Anthology 1968–2000*, edited by Hilary Robinson. Blackwell Publishers.

Krauss, Rosalind. 2000. *"A Voyage on the North Sea": Art in the Age of the Post-Medium Condition*. Thames & Hudson.

Kristeva, Julia. 1980. *Desire in Language: A Semiotic Approach to Literature and Art*. Translated by Thomas Gora, Alice Jardine, and Leon S. Roudiez. Columbia University Press.

Kristeva, Julia. 1984. *Revolution in Poetic Language*. Translated by Margaret Waller. Columbia University Press.

Kristeva. Julia. 1989. "Jackson Pollock's Milky Way: 1912–1956." *Journal of Philosophy and the Visual Arts* 1 no. 3: 33–38.

Lee, Rosa. 1987. "Resisting Amnesia: Feminism, Painting and Postmodernism." *Feminist Review* 26 no. 1: 5–28.

Mulvey, Laura. 1975. "Visual Pleasure and Narrative Cinema." *Screen* 16 no. 3: 6–18.

Nochlin, Linda. 2007. "Women Artists Then and Now." In *Global Feminisms: New Directions in Contemporary Art*, edited by Linda Nochlin and Maura Reilly. Merrell Publishers.

Pollock, Griselda. 1988. *Vision and Difference: Feminism, Femininity and Histories of Art*. Routledge.

Pollock, Griselda. 1999. *Differencing the Canon: Feminist Desire and the Writing of Art's Histories*. Routledge.

Pollock, Griselda, and Alison Rowley. 2003. "Painting in a 'Hybrid Moment.'" In *Critical Perspectives on Contemporary Painting: Hybridity, Hegemony, Historicism*, edited by Jonathan Harris. Liverpool University Press.

Ring Peterson, Anne. 2010. "Painting Spaces." In *Contemporary Painting in Context*, edited by Mikkel Bogh, Hand Dam Christensen, Peter Nørgaard Larsen, and Anne Ring Petersen. Museum Tusculanum Press.

Rosler, Martha. 2006. "Subverting the Myths of Everyday Life." *n.paradoxa: International Feminist Art Journal* 19: 98–109.

Schor, Mira. 1997. *Wet: On Painting, Feminism and Art Culture*. Duke University Press.
Schwabsky, Barry. 2011. "Everyday Painting." In *Vitamin P2*, edited by Barry Schwabsky and Michele Robecchi. Phaidon Press.

Figure 12.1. Danielle Hamilton (née McCarthy), *Entanglement*, 2014, acrylic paint on fabric, plexiglass, dimensions variable, detail of gallery wall, exhibited at fortyfive downstairs, Melbourne, 2014, Photographer: Andrew Curtis. *Source*: Courtesy of the artist. Used with permission.

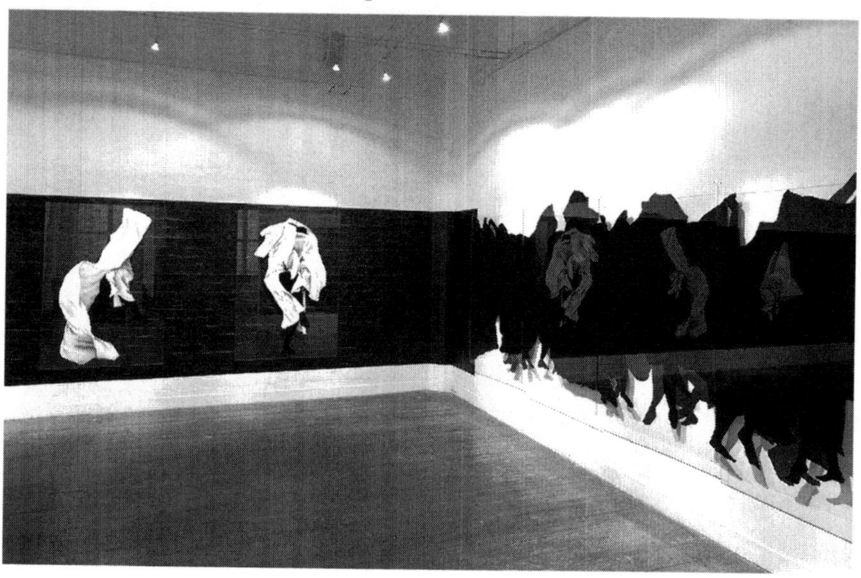

Chapter Twelve

Irigaray and the Baroque

Exploring Sexual Difference Through Creative Practice

DANIELLE HAMILTON

In *This Sex Which Is Not One*, Luce Irigaray asserts, "[i]f we don't invent a language, if we don't find our body's language, it will have too few gestures to accompany our story" (TS, 214). With this statement Irigaray conceptualizes sexual difference as a creative project that has more to do with embodiment, becoming and process than it does with static objects and end products. By exploring the specificity of our body's language and its truths, Irigaray interrogates the primacy traditionally accorded to sight. Reading Irigaray leads me to think of language in terms of full-bodied communication practices untethered from the primacy of speech. We are, in this sense, positioned in the realm of embodied language—a language constituted through the body to express our needs and desires and to enable us to live. There is a call to action issued in Irigaray's writing that is palpable. She warns of the risk if we do not engage in practices of embodied creativity and invention, with the prediction that "we shall tire of the same [stories] ones, and leave our desires unexpressed, unrealised" (TS, 214). This exhortation urges women to explore and materialize morphologies appropriate to their own bodily becoming. For the creative artist, this is a tantalizing proposition: to reinhabit and to reinvent through the situatedness of one's own bodily experience. The art practice I shall discuss here explores this creative potential of sexual differing through the

Deleuzian operation of the baroque fold. In so doing, it seeks to elaborate, as Irigaray suggests, an embodied language that encompasses untapped and limitless reserves.

Language that Thinks Outside Itself

Before focusing on how we can "invent a language" through creative practice, as Irigaray provocatively challenges us to do, we should clarify what exactly we mean by language. It is in its broadest possible sense that language is understood here as embodied practice that has more to do with our ability to affect and be affected in a reciprocal material relationship with others and the world. For the visual arts, there are synergies between Irigarayan philosophy and a realist, materialist perspective for the arts. In their influential book *Realism, Materialism, Art*, Christoph Cox, Jenny Jaskey, and Sahail Malik situate realism and materialism as radically distinct from a "philosophical and cultural view dominant over the last half a century, a view that affirms the indispensability of interpretation, discourse, textuality, signification, ideology and power" (2015, 15). This is a "staunchly anti-realist" view, the authors argue, in as much as it sets up a conception of language that is only ever "for thought" and the experience of the "knowing subject" (15). Realism and materialism depart from this view of language and its construction, with the human henceforth decentered within the world's ordering—in this more than human world, they posit, "thought can think outside itself" (15). Rather than being situated as fixed beings, we are pushed into motion by other bodies that are both human and nonhuman. Both Irigaray and Gilles Deleuze concur with such a materialist conception through their dynamic and open-ended view of language that places us in embodied and reciprocal relations with the world.

Isabelle Stengers argues that reading Deleuze and Félix Guattari "while remaining on the ground, means misreading them" (2009, 28). This holds true when reading Irigaray: we must let go of all grounds and enter into a productive "horizon of possibilities within which the reader is implicated" (47)—thus allowing ourselves to be swept off our feet and put into motion. Stengers qualifies this point by quoting Deleuze and Guattari, "to think is always to follow the witch's flight" ([1991] 1994, 41). In the present essay, I would like to put Irigaray and Deleuze in motion beside one another, to see what might be generated from such flights and to contrast the *experiences produced* when mounting these two particular broomsticks. For this undertaking, language is best conceived—to take up again a proposition by Stengers—as a kind of alchemy, "an immanent process requiring the action of something which has the power to dissolve, to separate what resists its action and what does not" (2009, 29). This is to say that language is enacted through a testing process that has much to do with the sensual realm. It is, accordingly, intimately related to becoming and the materiality of bodies, such that "it is 'sense' which becomes the most important element" (49). Language becomes less about the knowing individual subject and more related "to a concrete operation" (28). When language is connected to the senses in this manner, the productive and inventive potential of bodies in motion may be realized. The witch's flight of thought and the alchemical qualities of language (as proposed by Stengers) provide a boundary or space between sense and sensing. Irigaray upholds the necessity of a similar space between bodies with her conceptualization of the interval. Through attentiveness to one another's differences, Irigaray sketches a silence—a space/time, an interval—within which lies the possible conditions for a "respect for myself and the other within our respective limits" (ILTY, 116–117). Irigaray's conceptualization of the interval entails, as Elizabeth Grosz underlines, the recognition that one can never completely occupy the space of another. There is always a remainder that we cannot access, "insofar as it involves, for each subject in the relation, the recognition and valuation of the other as other" (Grosz 1989, 183). Grosz interprets the Irigarayan constitution of language as meaningfully enacted through bodies that are not "biologically or anatomically given, inert, brut objects, fixed by nature once and for all" (112) but, rather, bodies that are dynamic and in a constant state of flux and movement.

Irigaray places great emphasis on the specificity of human bodies. She writes that woman cannot be reduced to an entity of one: "She is indefinite, in-finite, *form is never complete in her* [. . .] This incompleteness in her form, her morphology, allows her to continually become something else" (S, 229; emphasis in original). Such incompleteness and constant becoming render the notion of the natural or the universal body meaningless. Artist and art theorist Caroline Phillips explores Irigaray's concept of the interval for the arts, writing that it is "a threshold of open potentiality, exchange and relation" (2017, 34). She frames the interval as *always already* in motion, revealed through the processes and practices of art and art making. These movements are generative of new creative languages, and they require the whole body in connection with other bodies. Grosz elaborates that movements are both "tactile and corporeal as well as conceptual, [reverberating] in their plurality and polyvocity" (1989, 132). In the creative and conceptual space of the interval, difference gives way to ever more differences; new space/times can open up, and new senses and sensitivities can be given voice. The presupposed individual or universal human is displaced, leaving instead an interval in which Irigaray stipulates "one will never exactly occupy the place of the other—they are irreducible to one another" (ESD, 13). Most importantly, the constitution of language within this space/place entails the elaboration of embodied difference through the expression of a body's specificity. Irigaray carefully refers to sexual difference in terms of a feminine *morphologic* rather than of a female anatomy. She stipulates that "we must go back to the question not of anatomy but of the morphology of the female sex" (WE, 64). As Grosz elaborates, the construction of women's bodies in culture is not, therefore, the "result of biology, but the *social and psychical meaning of the body*" (1989, 111; emphasis in original). Hence, language displays a much greater complexity: "Systems of language and representation must be internalized, taken on as one's own, in order that speech and language are possible, and that the subject's perceptions and experiences acquire meaning and thus value within its terms" (111). Hilary Robinson adds to this from a creative arts perspective, arguing that the concept of a feminine morphologic "opens up the possibilities of different legibilities" (2006, 97). What is involved, as a result, is a different order of thinking in which the "morphological relationship disrupts the clear-cut binary relationships found so frequently within phallomorphic thinking" (99).

Feminine morphology is situated in the space/time between women and grounded in the specificity of women's bodies. Of the endlessly folding, feminine morphology of "two lips," Irigaray writes: "Between our lips, yours and mine, several voices, several ways of speaking resound endlessly [. . .] One cannot be distinguished from the other; which does not mean that they are indistinct" (TS, 209). Such open and reverberating relations between bodies bear a striking resemblance to the baroque operation of the fold to which we shall now turn. As we shall see, Deleuze's writing presents us with a particular line of flight that requires a broadening of language and gives agency to human and nonhuman bodies, whereas for Irigaray, as I understand her, the invention of language is grounded in the sexual specificity of human bodies. Deleuze and Irigaray posit a dynamic capacity for differing that is found in the enactment of language. As such, the invention of language is understood throughout this chapter as linked to action and to the combination of materiality, ideas, and (human and nonhuman) bodies in motion.

Irigaray maps out a world of infinite expansion, "an energy, a morphology, a growth and flourishing still to come from the female realm?" (ESD, 19). She suggests that "I ought to reconstitute myself on the basis of a disassimilation [. . .] rise again from the traces of a culture, of works already produced by the other. Searching through what is in them—for what is not there" (ESD, 17). As regards the creative arts, this becomes a provocation for the woman artist to make art with 'all she has' and requires, therefore, an exploration of what already exists, while anticipating a future that may be realized through creative processes. In the discussion that follows, I take up this challenge of exploring modes of art making that foreground sexual difference and the production of bodily becomings through gestures appropriate to one's own body. The focus will be on communication practices that give form to sensations and emotions from one body to another.

This may be explored through mimesis, a process of reproducing or imitating through repetition. Irigaray describes mimesis as "play" and suggests that "if women can play with mimesis, it is because they are capable of bringing new nourishment to its operation" (TS, 76). Robinson calls this strategy "productive mimesis," which is "never purely cerebral but can also be found, either substantively or as a trace, in the body" (2006, 44–51). Mimesis is used to reinhabit the works of others and eclipse, through excessive repetition, the rigid confines of their languages. Ultimately, visual structures may be inflated beyond all recognition to elaborate the sexual specificity of the feminine. One possible mimetic strategy Irigaray suggests is that women work toward "repeating/interpreting the way in which, within discourse, the feminine finds itself defined as lack, deficiency, or as imitation and negative image of the subject"; with respect to this logic, women "should signify that [. . .] a *disruptive excess* is possible on the feminine side" (TS, 78). My aim is to deploy this strategic mimetic practice and reinhabit painting through the baroque operation of the fold, with a stress on process, society, and the body. To write from within creative practice expresses what is happening . . . and things do happen!

The Infinite Manifestation of the Fold

In *The Fold*, Deleuze charts a vision of the world in flux and movement. Going beyond representational and linear readings, he characterizes the baroque operation of the fold as the multiplication of openings and "pure emission of singularities" ([1988] 1993, 60). The Cartesian distinction between an ideational realm and the material world is splintered thereby into a cosmology of singularities, differences, and a univocal plane of folds, unfolds, and refolds. We see a world in infinite expansion, with the baroque fold as the figure that exceeds all attempts of limitation and constraint. The fold envisions life in all its complexity from one thing to another, in endless becoming.

Deleuze writes of baroque paintings that are so replete with folds that they simply refuse the containment of the frame. Renowned Italian Renaissance artist Jacopo Tintoretto's painting, *The Miracle of St Mark Freeing the Slave* (Tintoretto 1548) is an example where massive drapes distend and connect all manner of bodies and their various contradictions. They spill outward, upward, and beyond through the elaborate gilded frame and the overly decorative wall features, becoming part of the architectural folds of buildings and cities, then into the elemental folds of earth, wind, and water. We see billowing fabrics inflated by the invisible forces of the air; "in every instance folds of clothing acquire an autonomy and a fullness that are not simply decorative effects" (Deleuze [1998] 1993, 122). I want to consider this baroque operation of the fold through an Irigarayan frame, interwoven with bodily processes. These processes are inherently social and, as we see with Deleuze, they include both human and nonhuman bodies.

The baroque operation of the fold foregrounds the differencing processes experienced by all beings. Deleuze gives us to understand, as Claire Colebrook judiciously remarks, that all manner of beings occupy a "plane of immanence" within an "infinity of folds;" all manner of beings occupy this plane with "differing perceptions, different folds or inflections that create different vectors of becoming" (2002, 54). We might consider, then, in relation to artistic creation, that I perceive the paint on my palette and, in the same instant, the paint perceives me. Deleuze and Guattari elaborate this point, writing that "the plant contemplates by contracting the elements from which it originates—light carbon, and salts—and it fills itself with colours, odours that in each case qualify its variety, its composition" (Deleuze and Guattari [1991] 1994, 212). This is the great value of the baroque operation of the fold and its ability to set the world and all its processes in motion.

Irigaray's depiction of feminine morphology offers the same kind of momentum in its positioning of the voluptuous folds located in human bodies and between them. She writes of bodies that are always open and never closed and of the multiple as opposed to the one or the other of sexuality, stipulating that "[b]etween our lips, yours and mine, several voices, several ways of speaking resound endlessly" (TS, 209). The morphology of the fold is evident in the two lips that are never simply two. They are many and more; they are simultaneous. Where one body ends and another begins is never clear. This folding defies binary positions because it is both genital and oral and it oscillates between these states and beyond. Irigaray writes of the folds of sexual difference as an untapped reserve of infinite expansion "still to come from the female realm" (ESD, 19). This offers a way of thinking about art where the hand of the master is replaced by the interactions of societies, bodily realities, and the environmental impacts on those bodies.

In Irigaray's writing, sexual difference is situated as a complex web of internal and external relations comprising a topography of environmental, psychical, and biological forces, inseparable and interwoven. Unlike Deleuze, Irigaray stresses the importance of the elaboration of the sexual difference as the most urgent part of the differing process, focusing her philosophy on the blind spots of human bodily experiences that have excluded women throughout history and to the present day. The Deleuzian conception of the fold broadens our focus beyond the specificity of women's bodies to include all the material bodies of the cosmos.

The Passage from Sight to Touch

Contemporary artist Jenny Saville's monumental painting *Fulcrum* (Saville 1998–1999) occupies a liminal space, being neither open nor closed. A purely visual or "representationalist" reading of the work may preclude the comprehension of such a space. Barbara Bolt argues that representationalism "sets in place intentions and preconceives the outcome in such a way that we are no longer open to what could emerge in the process," underlining that "through man's ability to represent or model the world, he secures the world for his own use" (2011, 61). This constitutes the closed state of a painting. In its closed state, Saville's work shows an image of large naked bodies in a heap and bound together by rope. The soft pastel colors and application of paint, in combination with the meaty violence of the scene, converge to create a striking visual experience. A representationalist reading of *Fulcrum* might discern, for example, the big naked women to represent the bodies of all women, or might use the painting to discuss an artist's mastery over the medium of paint to depict living flesh. It might even contend that Saville's large women and their painterly treatment have much in common with the gigantic baroque paintings of the sixteenth century, well known for their use of great fleshy women, draped across all manner of scenes, perhaps to represent moral states or ideal beauty. Under representationalism, artwork is seen as an object with language as its only vehicle for its translation. It is viewed as an object that corresponds to something else in the world as a metaphor or symbol. Framed as a representation, the artwork can be deciphered through a "correct" interpretation or reading, which limits the performative potential of a work of art.

From the perspective just outlined, nature has a fixed essence that is frozen in place for all time within the work of art. Deleuze undoes this representationalist approach to art through the baroque operation of the fold. The latter, he writes, "stretches beyond its precise historical limits" and opens infinitely, carrying with it all manner of material bodies ([1988] 1993, 33). As such, "[f]olding-unfolding no longer simply means tension-release, contraction-dilation, but enveloping-developing, involution-evolution" (8). Rather than Saville's painting being viewed as a fixed object, it is set loose through the baroque operation of the fold. It confounds and exceeds the categories of representation, which recalls Irigaray's mimetic strategies and her provocative claim that the invention of women's language might emerge through the reinhabiting and repeating of works from the past. *Fulcrum* counteracts, in this respect, the static tropes of the naked female prevalent throughout Western painting. Irigaray's claim that "a disruptive excess is possible on the feminine side" wherever woman has been "defined as lack, deficiency, or as limitation and negative image of the subject" (TS, 78) finds here a confirmation. Saville's work shows how a painting can effect such a disruptive excess of representationalism through a resistance to closure.

There is much more circulating in this work than the visual experience of it. Robinson calls this "something akin to love," citing Saville herself: "I'm not painting disgusting, big women. I'm painting women who've *been made to think* they're big and disgusting" (2006, 123; emphasis in original). Saville is not painting a self-portrait, nor are these women her objects. She identifies with their lived experiences and articulates this through the medium of paint. Robinson sees this as a gesture of "attending to the interrelation of subjectivity and the body, and of restoring sight to touch" (123). I read this as a different kind of legibility that positively marks the relations between women. Saville moves us beyond a purely visual reading of this work to engage with its processes and internal structures. Excess abounds in this work, from the enormity of its visual impact to the effects generated from such a stupendous amount of paint. She restores "beauty to that *which has been regarded* as surplus substance" (123; emphasis in original). In my own viewing of this work, I have experienced this transformation through an embodied response.

Fulcrum is a painting that commands attention. The impact of my first viewing of this work remains with me still. I turned a corner and entered a large gallery where, even from a distance, the work filled my vision. However, in the space of a few steps, visual continuity disintegrated into pure abstraction and sense of touch. The image collapsed completely into a surface that had more in common with standing at the base of a cliff, looking into a pure rock face, than facing a human body. My senses were filled with its crags and jagged edges. There were lush gestural surfaces, textures, and tones that provoked memories of handling paint, and yet it was applied on a magnitude that I have never known. The initial vision of bodies, their curvatures and their folds, merged with the sensual experience of the work in the space of a few meters. The middle ground held the sensation of the work in a zone of indeterminacy, an interval and a passage from sight to touch. In this space a third term had been created, "where the painting is neither open nor is it closed" (Robinson 2006, 118). In *Fulcrum*, this resistance to closure operates through proximity to the work. A shift occurs that takes us from visual experience to physical encounter, and in this interval, it is impossible to separate these two experiences of the work. Rather, they oscillate between states and inflect one another as both visual *and* sensual states. This operation returns us once again to the morphologic of the two lips that Irigaray positions between and within women, as a site "which keeps woman in touch with herself, but without any possibility of distinguishing what is touching from what is being touched" (TS, 26). *Fulcrum* operates in a register that is resistant to a single reading or meaning and remains open as a space for mediation.

A Creative Language of My Own

I recall the anticipation I felt prior to attending a dear friend's musical performance. Three days prior to the event, she had experienced a significant romantic trauma that had knocked her off her feet. We had a coffee prior to the show, and she explained the story behind the flute solo she was about to perform. It was from the Greek myth of Pan and Syrinx. She explained that Pan fell in love with and pursued the nymph Syrinx. Having no desire for the satyr, she rejects him by fleeing to the edge of a river. Trapped between the amorous advances of the satyr and the water, she prays to the river nymphs to save her. They do so by transforming her into a bed of marsh reeds. In his frustration to possess her, Pan slashes and slices his way through the reeds searching for Syrinx. In his frenzy he noticed the beautiful melodic sound made when the air passed through the broken hollow reeds. So he bound pieces together to create a musical instrument that he named "syrinx" in memory of his lost love.

My friend was candid about how hard this performance was going to be and how difficult it would be to get through. The story and the timing had struck too close to the bone. By the time she walked into the middle of the stage and the flute was raised to her lips, I was aware of a palpable energy in the hall. After one deep, steadying breath she began to play a most impassioned and beautiful rendition of the musical composition. Yet there was something more happening than just the music. In that moment something circulated between us that I hadn't caught in the conversations leading up that moment. I felt compelled to contribute to this emerging language between us.

I worked for a year on my response to this event. It came in the form of an art installation, *Entanglement* (fig. 12.1). Throughout its development, I invited my friend to visit the studio and compose a flute piece in response to the emerging work. We did not mention the impulse that I had to create the work, but she was well aware of why I had begun the project. However, the language was changing as we were creating it, following where the work was leading us, with each of us attentive to the other's being in the world. As Robinson argues, "[a]ttentiveness here is about the society of creative practice, the communal and community nature of it. Art then is an object of mediation" (2006, 85). Neither of us was diminished by what passed between us, nor could we fully consume the other within the dialogue; the work generated between us acted as an object of mediation. In Irigarayan terms, what passed between us was a noncapitalized gift/space object "that neither reduces the other to an object, nor uses them [the other] to reflect back one's subjectivity" (84). A salient point that underscores the creativity and invention . . .

In *I Love to You*, Irigaray illustrates this offer of exchange and mediation in the following terms: "I do not take you for a direct object, nor for an indirect object by revolving around you. It is, rather, around myself that I have to revolve in order to maintain the *to you* thanks to the return to me" (ILTY, 110). My friend and I communicated in languages that exceeded the spoken word as we interacted in the modes most appropriate to our bodies, hers with wind through flute playing and mine with earth through painting. We were drawing on our lived fields of experience, capturing remembered sensation, as experienced through the body and materialized through art. There was a remainder, where my friend held something to herself that I had no access to, just as I held something to myself alone. To me, this experience felt akin to Irigaray's call that a woman must "resubmit herself—inasmuch as she is on the side of the 'perceptible,' of 'matter'—to 'ideas,' in particular to ideas about herself" (TS, 76). This communication between myself and my friend, in the midst of creating artistic work, enabled new forms of language and expression to be realized, documented, and shared. We were making work from what one is (a sexuate being), passing through and elaborating further with "a disruptive excess" (TS, 78).

My friend and I communicated the shared comprehension of romantic grief through gestures and collaboration. I was infected by affect, like a virus, becoming aware of how we can catch feeling/sensations (interactions that can only be accessed through our own field of understanding) from someone else and the ways they can pass through artwork and out and on. *Entanglement* was haunted by forms and feelings that came from my friend's flute performance, and in it I found a language of my own to add to this conversation. As feeling passed between us, it left a trace and enabled a space for something new to be added. Deleuze and Guattari write, "the artist is always adding new varieties to the world. Beings of sensation are varieties. [. . .] They not only create them in their work, they give them to us and make us become with them, they draw us into the compound" ([1991] 1994, 175). Thus, the work of art anticipates a world and a people yet to come because of its orientation to the future and a world that does not yet exist—but might.

This field of affect is the best way to give the sensations that passed between my friend and I the materiality they deserve: an agency of their own and a presence as real as you or I. And yet, there was more: even in the confines of the studio, a painting never simply appears; it is willed into existence. No matter how choreographed, how staged, or how much it is considered before its beginning, a painting goes at its own speed and determines its own outcomes. Multiple forces wrestle and resist, compete and coalesce. Paint with brush and ground; hand with eye and paint; ground with mediums, pigments, and paints. Competing forces enable or inhibit a painting in its becoming. While the artist sets the scene, enabling the work to happen, there are other multiple happenings occurring at the same time. I need to be moved to paint; I am not able to just do it for pleasure. I put sensations (which are often contradictory) that cannot find proper expression into my work. It is a feeling of being overfull. I am a painter; I talk in paint and with paint. I prefer solid grounds that allow more robust discussions. Often the paintings push back to tell me what I can and cannot do.

Entanglement began in the studio with a nightie and some bed sheets, a camera and a remote control, to record my movements. The photographs and the actions happened simultaneously, which made the choreography difficult and awkward. I chose the Perspex to paint on, the color range, the brushes, and the mediums; yet my borders were breached at every turn. Everyone I have ever known accompanied me into the studio; politics followed; the Perspex pushed back. The paint mixed into colors I did not dictate and took on body and textures I could not control. I could only allow or resist. This is the language of paint as it wrenches free of the artist to "become" and stand on its own (Deleuze and Guattari [1991] 1994). My voice is present, but there are others too, elemental voices of air, earth, and water. Deleuze and Guattari write that art is a "being of sensation" (164). In my view, there is a field of experience that these paintings have been drawn from and reach out toward; a whole field of experience drawn from the sexual specificity of my body in communication with other material bodies, experience that enables living sensation to take on form. The language of the painter is the language of multiplicity par excellence. It carries within it the cooled sediment of once fluid movement, captured and coagulated into the surface of paint, which then leaks from its ground out to the environment, architecture, and beyond. Deleuze articulates this same point when sketching the operation of the baroque fold: "we witness a prodigious development of a continuity in the arts, in breadth or in extension: an interlocking of frames of which each is exceeded by a matter that moves through it" ([1988] 1993, 123).

There is an invisible milieu surrounding a work of art to which we must be attentive when we stand within its field. We are called to the contemplative "action" of silence, patience, observance, and consideration. Given this attentiveness, the work will gradually unfold, revealing hidden parts. This will inevitably include sound, temperature, light, and physical environment. Mimetic practices and repetitive gestures were not deployed to maintain something already existent or given but to create a space for something new to occur, the invention of language between women. My way of achieving this was to create an opening between the plane of painting and the plane of reflection, where the work hovers between the familiar and the unfamiliar. Thus, the painting becomes a space that refuses to keep still, leaving the viewer with "nothing to hold on to" (Robinson 2006, 118). My installation was aimed at expanding the physical confines of the gallery and to broaden and distend the paintings so that they overwhelm and transform the physical spaces they are held within, perhaps even exceed them. This was achieved through the use of repetition, mirroring, transparent reflective surfaces, and play with surfaces and textures. The paintings in *Entanglement* featured flailing fabrics that appeared to hover in space, as the supporting body had been replaced by a black mirror silhouette. This tension between paint and slippery, reflective, mirrored surfaces meant that the paintings were constantly undoing themselves. These were paintings that were unsure of their authority, trying to be solid yet constantly undermined by their own reflections. There was more at play than the end product inasmuch as the paintings and all the materials were gathered together, assembled, exhibited, and, in excess of their materiality, present in loving support of my friend in her grief.

Conclusion

If we return to Stengers and the pursuit of the "witch's flight," the testing of those flights, and the invention of language, it is worth restating that this has not been an exercise in pitting Irigaray against Deleuze. Rather, their ideas have been put into proximity to see what might be generated from their philosophies through practices and approaches in the visual arts. Artistic events have been charted that have shown how the elaboration of Irigarayan sexual specificity might be considered in the light of the Deleuzian operation of the baroque fold. Both theorists offer limitless folds that are in perpetual, outgoing motion. In Deleuze, we see great sixteenth-century artworks transfigured and forming an interlocking chain of folds, unfolds, and refolds that exceed artwork, architecture, the environment, and even the cosmos. Saville's gigantic painting made legible a passage from sight to touch. Each artwork created a space and showed us something that was previously imperceptible. Thus, new languages were invented to shape themselves around these corporeal encounters.

These ideas have reverberated and transformed my approach to creating artworks. Within this philosophical frame, the invention of language becomes more and more about attentiveness to differences in life and the lives around me. *Entanglement* was a budding investigation into these ideas that materialized in the form of large-scale gestural paintings on plexiglass sheets that shifted and transformed according to proximity. The work was a response to another woman's experience of personal grief, expressed through a flute piece. Without Irigaray and Deleuze my flight would not have been articulable. Irigaray provides the momentum through her formulation of the sexual specificity of women's bodies and their hidden reserves, which is put in motion by Deleuze's human and nonhuman bodies that fold, unfold, and refold through all time and space.

Through encounters with the creative works of others, I have been swept off my feet into new space/times and have become sensitive to more and more differences. Direction is extremely important to me. It is true that we can all become "more" than what we are now, but time is not reversible, and sexual difference has determined a field of experience that I come to painting from, and there is no telling where this becoming might lead. The stakes are particularly high for the woman artist who hazards, with each work, a folding over and into the phallic regime (even one that does not declare itself directly). Irigaray's radical philosophy of sexual difference posits that the feminine must be fully articulated for the full-bodied articulation of *all* differences.

I am buffeted on all sides by other bodies and the environment, and yet, it is my body that is the locus for these experiences. At this point, reflective surfaces and gestural paintings are able to express a certain temporality, multiplicity, and sociality. But, I want more . . . more paint, more mirrors and reflective surfaces, my own style of dress and the way I act and speak in the world, the choice of whom I engage with and how it is done. I want a full-bodied language that speaks of a whole being and to create works informed by my own bodily particularities that speak beyond a purely psychological account of life. The process is about the forces circulating around me and through my body. Everything I think and do needs to be reconsidered, relived, and re-experienced to live and create in the world, and to extend my fold and my becoming.

References

Bolt, Barbara. 2011. *Heidegger Reframed*. I.B. Tauris.
Colebrook, Claire. 2002. *Understanding Deleuze*. Allen & Unwin.

Cox, Christoph, Jenny Jaskey, and Suhail Malik, eds. 2015. *Realism, Materialism, Art*. Sternberg Press.

Deleuze, Gilles. (1988) 1993. *The Fold: Leibniz and the Baroque*. Translated by Tom Conley. University of Minnesota Press.

Deleuze, Gilles, and Félix Guattari. (1991) 1994. *What Is Philosophy?* Translated by Graham Burchell and Hugh Tomlinson. Verso.

Grosz, Elizabeth. 1989. *Sexual Subversions: Three French Feminists*. Allen & Unwin.

Phillips, Caroline. 2017. *Materialising Feminism: Object and Interval*. Minerva Access.

Robinson, Hilary. 2006. *Reading Art, Reading Irigaray: The Politics of Art by Women*. I.B. Tauris.

Saville, Jenny. 1998–1999. *Fulcrum*. Oil on Canvas. Gagosian Gallery. New York. https://gagosian.com/artists/jenny-saville/

Stengers, Isabelle. 2009. "Thinking with Deleuze and Whitehead: A Double Test." In *Deleuze, Whitehead, Bergson: Rhizomatic Connections*, edited by Keith Robinson. Palgrave Macmillan.

Tintoretto, Jacopo. 1548. *The Miracle of St. Mark Freeing the Slave*. Oil on canvas. Gallerie dell'Accademia, Venice.

Figure 13.1, a and b. Rebekah Pryor, *Performing the Icon (Choreographic Notes 1–12)*, details 4 and 5, 2015, paper collage 30 × 42 cm © Rebekah Pryor. *Source*: Courtesy of the artist. Used with permission.

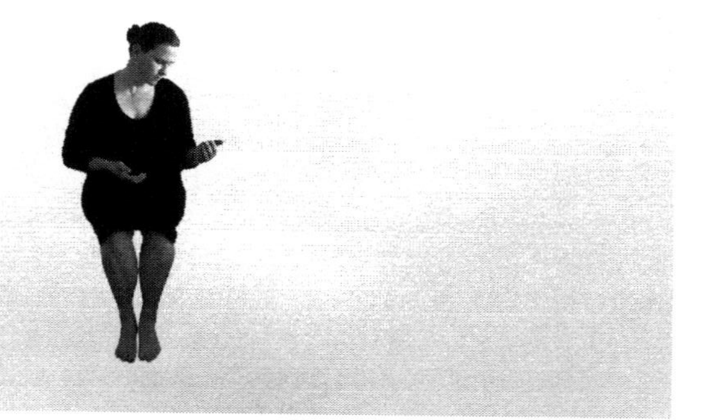

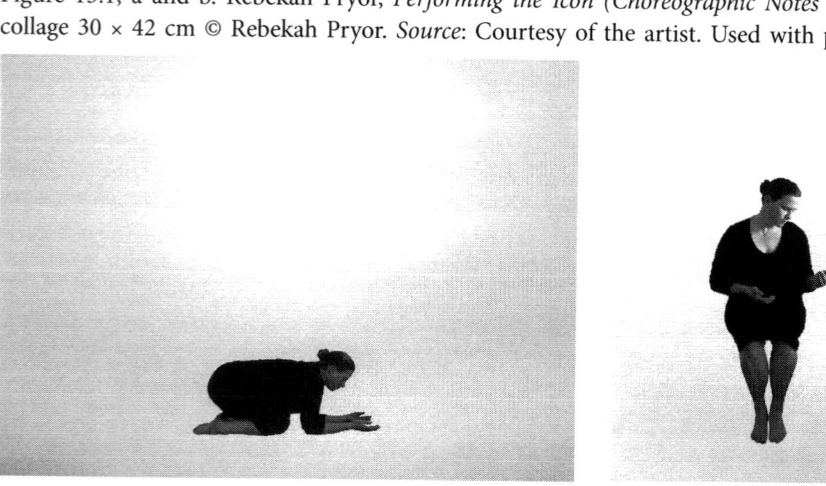

Chapter Thirteen

The Icon and the Absent Other

Rebekah Pryor

> . . . returning to the most simple of the everyday life is essential in order to pursue a spiritual path. This most simple is, in fact, always relational—whether it is a matter of the relation to nature, to things, to the other. The relation to oneself always goes through the relation to the other.
>
> —Irigaray (BTI)

In pursuit of our spiritual becoming, we return to a familiar place, a first space where our human being is most unmistakable: the maternal body.[1] While Western art has long represented the mother, the fact of our origin in the body of an other (a female other, no less) is problematic in a culture imagined and prescribed in/by the masculine. As philosopher Luce Irigaray contends, according to this imaginary, woman is understood only in terms of her corporeality—she is a body. Forgetting the relational nature of both his origin and any possible future spiritual becoming, man appropriates her. She is defined according to him and not with respect to her difference. In denying woman's subjectivity and the spiritual and physical capacity that enabled her to share life and breath with him from the beginning (the "maternal mystery," as Irigaray calls it), man reduces her to virgin or mother (BTI, 357). She is made passive; an idol, but one sacrificed time and again to his so-called God-ordained duty to deny the energy of desire (induced by difference) and take her for the purposes of procreation. As Irigaray writes, "his life thus unfolds in constant sacrilege" (BTI, 358).

Mary, the mother of Jesus, is one such woman who has suffered this fate. In historical and contemporary Christian iconography and devotion, while she is revered, adored, and prayed to on account of her imagined power, she is also held captive by a range of doctrines and iconic renderings that allow her to be known only as virgin or mother, sometimes queen, but never fully as woman. Accordingly, as Irigaray observes, Mary is relegated to back chapels or seasonal Christmas appearances, despite her real significance in the event of the Incarnation: "And yet Mary marks the entrance into the Christian era. Without her, the Good News of Christianity would simply not exist. She is the necessary condition for the Incarnation, the first mediation, the first mediator, between divinity and humanity, between God and humans, in order that a possible redemption of the world could happen" (NCE, 91). Interpretations of the Incarnation handed down in the form of dominant patriarchal Western Christian theologies see Mary's role and agency in the story as entirely contingent on "the goodwill of man" (NCE, 100). On behalf of God, man permits and mediates her involvement, even in the ecclesial community. But such limitations on the basis of sex and gender—limitations that ignore and erase the depth and breadth and breath of woman's capacity, including spiritual—surely undermine the very credibility of the Incarnation as a divine event with potential to transform the world. For Irigaray and from a feminist theological position, to recognize Mary as woman is to anticipate and so preserve "her spiritual virginity for a natural or a spiritual birth giving," including her own (NCE, 100). In "The Mystery of Mary," Irigaray emphasizes the importance of recognizing Mary's ability and autonomy to maintain and thus "ensure her own spiritual becoming and a spiritual exchange with the other, in particular with the different other—be this other a father, an amorous partner, or a son" (NCE, 101). As the philosopher asserts, the implications for Christian theology (and, by implication, practice) are not to be understated: "In order to render the mystery of Incarnation credible and respectable, the virginity of Mary—like that of any woman—must correspond to her ability to keep her breath autonomous and partly available for the advent of a not yet come to pass future and the encounter with an other respected in their transcendence" (NCE, 100–101). The cultural legacy of prescribing Mary and, after her, all women in certain, limited ways evidences a lack of understanding of the other as other, as transcendent—which is to say, as "forever irreducible to me or to mine because he or she is different from me . . . [and] dwells in a different world from mine" (BTI, 358). To liberate Mary from the long-held and doctrinally instituted assumptions that she can be fully known and thus contained and, indeed, to remain in pursuit of our own spiritual becoming, what is needed, Irigaray proposes, is a cultivation of sexuate energy (that springs from difference rather than the act of sex). Without it, we risk denying the very possibility of the kind of mystery Mary (and indeed the very event of the Incarnation) embodies; we underestimate and diminish ourselves and each other when we do this; we risk making idols of each other, such that we can only ever be sacred and superior or imperfect and forbidden. The consequence is a relation between us that is characterized by either worship or rejection.

In her essay, "Beyond Totem and Idol, the Sexuate Other," Irigaray distinguishes between totemic cultures in which difference is preserved (for example, via rules that require marriage across bloodlines and totem groups, effectively across clans and cultures) and patriarchal cultures in which difference is canceled (most particularly by rules that ensure marriage beyond the bounds of the family unit but within the same religious culture). In art, as in other modes of thought and expression in the West, this cancelation of difference has led to a taboo on both sexuality and spirituality. People have long generated images to signify their revelations of and encounters with "the divine," producing representations that affirm what is known, idealized, or desired within the communities in which they are generated. Spiritual becoming is stunted, however, when such images become fixed (that is, when they become idols or totems), limiting the divinity they mean to represent. In totemic cultures, the strength or fragility of a living being depends on the totem; more specifically, it is contained by it. The individual cannot contain the self or his/her/their sexuate energy. Only the totem observed, revered, and allowed to remain intact can preserve and protect the uniqueness and belonging of each person. In patriarchal cultures, on the other hand, difference is identified only in terms of physiology rather than also according to uniqueness. Zealous in his pursuit of divine illumination, man has upheld the right and strength of mind and spirit while separating himself from the body, whose weakness and impulsivity he relegates to woman. The value of the differently sexuate other and the integrity of belonging together in difference are lost and, worse, ignored in favor of a culture in which the other is considered as an idol of desire to be resisted and pulled down.

In each case, fixed images of the divine (however energetic or incarnate, according to our various definitions of it) can limit not only our conception of "God" but also our capacity to understand and relate to the human other as different and transcendent.

Reimagining the Maternal Body

By way of critiquing the Christian church's fixations on the maternal body and doctrinal limits on Mary and women after her, my artistic and theological research has to date focused on developing alternate motifs that might more fully and ethically represent the woman in the mother. I have aimed to generate images that contribute to a contemporary and feminist religious aesthetic and that, hence, disrupt the idol of motherhood perpetuated by the deep cultural dependency on Mary's intact hymen rather than on her spiritual virginity, as Irigaray identifies. I have sought to depict the feminine subject in her complexity and multiplicity, with regard to her sexuate difference. Early attempts circled around the tradition of the orthodox icon to produce figurative, replicable patterns of relation between mother and child. *Triptych* (2014) comprises three clear acrylic, figural shapes, each edged with 24-carat gold leaf and installed one in front of the other on steel pins, with a small gap in between.[2] Its place in the long lineage of orthodox iconography may be traced through the work's repetition of forms as well as its materiality (where transparent acrylic is used to evoke the portal-like quality of the orthodox icon, along with gold leaf, to signify the object's durability and sacredness) (Zaunschirm 2012). However, *Triptych* diverges from tradition in the way that it represents the maternal body. Not only is the whole body of the woman depicted but her facial features and expression are not illustrated, and she is depicted alone. The only suggestion of her maternal relation to a child is given by her posture, bent over and extended toward an absent other. In this way the work reaffirms the centrality of the body in Christian narrative: God incarnate, born of a virgin's womb; church as body with many parts; loving God and neighbor with the whole self: heart, soul, mind, strength—all key examples of the body understood theologically and symbolically as revelation and agent of divine love.[3] In its depiction of a bent-over maternal body, a body changing shape to meet the (albeit, in this work at least, absent) other, *Triptych* mimics the divine gesture of which the author of

John's gospel writes in the Prologue: "And the Word became flesh and *dwelt* among us" (John 1:14). Here, a derivation of the Greek σκηνόω (*skénoó*) is used, meaning literally "to tent or encamp."[4] Theologian Elizabeth Johnson describes this as the event of "deep incarnation"—the "divine reach" of God when "the Word/Wisdom of God joins the material world, sharing in the conditions of the flesh in order to accomplish a new level of union between Creator and creature" (2014, 196).[5] God pitches a tent—in the person of Christ but first, as Irigaray proposes, through relation with the person of Mary. The language suggests a flexible, intimate, relational, if also architectural gesture—a divinely maternal gesture—and figures (to appropriate the sociologist Peter Berger's [1969] phrase) a "sacred canopy."[6]

The Body Between Life and Word

Irigaray further elaborates the necessity of respecting sexuate difference for spiritual becoming when, having already outlined the distinctions and effects of totemic and patriarchal images of the divine, she queries whether Christ can be understood to mysteriously connect these cultures. She writes: "Christ seems to be, to some extent, a bridge between totemic cultures and patriarchal cultures, the cultures of life and the cultures of the mind, confused by the patriarchy with the Word. Christ represents in some way a human totem, but a totem between life and the Word in which a cultivation of desire and of loving breathing is missing, at least according to the testimonies we have at our disposal" (BTI, 362). In her speculative figuration of Christ as a bridge, Irigaray contests the Christian tradition's preoccupation with "the Word" (traditionally, of "God the Father") and its related neglect of Jesus of Nazareth's origins in the love and breath—the relational, living, moving body—of an other: a maternal other. In "The Mystery of Mary," Irigaray repeats the bridge motif to position Mary in a similar way, describing her as: "A woman capable of being a temporal bridge between the past, the present, and the future, and a spatial bridge between all the cultures of the world, thanks to her spiritual virginity—a safeguarding of a living and free breath, irreducible to anyone or to anything" (NCE, 121). Mary becomes mother to Jesus because of her "ability to sense and open up to the most delicate vibration" (ML, 176). Something is recovered or created through that opening. The Beginning begins again and again through breath and word: "The presence that had been buried and paralyzed in the text of the law is made flesh once more in the body of a woman, guardian of the spirit of divine life" (ML, 176). Mary's is "a divine that does not need to erect any capital letter" (ML, 172). Her attentive, corporeal, generative love precedes and exceeds the law. And after her, Christ "manifests the miraculous power of that love" (ML, 176), demonstrating the incarnate and uniquely (but not exclusively) cosmic nature of the logos, as theologian Catherine Keller has emphasized (2003, 226). Irigaray is critical of the patriarchal traditions of Christianity that have forgotten both this and the desire and loving breath that characterizes Christ in relation to different others. The figure of Christ—a potential bridge between cultures—has thus been curtailed by the closures of religious law and Word. Christ's body which, like Mary's, once held space (an interval) open for different others, is constricted by the language of gospels, institutions, icons, and dogmas.

For Irigaray, the "third space" of the interval is vital to our speaking and being together in difference. Indeed, it is our difference that gives rise to desire ("the source of energy, in us and between us"), and this, Irigaray writes, "can transport breath and energy from the centers of elementary vitality to the centers of the heart, of breathing, of listening, of thought" (BTI, 363). An understanding and cultivation of desire through difference is key to our unfolding and our spiritual becoming, and an interval between two subjects safeguards this difference, allowing each one to become without reducing, absorbing or appropriating the other.

As Hilary Robinson's (2006) discussion of art and Irigarayan philosophy suggests, the material object of art functions as an interval in intersubjective relationships. *Triptych* may be understood to operate in this way. The work hangs between artist and viewer, proposing a philosophy, sharing an experience, inviting an interaction, all the while maintaining the separation between the two. Even the gap between each of this work's layers serves as a visual reminder of the interval: the interval by which the woman and the child maintain their uniqueness in terms of each other; the interval by which (a/the) maternal experience is defined. In its repetition of shapes and materials, *Triptych* indicates something of the longevity of the maternal relation, and in figuring the motherly body alone, the work also succeeds in asserting the uniqueness and transcendence of the woman. By fixing her in a single posture, however, it fails to convey her multiplicity. Her body is, after all, more than just maternal. It is sexuate, constantly animated, changing, and becoming in relation to herself and the other.

The Multiple, Relational Body

I wanted to generate an image of the maternal body that evoked Irigaray's figuration of Christ (and Mary): bridgelike, between totem and idol. And so I sought to depict the body in action on the basis that its multiple movements might better represent woman's own desire, energy, and autonomy in the maternal relation. Contemporary dance informed my visual art exploration of multiplicity at this point, and Trisha Brown's *Roof Piece* (1971; recreated 2011) was a strong influence.[7] In Brown's work, dancers were positioned on various rooftops within a ten-block area of New York City, each wearing red and mimicking the movement of a nearby dancer until the choreography encircled the area. *Roof Piece* evoked themes like those in my own project: the ecstatic, energetic, and multiple nature of the body and the relational and architectural potential of gesture. I was also inspired by the nontraditional setting of the *Roof Piece* performance and the way that the architecture itself helped maintain an interval between dancers. I liked too how each dancer adapted their body and the choreography according to their rooftop setting and their relation to all the others. Bearing traces of these impressions, my next work, *Performing the Icon (Choreographic Notes 1–12)* (2015), aimed to explore and convey the versatility of contemporary images that represent the various movements of the maternal body. This series of twelve collages, each depicting a single, gesturing figure on a blank white background, resembles a kind of choreographic notation: a sequence of imaged gestures that can be mimicked, repeated, and reordered to create endless iterations of the subject. As such, they move beyond their domestic origins, adapting in ways that make them performatively and symbolically meaningful in different contexts—the liturgical space of the cathedral, for example, or the cultural institution of the gallery—places where they might interrupt and expand conceptions of the body, the woman, the mother, and the divine.

Performing the Icon aims to recover both the "cultivation of desire" and the "loving breath" that Irigaray argues is absent from Western Christian representations of the divine (BTI, 362). By depicting an ordinary human body in a range of familiar postures (at least to a Western spectator), the work affirms the divine nature of maternal love and relation and imagines the embodied—and, in light of the Johannine theology of the Incarnation, the architectural—possibilities of God's "divine reach." The divine is "conjured up," as Irigaray has said, "among us, within us, as resurrection and transfiguration of blood, of flesh, through a language and an ethics that is ours" (ESD, 129). This "sensible transcendental," which, in intersubjective relationships, is conditioned by each one's recognition of the other's irreducible difference, amounts to an event that is revelatory and liberating. The image of the maternal body (cast as energetic, material, and incarnational) revives, as it were, the Christ-like subject (figured by the maternal body) with the "desire and loving breath" identified by Irigaray as missing from the biblical tradition to which we have, until now, had access (BTI, 362). In her imaged action, the maternal body thus breaches the boundaries of historically gendered expectation by moving with such autonomy as to deny the fixative effects of any gaze. She eludes objectification in the process of making space for relation. Hers is an apophatic body whose loving, breathing, folding over, enfolding action says and unsays itself, in the context of interrelation—with divine capacity—allowing "every other, including the self, its margin of unknowability" (Keller 2008, 928). (Transcendence, in Irigarayan parlance.) Indeed, in the intimate encounter between bodies, each one is returned to itself via "the touch of the caress" of the other, as Irigaray describes it (ESD, 187). In such a "gesture of love," one body recognizes the other body as transcendent. Each one's "living presence" is revealed and reveals itself, before and beyond Word or language. Similarly challenging the limits of Emmanuel Levinas's thinking on the face as the site of revelation, Keller emphasizes that the kind of "sensitivity" or "spirited connection" Irigaray likewise suggests will aid the preservation of difference and expand our sense of the divine: it "will with courage negate each attempt at a totality that closes down the 'infinite in the face of the other'" (2008, 928).[8]

In *Performing the Icon*, this revelation of relation and transcendence takes place even in the absence of the other's body. In contrast to other Christian icons that portray the mother (the *Eleousa*, for example), this image of relation also succeeds without the clear expression of the face. The moving body is the face—the irreducible expression of living presence that resists the fixative effect of any icon-like form. And the whole body of the woman as mother constitutes the epiphany, the revelation of love.

Conclusion

In pursuit of our spiritual becoming, we return to a familiar place: the maternal body, the body that "ventures to share love" as a result of desire rather than sheer instinct (TBB, 76). Rejecting the mind-body divide so long perpetuated in Western culture, Irigaray urges a new and unified approach to being, desire, and relation, in and with our self and each other. "Desire wants reconciliation of the body and the soul, of the body and the spirit," she writes (TBB, 75). Contemporary art that reimagines the maternal body—that productively critiques and elaborates on the images inherited from Christianity in our culture by recognizing the whole body of the woman in the mother—serves this desire in difference. Through its remembrance and representation of the breath and bodies at the center of the maternal relation, such art reminds us of the uniqueness and agency of each person and the possibilities for "uniting here and now with a beyond, within ourselves and between us" (TBB, 75).

The ongoing practice of making and remaking the image (this is the work of the artist) constitutes a gesture of care for desire and its life-giving potential. It is a patient gesture, worked and reworked over time to avoid the idolatrous fixations of ideology and dogma. Most importantly, it is an embodied gesture (rather than simply a theoretical one), worked out materially and relationally, beyond the limits of language and speech and with an awareness of the sensible transcendence of bodies. This is the most powerful kind of gesture and perhaps the kind most necessary to help us meet our immediate human challenges. Indeed, a return to the breath and energy of our bodies is necessary if we are to collaborate in developing words and actions adequate enough to help us face our present realities. After all, "[n]o word exists from time immemorial that could be substituted for the words that we have to discover to speak to and love one another here and now" (NCE, 75).

With regard to contemporary Christian visual culture and theology, new images of the mother—more precisely, the woman in the mother—offer us a way of understanding the "deep incarnation" of Christ and our part in it (Johnson 2014, 196). Further, such images remind us of the expansive capacity in us and between us to wholly, divinely participate in what Irigaray envisions as "the passage from a past humanity to a new humanity" in which relation is "the source of the word," the originary source of divine being and knowing (TBB, 85).

Notes

1. The work presented in this chapter is part of a larger project concerning representations of the maternal body, now published in my *Motherly: Reimagining the Maternal Body in Feminist Theology and Contemporary Art*.

2. To view this work, visit www.rebekahpryor.com/icon.

3. Several key biblical texts are noteworthy here: Luke 1:26–38, where Jesus' birth is foretold to Mary; John 1:1–18, where Jesus is named "the Word" who was "with God" and "was God" "in the beginning" (1:1) and who "became flesh and lived among us" (1:14); 1 Corinthians 12:12–31 and Ephesians 4:4, 12 in which the Christian church is referred to as "the body of Christ;" Mark 12:29–31 where Jesus himself pronounces love (of God, neighbor, and self) as the first and greatest commandment.

4. *Strong's Exhaustive Concordance*, "skénoó," accessed March 21, 2019, http://biblehub.com/greek/4637.htm.

5. According to Johnson, the phrase "deep incarnation" is attributed to theologian Niels Gregersen.

6. Notably, Berger first coined this phrase to describe the sheltering function of religion that orders and protects against chaos by constructing and maintaining an artificial divide between the sacred and profane through myths, rituals, theologies, and doctrines. Setting his sociological application of it aside, I appropriate the term here for its usefulness in describing the theological idea of incarnation and my artistic approach in representing it. See my chapter "Sacred Canopy" in *Motherly*, 92–120.

7. *Roof Piece*, choreography by Trisha Brown, dance performance, approximately 30 minutes, 53 Wooster Street to 381 Lafayette, New York, 1971 and 2011.

8. See also Levinas, *Totality and Infinity*.

References

Berger, Peter L. 1969. *The Sacred Canopy: Elements of a Sociological Theory of Religion*. Anchor Books.

Johnson, Elizabeth A. 2014. *Ask the Beasts: Darwin and the God of Love*. Bloomsbury.

Keller, Catherine. 2003. *Face of the Deep: A Theology of Becoming*. Routledge.

Keller, Catherine. 2008. "The Apophasis of Gender: A Fourfold Unsaying of Feminist Theology." *Journal of the American Academy of Religion* 76, no. 4: 905–933.

Levinas, Emmanuel. (1961) 1979. *Totality and Infinity*. Translated by Alphonso Lingis. Martinus Nijhoff.

Pryor, Rebekah. 2022. *Motherly: Reimagining the Maternal Body in Feminist Theology and Contemporary Art*. SCM Press.

Robinson, Hilary. 2006. *Reading Art, Reading Irigaray: The Politics of Art by Women*. I.B. Tauris.

Zaunschirm, Thomas. 2012. "The Invention of the Gold Ground." In *Gold*, edited by A. Husslein-Arco and T. Zaunschirm. Hirmer.

Contributors

Francesca Brezzi is Professor Emerita of Moral Philosophy at the University of Roma Tre. She has published widely in contemporary French philosophy and feminist philosophy.

Louise Burchill works mainly in contemporary French philosophy, feminist philosophy, aesthetics, and space studies. She has published numerous articles in these fields of which several bear on the work of Luce Irigaray. Among the latter, the most recent are "Reconsidering Chôra, Architecture and 'Woman' " in *Field: A Free Journal for Architecture*; "Of a Universal No Longer Indifferent to Difference: Badiou (and Irigaray) on Woman, Truths, and Philosophy" in *Philosophy Today*; and "Life-Giving Sex Versus Mere Animal Existence: Irigaray's and Badiou's Different Conceptions of 'Woman' and Sexual Pleasure" in *Thinking Life with Luce Irigaray: Language, Origin, Art, Love*. Burchill is equally the translator of three books by Alain Badiou, various articles by Julia Kristeva, and—most recently—Michel Serres's *Hermes I: Communication*.

Jennifer Carter is a Lecturer in Philosophy at Stony Brook University in New York. Her research focuses on continental philosophy and phenomenology, especially the philosophy of Luce Irigaray, philosophy of touch, and philosophy of science and technology. Her recent publications include *Approaching a Sensitive Thinking with Luce Irigaray* (co-edited with Andrea Wheeler, forthcoming); "An Uncontainable Subject: Thinking Feminine Sexuate Subjectivity with Irigaray" in *What is Sexual Difference?*, "On Peaceful Political Relations Between Two in Luce Irigaray's Work" in *Sophia*, "How to Lead a Child to Flower: Luce Irigaray's Philosophy of the Growth of Children" in *Towards a New Human Being*, and "Touch and Caress in the Work of Luce Irigaray" (dissertation).

Athena V. Colman is an Associate Professor of Philosophy in the Faculty of Humanities at Brock University in St. Catharines, Ontario, Canada, where she is also core faculty on the program committee of the Centre for Women's and Gender Studies in the Faculty of Social Sciences. Her interests are transdisciplinary and include social and political thought through phenomenology, psychoanalysis, contemporary continental philosophy, and critical theory: the Frankfurt school. Her publications include work on Irigaray, Merleau-Ponty, Fanon, Freud, Lacan, Butler, Kristeva, and the field of transfeminism.

Annu Dahiya is a Doctoral Lecturer of philosophy and interdisciplinary studies at York College, City University of New York. Her work focuses on feminist philosophy, philosophy of science, philosophy of race, and anticolonial philosophy. A central question that runs through her research and teaching is examining how systems of oppression—which deploy a colonial, sexist, and anti-Black logic—have shaped what we know, how we understand our world, and our relationships with one another. You can learn more about her work at annudahiya.com.

Danielle Hamilton is Senior Lecturer in Learning Futures at Deakin University. Her research interests include new materialist approaches to contemporary art informed by posthuman feminist perspectives, applied ethics, and process philosophy. Her PhD exegesis "Folding into AI: An Ethical Relationship with Technology Through the Arts" explores how ten years of creative arts practice led to the training of an artificial intelligence, resulting in a collaborative approach to creative practice generative of expanded modes of drawing with technology. Her current research pursuits center on experimental projects that explore the ethics of relationships at the interstices of bodies and technologies.

Rebecca Hill lives in Melbourne/Narrm. She is Senior Lecturer in the School of Media and Communication at RMIT University, and she conducts research in decolonial theory, critical Indigenous studies, and feminist philosophy. Hill has published widely on Luce Irigaray's ontology of sexual difference. Her recent publications include "Intuition and Feeling: Reading Bergson with Neidjie and Country" in *Parrhesia* and "Chauka's Voice: Resistance in the Art of Behrouz Boochani" in *Overland*.

Marguerite La Caze is Professor of Philosophy at the University of Queensland, Australia. She has research interests in European philosophy,

philosophy of the emotions, and philosophy and film. Her publications include *Film and Everyday Resistance*; *Ethical Restoration after Communal Violence: The Grieving and the Unrepentant*; *Wonder and Generosity: Their Role in Ethics and Politics*; and the edited collections, *Hannah Arendt and the History of Thought*, *Truth in Visual Media* with Ted Nannicelli, *Contemporary Perspectives on Vladimir Jankélévitch* with Magdalena Zolkos, and *Phenomenology and Forgiveness*. Her articles have appeared in venues such as *Angelaki*, *Contemporary Political Theory*, *Derrida Today*, *Hypatia*, *Philosophy and Social Criticism*, and *Philosophy Today*.

Ellen Mortensen is Professor Emerita in Comparative Literature at the University of Bergen, Norway. She is the author of *The Feminine and Nihilism: Luce Irigaray with Nietzsche and Heidegger* and *Touching Thought: Ontology and Sexual Difference*, and she is the editor of *Sex, Breath and Force: Sexual Difference in a Post-Feminist Era*. In addition, Mortensen has published numerous articles on literature and feminist/queer theory in academic journals and books. Her latest publication (in *Scando-Slavica*) is an ecofeminist study of Olga Tokarczuk's novel *Drive Your Plow Over the Bones of the Dead*.

Elizabeth Presa is an artist living in Dja Dja Wurrung country in Central Victoria. She lectures in Sculpture and in Critical Art Theory at the Victorian College of the Arts, the University of Melbourne. Her work often explores translations of philosophical concepts through experiments in materials, processes, and form. Currently she is working with art students in Melbourne and Tokyo on seminars and exhibitions addressing the most difficult task of maintaining belief in this world despite the violence of wars and environmental destruction.

Rebekah Pryor is an artist and academic at the School of Graduate Research, University of Divinity, Australia. Her art practice and interdisciplinary research focus on embodiment and how this is experienced, constructed, represented, and renegotiated in material cultures and communities of belief. Her publications include *Motherly: Reimagining the Maternal Body in Feminist Theology and Contemporary Art*, *Contemporary Feminist Theologies: Power, Authority, Love* (coedited with Kerrie Handasyde and Cathryn McKinney), and *Feminist Theologies: Interstices and Fractures* (coedited with Stephen Burns).

Kristin Sampson is Professor of Philosophy at the University of Bergen, Norway. She works mainly within the areas of ancient philosophy—primarily

Plato and early Greek thought going back to Homer and Hesiod—and feminist philosophy, with a particular focus on the thought of Luce Irigaray. She also combines these two areas of interest by reading Irigaray together with early Greek thinking, something of which her contribution to the present volume is an example. Her latest publications in English include "Thinking Life through the Early Greeks" in *Thinking Life with Luce Irigaray: Language, Origin, Art, Love*, "Conceptions of Temporality: Reconsidering Time in an Age of Impending Emergency" in *Theoria*, and "The Art of Politics as Weaving in Plato's *Statesman*" in *Polis: The Journal for Ancient Greek and Roman Political Thought*.

James Sares is a Lecturer in Philosophy at the University of Kentucky. He researches at the intersection of the history of modern philosophy and contemporary continental philosophy. He is the co-editor of *What is Sexual Difference?*, and his recent articles on sexual difference include "Beyond the Neuter Universal: Hegel and Sexual Difference" in *Hegel Bulletin*.

Gail Schwab—one of the original co-directors of the Luce Irigaray Circle, along with Professor Mary C. Rawlinson—is Professor emerita of French at Hofstra University in Hempstead, New York, where she also served for many years as Associate Dean of the Hofstra College of Liberal Arts and Sciences. A reader of the work of Luce Irigaray since the 1970s, she has translated Irigaray's *To Speak Is Never Neutral*; edited the scholarly collection *Thinking Life with Luce Irigaray: Language, Origin, Art, Love*, and authored many articles on various aspects of Irigaray's work, including psychoanalysis, law, spirituality, linguistics, Greek tragedy and mythology, pedagogy, film, nature and sustainability, and Irigaray's philosophical relationship to the French existentialists Simone de Beauvoir and Jean-Paul Sartre.

Jacqueline Taylor is an artist, writer, researcher and educator who is currently the doctoral education lead at the Faculty of Arts, Design and Media, Birmingham City University, United Kingdom. Jacqueline's research traverses the fields of painting, art writing, and performance although she is particularly interested in the spaces at the edges or in-between multiple artforms. Located at the intersection of aesthetic practice and poetics, her research explores the ways in which nonrepresentational art practices signify and enable meaning-making. She exhibits, presents, performs, and publishes her research practice on language and art globally, often in alternative hybrid academic forms, which expand the parameters of the written text.

Index